THE FORGOTTEN LETTERS

World War II Eyewitness Accounts of Survival and Loss

Sia Arnason

First published by Dog Ear Publishing
4010 W. 86th Street, Ste H
Indianapolis, IN 46268
www.dogearpublishing.net

ISBN: 978-1-4575-2877-4

Library of Congress Control Number: has been applied for

This book is printed on acid-free paper.

Printed in the United States of America

For Lise and Frank –
Warm regards,
Tia

For Frits and Jan
and all the other very dear members of my family and for Jon,
who encouraged me throughout the years of writing.

The book is based on letters that were written by our family shortly after the end of World War II. The letters had been carefully saved, we don't know by whom, and had been stored later in cardboard boxes in our mother's basement room. Then they were forgotten for decades. Our parents and the other family members who wrote these letters are all gone, but their writings continue to live and to tell a vivid story of courage and fear, of survival and loss. Without these letters, the book could not have been written and our family's story would have been forgotten forever.

TABLE OF CONTENTS

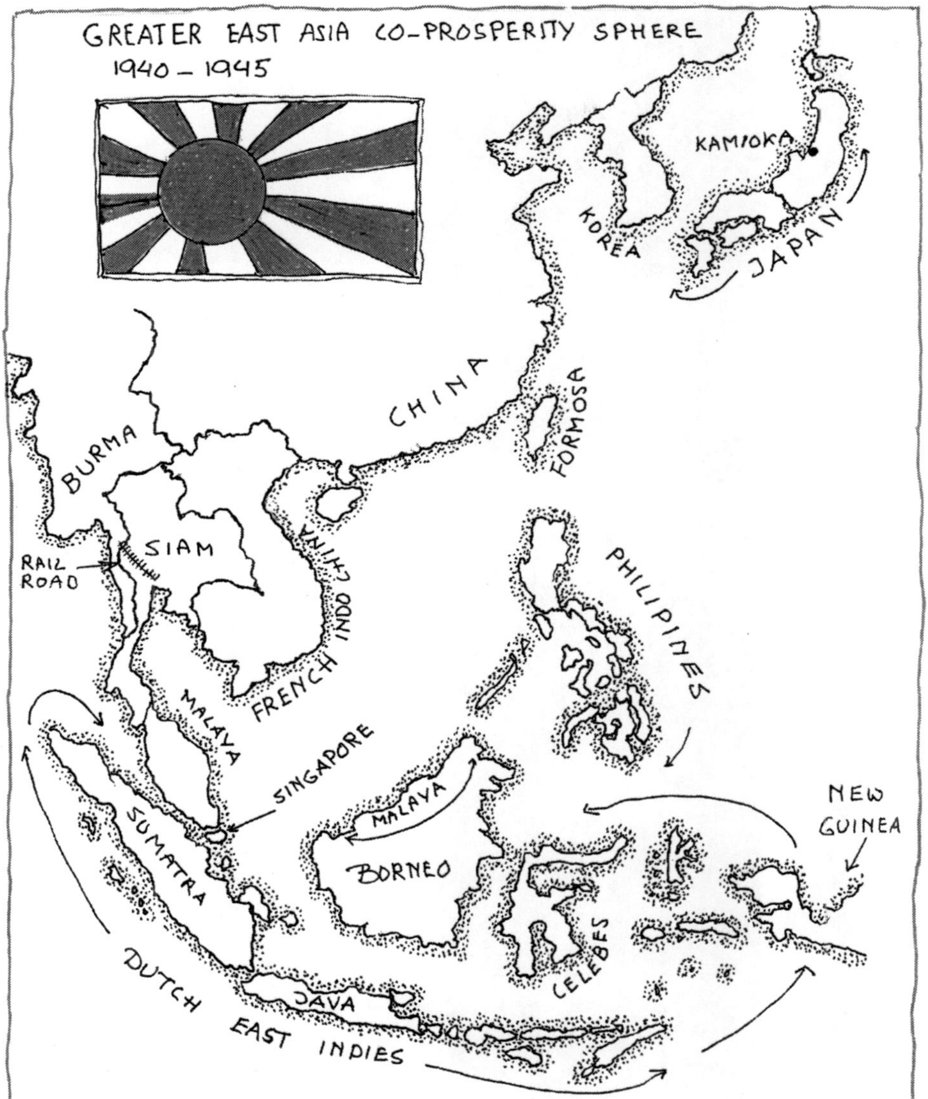
GREATER EAST ASIA CO-PROSPERITY SPHERE
1940 – 1945
KAMIOKA
KOREA
JAPAN
CHINA
FORMOSA
BURMA
SIAM
RAIL ROAD
FRENCH INDO CHINA
PHILIPINES
MALAYA
SINGAPORE
MALAYA
BORNEO
NEW GUINEA
SUMATRA
CELEBES
JAVA
DUTCH EAST INDIES
SCALE: 0 250 500 750 1.000 KM
SIA

INTRODUCTION

FINDING THE FORGOTTEN LETTERS

Today we expect the arrival of the airplane from Holland and I hope so very much that there will be a letter for me, so that I will know exactly how you all are and who I will see again. I heard by way of Francine ... that you are well, Mam, but that Father has died. Is that true? I cannot yet believe it—it is such a terrible thing, because there was so much I needed to set right .... Kuk is married to Cor van Nieuwland and then, Francine writes: "Your brother is doing well," forgetting that I have two brothers. Oh, the terrible uncertainty ...

Didi's first letter home to her family, November 12, 1945

My mother, Didi de Jong, wrote these words in her first long letter home to her mother in Holland while we still were in a Japanese internment camp for women and children on the island of Java, on the other side of the globe from Holland, waiting to hear when we would be repatriated to the Netherlands. This is one of many letters my mother and I found in Holland that were written weeks after the end of the Second World War.

We found this one and dozens of other old letters in January 2000 while we cleaned Didi's small basement room of the clutter that had accumulated there ever since she had moved to the apartment twenty-five years before. The letters had been stored in cardboard boxes among old furniture, empty suitcases, decades-old tax records, and broken flowerpots. Swept up in the spirit of clearing away so much unused and long-forgotten stuff, my mother's immediate reaction was "Let's throw out all those dusty papers! After all, who would want to read those old letters anyway?"

Of course I did not agree. "But Mam, who knows what's in there? We cannot get rid of these letters until we know what they are about!" Sitting on old suitcases, we sorted through the old letters, brittle with age and written with soft pencils on both sides of onionskin paper. They are difficult to decipher and at times emotionally wrenching. We agreed that I should take the letters to the States with me.

It is a miracle that these old letters still exist. After all, we moved back and forth to Indonesia at least every three years until 1958 while my second father was still working in Indonesia for a Dutch trading firm. Had they traveled with us, or had they been saved by my grandmother in Holland? My mother did not remember.

One thing is clear: Some of the letters and cards Didi received during the war or that were returned to her must have traveled with us in the bottom of the duffel bag in which we carried all of our belongings during the three years we were living in various Japanese internment camps. After having read the letters, I now realize something else: Some of the letters never reached their destinations during the chaos of war and were eventually returned to the sender, another reason why some of them still exist today.

Many of these long-forgotten letters, written in the fall of 1945, were the first letters my mother and grandmother wrote to each other after a war-imposed silence of more than four years. They wrote about how they had survived the war years in the East Indies and in the Netherlands and who had survived and who had been lost during those terrible years during which they were both widowed.

Didi's letters home announce the wonderful news of my brother Frits's birth in 1942 and how she, Frits, and I survived the internment camps during the Japanese occupation in Java. Oma's letters describe the 1943 death of my grandfather from tuberculosis that ended in meningitis, and how she and her younger daughter and two sons had survived the war in Deventer, a small provincial town in Holland, during the German occupation.

Didi also wrote her mother about my father's death in 1944. My father, Daan Engelberts, whom Frits and I called Papa Daan, had died during a bombing raid by our allies on the steel railroad bridge spanning the River Kwai Noi near POW camp Tamarkan in Siam (this is the bridge featured in the movie *Bridge over the River Kwai*). The bombs destroyed the large bridge, but several stray bombs also fell on the camp and killed sixteen young men, prisoners of the Japanese, my thirty-three-year old father among them.

The collection of long-lost letters includes many loving letters from my mother to Jan Borgerhoff Mulder, who became my second father after the war. Written in the spring of 1946, while he was still in Batavia, now Jakarta, waiting to be repatriated and Didi was at home in Holland, my mother's letters to Jan are full of hope for the future and love for the man who had been her best friend before the war and whom she would marry that summer.

A Letter Brings Papa Daan Alive

One of the oldest letters we found was written by both of my parents on November 25, 1938. At the time, they lived on Donowarie, a rubber plantation in East Java, where my father was employed in the administration of the estate and the supervision of local workers who tended the rubber trees. The letter is, of course, in my parents' own handwriting. My father wrote about their plans for the future and asked for investment advice from his father-in-law, while my mother wrote about their life in the tropics. I was surprised about my reaction to this letter, which is one of the few things I have that was actually touched by my father's own hand. With this letter in my hand, I felt a surprising and unexpected connection with my father, a connection I had not felt for many decades and one I had avoided for a long time.

In addition to the many letters we found in Didi's basement storage room, we found an account written by Herbert van Oyen, Oom Heb, a friend of my parents with whom my mother and I stayed in the early weeks of 1942 when the war with Japan was expected and Papa Daan was already garrisoned in Soerabaja as part of the Dutch colonial army, preparing for the Japanese invasion of the north coast of Java.

Oom Heb was the leader of our small group of eight who fled into the mountain wilderness to hide from the Japanese troops, which were rapidly advancing into the interior of Java, on March 3, 1942, only to find ourselves attacked by local insurgents. Our group consisted of Oom Heb and his wife, Tante Bep; their two young sons, Herbert and Loetje; the children of friends of the van Oyens, Meindert and Anke Bolhuis; and my six-month pregnant mother and I. The three adults and five children, between the ages of two and eight, hid in the woods from March 3 to March 17, when we finally walked into the town of Buitenzorg after having surrendered to the Japanese we met on the way. Didi gave birth to Frits in May, and months later, in December 1942, Didi, little Frits, and I were moved by the Japanese to an internment camp for women and children in Bandoeng. Our imprisonment lasted until the end of October 1945.

The other document was written decades later by one of the other children who participated in our flight into the wilderness of West Java early March 1942. Meindert Bolhuis was eight years old at the start of the war and the oldest child among us. Although written decades after the war and based on his childhood memories, his letter vividly captured the mood of the trek through the jungle.

The letters and documents we found in the basement on that cold January day encouraged me to start searching for more details of our family's story, so that I might write it all down.

One of the things that made it difficult to learn more about the wartime past was that the people who lived through it did not talk about the war after they had started new lives for themselves. In 1946, my mother's doctor in Deventer advised her to tell the immediate family all about what had happened to her—but only *once;* she was to stop talking about her wartime experience with the many interested family members and friends who came to welcome her back home.

Didi did just that. She apparently talked for two days and nights straight, and then she fell silent! So it was that our family stopped speaking about the war years, and most of the people who once could have handed the stories down are now no longer alive.

These letters still live, however, and they tell a vivid tale that should not be forgotten.

Acknowledgments

This book is based primarily on the letters that were written in the fall of 1945, when the wartime experiences of my mother and grandmother were still fresh in their minds. As a result, the book is largely based on eyewitness accounts that were written down by the people who lived through the horrors of the Second World War in Southeast Asia and in Holland, not long after the events they described had actually happened. The account by Oom Heb was written while he was recuperating from the ordeal of our flight into the wilderness, days after we had walked into Buitenzorg. Only Meindert Bolhuis's account of our flight is a true memoir, in the traditional sense of the word, having been written decades after the end of the war. I have added my own childhood memories where that seemed appropriate.

Writing this book has given me the unexpected opportunity to get to know my mother and two fathers through the letters they wrote, as if they are my contemporaries. I have come to know them as friends who lived during calamitous times and who tried in many different ways to survive and to overcome hardships through fortitude and plain decency, and who, in the final analysis, were much more multidimensional than I had thought as a child growing up. I have also learned to see myself in a different light and now feel compassion for the little girl I once was. My reawakened love for my parents and the new feelings of devotion and understanding have made the writing of this book a personal adventure and a pleasure.

Of course, Didi and Oma, my grandmother, together with Oom Heb, are the primary authors of this story. My two fathers, Daan and Jan, and Didi's siblings, Gerrit, Kuk, and Pieter are other key sources. Without their letters, this book could never have been written in the first place. Sadly, Didi died in November 2011, before I was able to finish the manuscript, but she did see an earlier version and enjoyed reading about her own distant past.

Many friends and family members have helped me during the years I was writing, by reading and reacting to parts of the story and encouraging me to continue.

Ian Burnet, the historian and author of *Spice Islands* (2011) and *East Indies* (2013) published by Rosenberg Publishing, read the entire manuscript and urged me to add historical context to the events I have described. I am grateful to Ian for his fine attention to detail and his suggestions for changes in the text and additions to the content of the story.

I am indebted to Lidwien, who transcribed the account of Heb van Oyen into Word. Oom Heb's seven-page, single-spaced, and faded carbon copy of a document, typed on a defective typewriter in 1942, describes our flight into the wilderness at the beginning of the war. Making sense of Oom Heb's account was a labor of love!

My brother Jan has given me helpful information about Pappie and the family Borgerhoff Mulder, information I needed to write the chapter on Pappie's wartime experiences. Jan also gave me copies of letters that Pappie's sister, Tante Tiek, had written to him at the end of the war. And I have copies of the pages of the guestbook maintained by the Borgerhoff family before the war, showing that a close friendship had been established as early as 1936 between Pappie and his family, and Didi and Daan.

My brother Frits showed me a letter written by a friend of Papa Daan's who was at camp Tamarkan when the bombs started falling; the letter describes Papa Daan's death in detail. I had not seen this letter before, and it gave me information I did not have until I read it recently. Frits also was able to get a hold of some old glass plates, negatives of photographs of the Engelberts family, including a wonderful picture of Papa Daan as a very little boy, standing among his parents and older sister and brothers.

Didi's sister, Kuk, who calls me her third daughter, has read the sections that feature Deventer during the war and has given me details and corrections about the experiences of my family during the Nazi occupation that were very helpful.

I also want to thank my friends Jane Waters and Peter Caldwell, Anne and Peter Putzel, Martha Zimiles, Emily Upham, David Plimpton, and Peter Ochs, who read the manuscript. Their suggestions have been invaluable, and their encouragement was important when the going got rough.

I owe many thanks to Stacey Moore of "Moore and More" in Millerton for touching up the photographs and making sure that they would show to best advantage. And I want to thank Patricia Horan, who edited the original manuscript and helped me to get it in order. Her interest in the Second World War and the questions she asked about the Dutch POWs and internees added to my own understanding of the history I have described in these pages.

Lastly, Jon has been there for me throughout the years I was writing. He often was in tears as he read some of the earlier chapters. Together with Jon, I found Papa Daan's grave in Thailand on November 29, 2004, on the sixtieth anniversary of his death. At his graveside, I reconnected with the father who left me when I was two years old, and to my great surprise, I didn't say good-bye to him once we had found him, but instead welcomed him back into my life. Jon's support has been heartwarming. I could not have finished this book without everyone's help and encouragement. Thank you, all.

Throughout this book, I have used the colonial Dutch spelling that was in use during the time before Indonesia's independence in 1949. For example, Soekarno, as it was written in the prewar period, is now written Sukarno. The name of one of our camps was Tjihapit, which today would be written as Cihapit. I have also used the Dutch colonial names for the cities and towns that were renamed after Indonesia's independence. For example, Buitenzorg, where my brother was born, is now called Bogor, and Batavia is now called Jakarta.

CHAPTER 1

YOUNG COLONIALS BEFORE THE WAR

Today we received your wonderful long letter, Mother, many thanks. Yes, time is beginning to fly for us.... It is fairly certain that I will leave for Holland on furlough on the 20th of September 1940—only 22 months from now. We so much look forward to it and cannot think about much else.

—Daan's letter to his parents-in-law, November 25, 1938

My parents celebrated their engagement just before my father was to leave for the Dutch East Indies. Daan had just graduated from the Koloniale Landbouwschool in Deventer and he and many of his school friends left immediately for the Dutch East Indies to look for work as assistant administrators on the coffee, tea, tobacco, rubber, sugar, and palm oil plantations in Java and the other islands of the Dutch colony. Daan left for Java in the late spring of 1935 and, like so many of his classmates, left on "de bonne fooi," as the saying goes in Dutch, to look for work.

Didi and Daan on a bicycle trip along the River IJssel in 1934, which took them over the dike to the village of Olst to visit family—a favorite Sunday excursion

Soon after his arrival in Java, Daan was hired by Harrison and Crosfield, a British firm, to be the assistant to the administrator of the rubber plantation Donowarie, located in the mountains, about fifty kilometers south of Malang, in East Java. Donowarie was managed by Douglas Smart, a Scotsman who was assisted by my father, whom Mr. Smart inexplicably called George. Of course, the social formality of those days required that Daan never call Mr. Smart by his first name. Mr. Smart and Daan were the only two Europeans in Donowarie, and before Didi's arrival, there were no European women on the plantation.

Mr. Smart and Daan preparing for a swim in Donowarie's pool. Because they had company that day, they wore their fashionable bathing suits.

One of Daan's daily tasks was to check on the workers who were engaged in tapping the sap from the rubber trees, a process that is similar to the harvesting of maple sap in the United States. The harvest of latex, as the rubber sap is called, is then processed in the factory on the plantation, where it is changed into large sheets of rubber.

The estate was run in a feudal manner by Mr. Smart, who not only decided what my father would do during his working hours but also dictated how Daan's free time was to be spent. When Mr. Smart wanted to play cards or Monopoly in the evenings, he would summon Daan, who could not refuse to come to the *besaran*, the big house on the hill, and play games with the *toean besar*, the boss.

Daan was paid the munificent sum of 3.25 guilders for a day of work, an ordinary low-end salary for a youngster, as the newly arrived Europeans were called. When one of my father's superiors announced with fanfare a year later that Daan was to get a raise and would be paid 100 guilders on a monthly basis, my father's reaction was tepid. The firm had probably expected surprise and delight on my father's part, but my father, who had to be very careful with his money and turned over every penny several times before he spent it, asked politely if the raise could be deferred until the following month because the current month had thirty-one days and would therefore yield a few guilders more at his current rate than with the raise.

Finishing High School, Preparing for Marriage

While Daan was beginning his career as a planter at Donowarie, Didi was finishing her final year at the gymnasium in Deventer. After graduating, she went to Den Haag to learn the housekeeping skills that were deemed appropriate for European women in the colonies. She learned Maleis, or Malay, the lingua franca spoken by most people in the Indies. She also learned how to supervise household employees, how to administer rudimentary first aid, and how to care for babies and young children alone, without the help of family or friends. And of course, together with Oma, she set about assembling her dowry, consisting of enormous numbers of sheets, towels, and other household items. Her linen supply was so large that she took only half of it with her in 1936. The remaining half was sufficiently ample so that Didi could share it with her sister, Kuk, when both of them started to establish households after the war, in 1946.

Didi in the garden in Deventer, standing on a small rug to model her wedding dress

I have several photos of my mother taken in 1936 in the old walled garden of her parents' home in Deventer. In one of the pictures, she is modeling her wedding dress, standing on a small Oriental rug to keep its train clean and pristine. The dress is lovely, with its narrow skirt cut on the bias so it falls sleekly down her hips into soft undulating pleats at the hem. The top is made of lace, with a high neckline and short sleeves. My grandmother and mother had seen this dress in Spanier, one of the few elegant shops in the Lange Bisschopstraat in Deventer. The dress was expensive at 100 guilders—the same amount as Daan's monthly salary.

My mother remembers modeling the dress for her father in the hope that he would approve its purchase. A man of few words and frugal with his money, he stood sucking on his pipe, looking at his lovely elder daughter, and then said simply, "I think you should get it." For Didi, who had always been in awe of her father and somewhat unsure in his presence, this gesture of love and pride for her was a surprise and a delight.

She remembered that golden moment throughout her life.

A Bittersweet Parting, a Gala Sail

Didi left home in early July 1936, days after her twentieth birthday. Her parents and eldest brother, Gerrit, brought her to the train station in Arnhem and helped settle her with her luggage on the international train that would take her to Genoa in Italy. There she planned to meet *The Marnix of St. Aldegonde*, the passenger liner that would bring her to Batavia, now Jakarta. Didi was in high spirits until the moment the train pulled away from the station and she saw her parents becoming smaller as the train accelerated. Dissolving into tears, she saw her father's face and his balled fist raised high, encouraging her to be brave.

It was the last image she had of him.

The Marnix of St. Aldegonde was typical of the ocean liners of that time. The ship was built in opulent art deco style with sweeping staircases, lots of polished wood, etched glass, and elegant wall decorations. The promenade decks were wide open to the sea air and were lined with comfortable deck chairs, where the passengers would spend a great deal of their time reading, talking, drinking, or walking around to see and to be seen. Twenty-year-old Didi, who had never been far from Deventer, looked at this luxury with wide-open eyes, but it did not take her long to love every minute of it.

The ocean voyages on the boats sailing from Holland to Batavia took close to four weeks, with the ships stopping at several exotic ports on the way. The first stop after Genoa was Port Said in Egypt, the gateway to the Suez Canal. For Didi, who was making the passage to the Indies for the first time, the visit to Port Said was an unforgettable glimpse of a world vastly different from Europe. She always remembered that she could smell the Far East upon sailing into Port Said's harbor!

Together with the other passengers, Didi shopped in the ancient bazaar, mingled with the colorful citizens of the old town, and marveled at the expensive European-style stores stocked with the latest Parisian fashions. In the harbor, she saw little boys dive from their skiffs to catch the shiny coins passengers would throw in the water for them. The next day, while the boat made its way through the Suez Canal, everyone lounged on deck to watch the camel caravans and the desert slide by.

While the ship was at sea, slowly making its way to the tropics, the passengers played games, swam in the pool, and lazed about in deck chairs during the day. In the evenings, they dressed formally and danced on the upper deck under the wide sky filled with unfamiliar constellations and stars. Didi was a popular girl. She loved to dance and was good at it, and she savored these few weeks of total freedom without a care in the world. The four weeks on board were one huge party; Didi had a glorious time and made several friends, among them Charles Drievoet, Miel de Mos and Jan Borgerhoff Mulder. Didi had noticed Jan on the sidelines, watching her while she played deck games with the others, but he had not spontaneously joined in. He was shy, but also dark and handsome, and she made the first move by asking, "What is your name?" From then on, she and the three young men spent most of their time together.

Snake and Tourist Charmers

In Colombo, the capital of Ceylon, now Sri Lanka, passengers again disembarked for a day. It was their first exposure to the sights, sounds, and spicy aroma of the real tropics. Didi marveled at the large variety of tropical fruits and flowers, and their intoxicating smell. In the streets, she saw snake charmers playing small flutes next to baskets, out of which snakes slowly uncoiled, but she and her friends also saw the terrible poverty of people on the street alongside the excessive luxury of the well-to-do, so common in the large colonial cities of that time.

Didi had vivid memories of a trip to the famous beach-side hotel Mount Lavinia, a converted nineteenth-century British governor's palace where most passengers ended up celebrating their last days before they arrived at their destinations. In the afternoon, high tea was served on the lawn in the gardens of the palace, where a riot of flowers, planted orderly in their immaculate beds, competed with masses of orchids hanging in abundant chaos from the trunks of trees. At Mount Lavinia, Didi saw little boys climb straight up tall palm trees to fetch coconuts for the guests. It was an iconic image of a tropical dream.

After Colombo, the boat started to drop off its passengers, first at Belawan, the harbor of Medan on the island of Sumatra, then at Singapore, and then finally at Tandjong Priok, the harbor town of Batavia. In Belawan, Didi and her three friends hired an *opelette*, a small bus with driver, to go swimming at one of the spectacular beaches of Northern Sumatra. They had such a good time that they lost track of the hour of departure and almost missed their boat. By the time they got to the quay, the gangplank had been pulled up and the boat was about to sail away.

On their last evening on board *The Marnix of St. Aldegonde*, Didi was brought to her cabin by her friends Jan, Charles, and Miel, who each gallantly kissed her good-bye. The next morning, she was met by Daan, whom she was to marry in two weeks' time.

Though Didi never said so, I have always imagined that this day must have been bittersweet for her. She had not seen her husband-to-be for more than a year, and for just these last few wonderful weeks, she had tasted the freedom of being on her own, without parental supervision, in a carefree, luxurious environment, surrounded by three charming young men who enjoyed her company and never left her side. Daan must have represented the end of that freedom and the beginning of a much more sober, adult life. For Daan, on the other hand, Didi's arrival ended the lonely bachelor existence of life at Donowarie with the toean besar, the boss, Mr. Smart. He had been looking forward to the moment of her arrival ever since he himself had arrived in the Indies a year before.

A Rude Beginning

Just married: Didi and Daan in Malang, August 14, 1936

Didi and Daan stayed in Batavia for a few days to visit friends before they traveled by train to Malang. Daan, who had immaculate manners that were not at all commensurate with his modest station in life at that time, decided that it would be proper to introduce his bride to the management and directors of Harrison and Crosfield while they were in town. Dressed for the occasion, eager to make a favorable impression on his superiors, the two of them must have looked stunning. Didi wore a smart linen dress, a hat, and white gloves; Daan was dressed in his sharkskin suit. But as they waited outside on the wide steps of the building to be invited in to meet the boss, a junior employee met them instead. "I am sorry," he said, "but the directors cannot meet with you this morning. I will be happy to tell them about your visit. Thank you very much for your visit. Good-bye." They were not invited in, and no one from management ever acknowledged the fact that my parents had made the effort to pay their respects.

During the two weeks before their wedding, Didi stayed in Malang at the home of Mr. and Mrs. Mulder, the parents of Jeanne Mulder, the wife of Papa Daan's brother Gerard. (The Mulders are unrelated to Jan Borgerhoff Mulder). Mr. Mulder had been an assistant resident in East Java, and he and his wife had recently retired. My parents were married out of the Mulders' home in Malang on August 14, 1936. One of the witnesses at the wedding was Buis Hofstee, one of Daan's friends, whom Daan had met on the boat coming out.

Didi and Daan spent a short honeymoon on the rocky south coast of Java with its isolated, white sandy beaches and rough surf, and then went on to Donowarie. My mother had been looking forward to going home with her new husband so she could show him their wedding presents, including the upright piano she had brought along, and the silver, the china, the Wedgewood tea service, the crystal, and the Oriental rug, a gift from Daan's parents. But it was not to be that first evening in their own home, because Mr. Smart invited Daan and Didi to come for a visit so he could meet my mother and to play cards. Daan must have used all his powers of persuasion to convince Didi that they had to obey the boss. And so they went, my mother protesting all the way.

Within weeks of her arrival on Java, Didi had learned some important lessons: first, junior employees and their wives had no standing among the "old hands" in the colonies, and their impeccable manners were not necessarily appreciated by their self-important superiors; second, they were expected to snap to when the boss called, whatever the time of day. It was Didi's introduction to an unpleasant reality: She and Daan and all "youngsters" like them were unimportant elements in the colonial hierarchy of that time.

Making a Home under the Rubber Trees

Didi and Daan's house in Donowarie was a modest, small cottage with a corrugated iron roof, covered in purple bougainvillea. The iron roof would clatter with the sound of huge raindrops of tropical storms and would shimmy and bang during earthquakes, which scared the living daylights out of my mother. Some of the inside walls had cracked during previous earthquakes, and although it was impossible to see through the walls into the adjacent rooms, you could always tell whether the light was on in them.

Bari and Ton cooked, washed the dishes, did the laundry, cleaned the interior of the little house, and served the meals

For Didi, who had grown up in a townhouse in Deventer, it took some time to get used to her new home, especially because they had to share it with a variety of animal life. At night, when they turned on the lights, tjitjaks, tiny transparent lizards, came out from their daytime hiding places behind the pictures on the wall to hunt for mosquitoes, while the larger tokèhs, geckos, which lived on the ceiling, started calling, "Tokèh—tokèh." Their new Oriental rug in the living room covered the exit holes of ants' nests in the cement floor, and every now and then, little mountains of sand, the debris of the ants' excavations, would build up through the wool of the rug. And then there was the occasional snake. A friend, Mieke Hofstee, once ran screaming from the lavatory because a snake had curled up inside it and had reared its head just as she was about to sit down. Although all this took a bit of getting used to, Didi loved their little cottage and its cozy *platje*, a covered patio attached to the living room, with its rattan easy chairs dressed up with chintz pillows, an embroidered tablecloth on the table, and flowering plants in pots all around.

In 1936, the income of the newlyweds was 125 guilders a month. With that amount, they were able to make ends meet and even employ a couple, Ton, the *Kokkie* who cooked, and her husband, Bari, the *Djongos*, who took care of household chores. Together, Ton and Bari were paid 13 guilders per month, and once a year, when the Muslim fast was over, they received new outfits at my parents' expense. A young boy employed and paid by the plantation administration, a *Katjong* maintained the yards around the houses on the estate and hauled water in large buckets from a nearby spring to fill the water cisterns in the bathrooms.

To Didi's delight, Ton and Bari had a baby boy soon after her arrival at Donowarie. The young couple and their cute little son added human contact that was so very scarce on the isolated plantation in the mountains.

Those first years at Donowarie must have been hard for my very young and lively mother, who was the only European woman for miles around. In a letter to her grandmother in Olst, near Deventer, Didi wrote about her daily schedule:

> *What should I tell you about our life here? There is not much to say. All days are the same. This morning I took a long walk in the gardens. It is now cold in the mornings and it was nice to walk; I imagined myself walking in the woods in Holland. And when I got home I made something nice for Daan; sometimes I write or read letters, and play the piano, and in that way the time flies by. Daan leaves the factory at 12 noon, visits the boss for a few minutes, and then comes home for lunch. In the afternoon he returns to the factory and works until 5 o'clock and during that time I read or do some embroidery and look forward to 5 o'clock when we can drink tea outside. In the evening we read the papers or we go visit our friend Tiedeman, and that way the day ends and we start all over again in the same way the next day.*

Carefree When the Party Was On

Didi and Daan were allowed to leave Donowarie once a month to go shopping in Malang or to visit with friends in the coastal cities of Semarang or Soerabaja. Those visits with friends became the highlights of their lives. On Saturday evenings in town, everyone went to the "soos," short for "society," the Dutch Club. With a large verandah with lots of comfortable furniture and broad lawns, it offered a home away from home. Outside, they would play tennis and swim in the pool. Dances were held almost every weekend, and the bar and spacious dining rooms were popular spots inside the whitewashed art deco building. The midday meal on Sundays was usually a *rijsttafel*, a splendid and very elaborate meal of rice surrounded by at least twelve or more different curries of all kinds. Although a rijsttafel is not an Indonesian tradition and is now considered a remnant of colonial excess, the Europeans living in the Indies before the war considered a rijsttafel the best example of the delicious cuisine of the Dutch East Indies. Each Kokkie had her own repertoire, and no two rijsttafels were the same.

At the end of the afternoon or on weekend evenings, the adults usually could be found at the bar or on the verandah, where they had drinks, called *borrels*. They danced to the most recent big-band records from America, gossiped about newcomers, watched the newly arrived young wives, talked about their plans and hopes for the future, and shared news from Holland.

My childhood memories of an afternoon at the soos are of a boisterous time, when parents became easier on us children and we could usually count on an *ijsje*, an ice Popsicle, from a parent or an "uncle" or "aunt," as we called my parents' friends. At those times, when the party was on, even money-conscious people became a bit more carefree, while we children ran around outside with our friends, playing hide-and-seek in the shady gardens until dark settled in. Then the lamps would be lit in the soos and the families would pile into their cars to go home, where their Kokkies would be ready with dinner.

Didi often told me that she was not unhappy at Donowarie, except when she and Daan returned after a weekend in town. Then it felt as if the prison gate closed again. But this feeling would not last long, and within hours, she would be happily settled into her life on the plantation. Although Didi was young and vivacious and constantly looked forward to their visits to town, she also had a knack for being alone, and she was very good at amusing herself by keeping busy in her little house, where Ton and Bari took care of their small household. She spent days sewing dresses from yards of fabric she had brought from Europe. She would make endless numbers of cakes and pastries—she gained ten kilo in one year—and she tended her vegetable garden planted with seeds from Holland. She chased the monkeys from the ripe tomatoes, walked on the paths under the rubber trees in the plantation gardens with Datiko, their dog, swam in the ice-cold water of the pool, and wrote her weekly letters home.

> *At the moment we have tomatoes, kale and cauliflower and radishes—pretty soon we will plant a kind of Chinese cabbage, called "petsai". I have also some boxes with seedlings of kale and cauliflower and some zinnias—the latter are not doing too well. It is raining a lot*

right now, and that makes planting the seedlings difficult. Once they are settled, they thrive however. The kale is delicious by the way. We eat it with Dutch smoked sausage, bought at "Toko Piet" in Malang—it is expensive because we get it frozen, but it is much better than the sausage we can get from the local butcher. It costs 75 cent for a half pound of sausage, you don't pay that at Stegeman's do you, Mother?

On the Patio at First Light

When I close my eyes, I can imagine my parents sitting on their platje in the early morning. They are both in pajamas, drinking their first cup of coffee and looking out over the valley and the mountains in the background. The sun is just coming up and it is still cool. The sky is brilliant, with its reds, oranges, and purples against which the mountains are outlined in dark blue. Fog and smoke rise from the river bottoms and the small wood-fires in the kitchens of the houses in the *dessa*, the small village near Donowarie. As they sit in silence, enjoying the cool of the early morning, they hear the monkeys chattering in the trees, and the cocks crowing and dogs barking from the valley below. A little later they hear the singsong of the workmen's voices as the men walk to my parents' yard, where they assemble, sitting on their haunches to await instructions about the day's work.

Didi and Daan under the rubber trees, having breakfast early in the morning, accompanied by Datiko, their dog

After Daan has left with the men, Didi gets dressed and prepares his breakfast and then brings it to him in the plantation gardens, where they sit on a big stone on the side of a path under the rubber trees and talk.

On the weekends, many of their friends who lived in the dusty, humid, and hot towns of the coast and low-lying plains liked to come for a visit to catch a breath of cool mountain air and enjoy the sights in the neighborhood of Donowarie. They made trips to the ancient Boroboedoer and Prambanan temples. They rode their ponies down into the sand sea of the extinct Bromo volcano and then climbed up to the top of the smaller cone in the center of the vast expanse of sand to see the fire and bubbling sulfur in its depths. They had fun together, swimming, playing tennis, and hiking the old footpaths in the mountains. Their friends from those days remained friends forever, quickly becoming more than friends—they were each other's extended family far from home.

Didi once wrote a little ditty in the guest book maintained by Jan's mother, when they spent a few days with the family Borgerhoff Mulder in Soerabaja:

Although there are often complaints
About jobs, bosses, the heat, and money
There is something that is far more important,
Something that counts for much more
That is a circle of true friends,
A small piece of home,
Of people you don't want to lose, ever,
Even if the world were to fall apart

Daan, Didi, and Jan on their way to Malang in Daan's secondhand car with license plate 1082. The car was often referred to as the "tien twee-en-tachtig."

One of the most frequent visitors to Donowarie was Jan Borgerhoff Mulder, who was employed in Semarang at the time. Didi, Daan, and Jan were frequently seen together in Malang, Semarang, and Soerabaja, and the colonial rumor mills were soon busy, wondering why Didi always could be found with her husband and accompanied by Jan, their bachelor friend. Jan had been engaged to a young Dutch woman earlier but had broken the relationship. When Didi asked him why he had done that, his answer had been "I don't like Anneke as much as I like you!"

Decades later, in a toast celebrating Didi's sixty-fifth birthday, Buis Hofstee fondly remembered the good times they enjoyed together when they were so young, more than forty-five years ago. Buis and Papa Daan had traveled together on the boat to the East Indies in 1935, and Buis had met Didi soon after she arrived in Java; he had been a witness at their wedding and had gotten to know Didi well when she and Daan lived at Donowarie with Datiko the dog, Bari the Djongos, Ton the Kokkie, and, of course, Mr. Smart. In his toast, Buis remembered the good times they often had in those days:

> *When we had to play the required Monopoly games with Mr. Smart at the besaran; the swimming parties at the South Beaches; the time Didi tumbled from my Harley Davidson—but she was young and flexible and did not break a thing; the trips to Malang; reunions with alumni from our student days in Deventer; weekends in Semarang after I too had married; swimming and sunbathing in Kopeng; traveling with ever more recent second hand cars, which overheated nonetheless; and when we had to stop the car to let it cool down and would put our gramophone on the road and dance to the music; and the Javanese residents of the local dessa who would come and watch those "gila orang blanda" [those crazy white folks]; and the tennis games at Kali Tello where Didi usually was an attractive observer at the sidelines…*

Not long after Didi's arrival at Donowarie, Mr. Smart decided to marry as well. His "mail-order" bride arrived in due time from Britain, but the two women didn't get along at all, particularly since Mrs. Smart remained aloof and was critical of my mother's freewheeling hospitality; she had been insulted when my mother and a girlfriend from Deventer, Ella Birnie, had paid her an unexpected visit so that my mother could introduce her friend. Didi was told that she should have waited for an invitation from Mrs. Smart.

While I was writing this book, Didi told me about another faux pas that occurred during a dinner party one evening when Mr. and Mrs. Smart had been invited to my parents' house. My mother probably had ordered Ton, the Kokkie, to cook something special, a solid Dutch meal or perhaps an Indonesian curry, and no doubt she had set the table with her best linen and family silver. Unfortunately, the effect was completely lost when their friend Bruno Tiedeman unexpectedly arrived from Kali Tello, the neighboring plantation. Bruno, a bachelor, had come unannounced in the hope of a borrel and the company of a young

Dutch woman, a rare commodity in the mountains. He arrived on his motorcycle and was dressed in dusty shorts. My hospitable mother, giddy with the excitement of so much company all at once, invited him to dinner as well and then did not pay attention to the proper seating arrangement at table, so that Mr. and Mrs. Smart did not end up sitting at my mother's right hand.

The next morning, Mr. Smart visited Didi at her house and scolded her: "Mrs. Engelberts, your behavior yesterday evening was abominable, and you make yourself cheap by inviting young men in shorts to your home!" Mr. Smart did not dwell too much on the fact that my father had been present during the visit by the young man in his dusty shorts. My humiliated and furious mother promptly ran out of her house, crying, leaving a startled Mr. Smart behind.

Weekly Letters Home

Didi and Daan's weekly letters home are full of stories about their life in the tropics, but they also show that they were homesick and looked forward to their furlough. One of my father's letters, written when he was twenty-seven years old, is full of his plans for the future, a future that would never be. My mother's part of the letter describes her life on the plantation and her longing for their vacation in Holland twenty-two months hence. The letter, excerpted below, was written to my mother's parents on November 25, 1938, and was mailed from the Donowarie Estate, Soember Poetjoeng, Java, Nederlands-Indie. Daan wrote:

> *Personal!*
>
> *One of these days I am expecting my annual share in the firm's profits, which I expect to be between 400 to 500 guilders. A large part of that will, of course, go to the Bank and together with what is already in the account will add up to about 1,600 guilders. It is too bad that I cannot make more with that money than 2.4% interest. I feel that that is too little. It should be possible to get 4 to 5% interest. That is why I am asking you for advice. I have recently been vested in a pension fund. The firm deposits 10% of my salary into that fund. This is paid on top of my salary. I will be eligible for my pension the moment I reach the age of 50. If all goes as expected, I can count on a pension of about 200 guilders per month when I am 50 years old. This is by no means enough, and if there are children in school or at university, it will be even less possible to live on that amount. I do have a life*

> *insurance policy of 5,000 guilders, which can be cashed when I turn 50 or upon my death. If that doesn't happen I will have that amount of money in hand as well. It is our intention to come back to Holland in 20 years' time. I must then be able to obtain my firm's pension of 200 guilders, but expect that I must add the same amount at a minimum to be able to live in Holland.*
>
> *You know that I would love to own or manage orchards. The question is this, Father, how much acreage does one need to earn 200 or 300 guilders per month, after expenses? And how would you advise us to invest the 1,600 guilders I spoke of before? I thought that it might be wise to buy some savings certificates but I don't really know much about them; do you happen to know? I would very much appreciate your reaction to this and if there is something that is not clear, please let me know.*

Unfortunately, my grandfather's reply is lost. Didi finished the letter:

> *Your letter, which we received yesterday, Mother, was wonderful and it made our day. Daan already has written that it was "Lebaran" yesterday, and I had given all the help a day off. I actually enjoyed having to do everything myself, even though I was not terribly thorough. I "did" the bedroom but not much else. In the afternoon I made pancakes, we still had some soup leftover, so dinner did not require a lot of work. Afterwards, Daan and I washed the dishes together—and we felt as if we were in Holland. Can you imagine? I think that it would not be so much fun if I had to run the household alone without help. That is a great advantage here in the Indies.*
>
> *Tomorrow we are off again—a pretty good week! The only thing is that we cannot leave because we are broke. We have to wait until next week for that. Darlings, do you know that we will be here one additional "Sinterklaas" [the Dutch celebration of the birthday of St. Nicholas on December 5] and then!!! .... I am not counting this "Sinterklaas" because this one is almost over. One more year plus ten months—is it not amazing? I can hardly believe it!*

After a page and a half of family gossip, Didi described the holiday of Lebaran:

> *During Lebaran the Inlanders celebrate a lot. They all buy new "baadjes" [tailored shirts for the women] and sarongs; hold many*

"slamatan" feasts; and have fireworks so that the noise is deafening. Our Kokkie also had a slamatan of course; she had cooked all sorts of delicious things. Among other things, she had made a kind of bread from flour, sugar and eggs. She made dough from these ingredients and then steamed the whole lot in a basket. She gave me one of these and it was delicious—it reminded us of the egg breads we eat at Easter time. It really was delicious—isn't it nice of her to do this? This is not something one hears much anymore—in the past this apparently happened much more, but not any more these days. I thanked her warmly of course, and it pleased me so much, because it also is an indication that they are happy here, that they are "senang." I am going to stop now—I just heard the whistle, which means that Daan will be home soon.

The Indonesian Muslim feast of Lebaran celebrates the end of Ramadan, the month-long period of fasting. It is tradition in Indonesia that Lebaran is celebrated with new clothes, fireworks and other lights, presents for the children, gifts for the poor, and visits with family and friends. Of course, in Indonesia, the feast also includes a slamatan, a huge festive meal, in which an abundance of food is cooked and consumed.

I remember going with Frits to such a slamatan after the war, when we were back in Indonesia in 1949 and lived in Makassar. The slamatan was given by our Baboe, Madja, who mostly took care of our little brother, Jan. Madja was much loved by all of us, and our parents trusted her completely with our safety; they had no concerns about leaving us in her care for the day. Frits and I, ages seven and nine, were treated like important guests in Madja's house and her village, and while we enjoyed the mountains of food and satays that were served, Madja and her family and neighbors looked on with pride. At the end of the meal, we drank a very grownup cup of *koppie toebroek*, strong coffee, diluted by lots of milk and sugar.

Well-made Plans, Slightly Adjusted

Didi and Daan had their lives well planned out. They would not have children right away but expected to wait at least five years. They would "go home" on furlough in the fall of 1940 and every five years thereafter, and they would save and leave the Dutch East Indies after twenty years to go back to Holland with their young family and some money in the bank. Of course, this plan was not as "fixed" as it seems at first blush. I was born in Malang on January 31, 1940, in the Roman Catholic Hospital Sawaan, three and a half years after their wedding. Didi and Daan gave me three names: Sytske because they liked that name, Aaltje after my maternal grandmother, and Dania after my paternal grandmother. Years later, when Jan, my little brother, was learning to speak and could not pronounce Sytske, he turned my name into Sia.

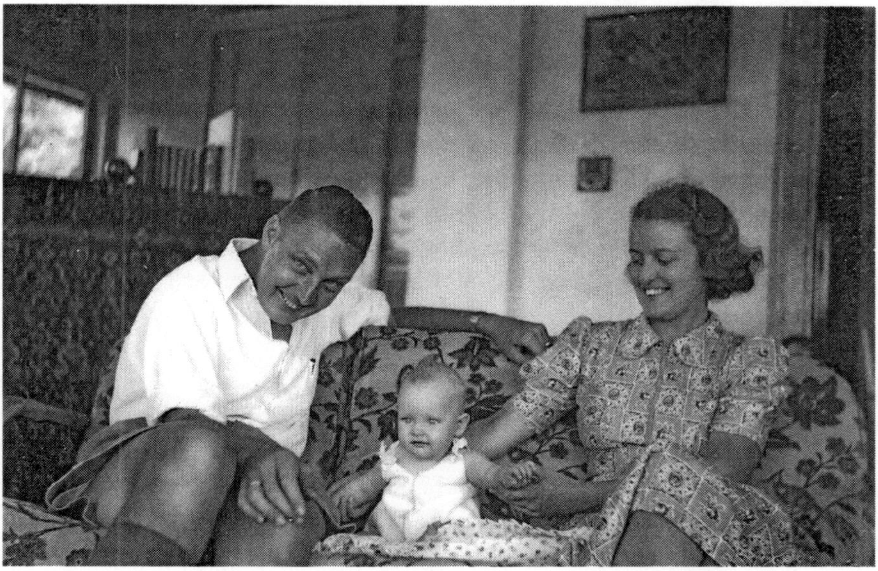

Proud parents and a happy baby—Sytske Aaltje Dania at six months, in Tjimatis, 1940

CHAPTER 2

PREPARING FOR WAR

Major events will take place any day now.

—Papa Daan's last postcard to Didi, written on February 26, 1942

The Dutch in Holland had remained optimistic throughout the decade of the 1930s; they hoped and expected that they would not be invaded by Germany but would remain neutral, just the way it had been during the First World War. But when I was just over three months old, my mother wrote about one awful day, a day that would never be forgotten: May 10, 1940, the day Germany invaded the Netherlands.

> *I was changing Sytske when Daan walked into the room to let me know: Holland had been invaded. The fear we had for the people there and when we would see them again! We had so much looked forward to show them our little love and now .... I cried with my head against her small little body and thought about the dangers for all little children, like ours, wanting to take her to a place where no one could ever find her.*

Soon after the invasion, the Germans discontinued regular mail service between Holland and its colony, and very few letters have survived that were mailed since then. On rare occasions, the International Red Cross was able to deliver mail and Didi and Daan were able to send at least one letter home to Deventer by way of the Red Cross. The letter arrived on June 11, 1941, and in it, Didi and Daan announced wonderful news—they were expecting their second baby. The letter made the rounds of the entire family, including also my grandparents Engelberts, who lived near the city of Leiden.

Sadly, the letter from Didi and Daan did not survive, but we know its contents from a six-page reply written by Didi's parents and their three other children: Gerrit, the eldest son, who was already at university in Delft, and the younger kids, Kuk and Pieter, who were attending high school and lived at home. The whole family had been excited about the new baby; they also wrote about their ordinary lives in Holland, without dwelling much on the German occupation. The primary topic was their joy in hearing my parents' "great news," even though my grandmother writes that the second baby followed me perhaps a little too closely and that it might have been better to have waited a little longer!

Opa and Oma de Jong and their kids wrote their long and cheerful reply on June 29, 1941. Their plan was to send the letter to a cousin, Ank Idzenga, who lived in Switzerland. Ank had agreed to forward the letter to Didi and Daan in Java; the plan was a perfectly good one because Switzerland had remained neutral and continued to maintain limited mail service between Europe and the Dutch East Indies. But none of the family in Deventer had considered the paranoia of the German censors in Holland. Their letter has survived because it was opened and read by the Germans and then returned to Deventer. The letter's envelope is stamped on both sides with German seals of the Oberkommando der Wehrmacht. According to the censors, the letter contained news and information intended for the enemy: "Nachrichtenvermittlung fur Feindland."

If my parents had received their happy letter, there would not have been much to celebrate back in the Indies, since my mother lost the baby in the summer of 1941. The little boy had been four months premature. Of course, if the letter had arrived in the Indies in 1941, it would have been lost with the Japanese invasion. Thanks to the Oberkommando der Wehrmacht, the letter was returned to the sender; it has been saved and is lying right here in Millerton next to me among the many other old letters that still exist.

Little Robert Fermin and Sytske going for a ride in the buggy pulled by a billy goat, the event supervised by a Djongos, dressed in the standard outfit of male house servants

Though Holland was now occupied by the Nazis, life for the Dutch in the East Indies did not change much initially.

In July 1940, my parents were transferred from Donowarie to Tjimatis in West Java, a plantation administered by Mr. Claassen. He and his wife became good friends of my parents, and I adored *Oom en Tante in de bergen*, uncle and aunt in the mountains, who maintained a farm with various farm animals. They even had Holstein cows with calves, and there was a flock of chickens that produced a daily supply of eggs, which I "helped" to gather in a little basket.

We lived in Tjimatis for a year, and in the summer of 1941, we were transferred to the small town of Djasinga, where my father managed an oil palm plantation. At Djasinga, I had playmates, among them Loetje and Herbert van Oyen and Robert Fermin, who had a room full of toy cars, a great rocking horse, and, best of all, a child-size buggy pulled by a real billy goat.

The Mobilization of All Able-bodied Men

Notwithstanding the Nazi occupation in Holland and the expats' worries about their families there, life in the East Indies remained idyllic for a while longer. Didi and Daan and most of their friends started second babies, but at the same time, with the increasing threat of war, all able-bodied male Dutch civilians were mobilized and required to prepare for war by participating periodically in defensive maneuvers with the Dutch colonial forces, het Koninklyk Nederlandsch-Indies Leger (KNIL), in preparation for a Japanese invasion of the islands.

Daan, second from right, and his friends preparing for war

The civilians were called up several times a year to participate in these war preparations; Daan was not very fond of these maneuvers, especially because they had to wear Dutch uniforms in the heat of the tropics—uniforms made of itchy, green wool! In any case, the maneuvers were not taken very seriously by the civilian recruits, especially because they had to work with far too few, and very antiquated, weapons.

During Papa Daan's absences from home, Didi and I would frequently stay with friends. When I was nine months old, we visited with Tante Mieke Hofstee, whose son, Jan Huug, was only two weeks older than I. We became friends later, but as babies, we were not entirely compatible, since Jan Huug was an agile baby who could stand and walk at nine months. While he ambled about in the playpen around me, I would lie on my back, contemplating the blue sky and the leaves moving in the trees overhead. For my mother and Tante Mieke, those were happy days, even though Papa Daan and Oom Buis Hofstee were both away, preparing for war.

In the years leading up to the war, few Dutch nationals had reason to wonder how the local population of Holland's 300-year-old colony, the thousands of islands known as the Dutch East Indies, would react to an invasion by the Japanese, and even though an independence movement had started among well-educated Indonesians years earlier, nobody expected that the people would turn against the Dutch if the country were ever to be invaded by another Asian power.

When Soetardjo, a prominent member of the *Volksraad*, People's Council, and one of the leaders of the independence movement, suggested that a roundtable meeting be organized in 1938 to discuss the possible parameters of independence under some sort of Dutch protectorate, the Dutch authorities had rejected that idea. Even when Soetardjo offered a national statement of loyalty to the Dutch government in case of war, the Dutch rejected that initiative as well "Since the desire of the people of the Dutch East Indies to remain an integral part of the Dutch nation was not in dispute, a statement of loyalty was not necessary."

Until the very last, the Dutch government, in its arrogance, refused to believe that the local leaders were ready to govern, and they continued to believe that the majority of Indonesians were happy with the colonial status quo. The Dutch would pay dearly for this attitude during the war and especially afterward, when thousands of young Indonesian men started an armed uprising against the Dutch, under the guidance of Soekarno, who declared Indonesia's independence on August 17, 1945, and became Indonesia's first president in December 1949.

Pearl Harbor and the Start of World War II in Java

The threat of war in the Indies must have been on everyone's mind in 1941, yet the prevailing wisdom was that the Japanese threat could be discounted because it was highly unlikely that an Asian nation would be so bold as to try to invade a well-defended European colony. And, of course, Pearl Harbor had not happened yet in the summer of that year.

The Dutch remained convinced that in the unlikely event the Japanese were to invade and any real fighting would take place, it would be in the coastal towns, where they expected that they could contain the Japanese and defeat them easily. To protect the interior sections of Java, the Dutch East Indies forces had placed barriers of rocks and trees on various strategic points on the roads leading into the mountains as an added safeguard.

On December 8, 1941, a day after the attack on Pearl Harbor, the Dutch government in exile in London declared war on Japan and the mobilized civilians entered military service. Papa Daan was stationed in Soerabaja with his unit, and since a Japanese invasion was anticipated within weeks, my mother and I moved in with their friends Oom Heb and Tante Bep van Oyen, who lived on the plantation of Simpang, an estate also owned by Harrison and Crosfield, near the village of Pasir Madang in West Java. Oom Heb van Oyen was an insulin-dependent diabetic and had therefore not been called to arms but had remained at home with his wife and two sons. The plan was that Didi and I would stay with the van Oyens on their plantation in the mountains for a short while until all fighting and unrest had stopped and Papa Daan could come home again.

Staying with the van Oyens was a feast for me. I adored their sons, Herbert and Loetje, who were a few years older than I was. In addition, there were Meindert and Anke Bolhuis, the children of friends of the van Oyens whose parents lived in Buitenzorg. The Bolhuis children and my mother and I lived with the van Oyens at Simpang for several weeks until the middle of February, when all of us moved to Tjileungsa, another plantation, located even farther away from civilization.

My Second Birthday and the Last Days of Peace

Didi and I traveled to Soerabaja in January 1942 to visit Jan's mother, Oma Borgerhoff, and to spend some time with Papa Daan. The weeks with Oma Borgerhoff were a last fling of normalcy during which we celebrated my second birthday on January 31, 1942, with lots of love and far too many presents, but the days in Soerabaja, an important harbor town and the main port of the Dutch navy, were also marred by the oncoming war. At the end of our visit, we experienced the first bombing of the city by the Japanese. For two hours, all of us hid under Oma Borgerhoff's bed for shelter, while I had a major tantrum because I had been promised a bath outside in the yard and could not understand why I could not have it. Papa Daan accompanied us back to our home that

Didi and two-year-old Sytske in Soerabaja weeks before the Japanese invasion

evening, but his stay was short. A few days later, when I woke up from my afternoon nap, Papa Daan was gone and none of my prayers to *Onze Lieve Heertje*, Our Dear Little Lord, were answered. We would never see Papa Daan again.

I have two postcards written by Papa Daan on February 26, 1942, two days before the Japanese invasion. He writes that he is glad we are safe with the van Oyens at Pasir Madang and that he is well. He is still in Soerabaja and mentions that he will send "the photo" to us now that he has a print himself. He has also given a print to Oma Borgerhoff. The photograph he refers to is probably the one of my mother and me, which Daan later had copied into two pencil drawings.

Daan also mentions that Oma Borgerhoff has been overwrought and that she, at his suggestion, recently left Soerabaja to join her daughter, Tiek, in Semarang. The second card, written on the same day, mentions that "major events will take place any day now" and that any mail from now on should be addressed to him as follows: D.L.A. Engelberts, Military Sergeant, First Class, 153011, IV Infantry III.

The Japanese Invasion

Daan was right. The Second World War became a reality for us in Java when a large Allied fleet, consisting of units of the American, British, Dutch, and Australian navies (ABDA), under the command of Dutch Admiral Karel Doorman, was attacked by the Japanese in the Java Sea on February 27, 1942. ABDA's fleet consisted of two heavy and three light cruisers and nine destroyers. The battle lasted two nights and one day but was fatally lost when the Japanese fleet used its underwater torpedoes to sink the Allied ships. Several subsequent encounters between the remaining elements of the ABDA fleet and the Japanese resulted in the nearly total destruction of that fleet, leaving Indonesia with no protection against the Japanese invading force. An estimated 2300 ABDA

A serious Papa Daan in the uniform of the Dutch colonial forces, days before the start of the war

men were lost at sea; among the casualties was the Dutch commander, Admiral Karel Doorman.

The destruction of the ABDA fleet meant that the Japanese had no trouble landing on the north coast of Java in the night of February 28. Three and a half years of the Japanese occupation began when the Dutch colonial government capitulated on March 8. The capitulation effectively ended three centuries of Dutch rule, which would be only briefly reestablished after the end of World War II. From then until August 1945, my mother, Frits, I, and my two fathers were all "Guests of the Emperor of Japan," a sarcastic term widely used by POWs and internees.

Though the invasion had been expected, the Dutch forces, poorly trained and using antiquated equipment, had been no match for the Japanese. In addition, the Dutch East Indies Army, consisting of some 140,000 men who had primarily acted as a police force and who had no military training, was spread over the entire archipelago of thousands of islands. Furthermore, the Dutch forces were seriously demoralized after the fall of Singapore in February 1942 and the debacle of the Java Sea.

CHAPTER 3

OUR FLIGHT INTO THE WILDERNESS

After the Japanese invasion we arrived in Buitenzorg on March 17th. We had lost everything—but we were alive and healthy. Nothing else mattered then and I couldn't care less. I was just very thankful that we had survived.

—Didi's first letter to her family in Holland, written on November 12, 1945

Taken in February 1942, the picture shows the five children who participated in the flight into the woods. From left to right: Herbertje van Oyen, Sytske, Meindert Bolhuis, Loetje van Oyen, and Ankie Bolhuis

Three days after the invasion, on March 3, our little group, guided by Oom Heb van Oyen, took flight into the jungles of Bantam on West Java in an effort to escape the Japanese troops. Oom Heb, Tante Bep, Didi—who was six months pregnant at the time—and the five children between the ages of two and eight escaped into the woods; I was the youngest, having just turned two.

In her first letter home after the war, Didi wrote:

I will tell you later the details of that trek to Buitenzorg—the most important thing is that we survived the ordeal and the rest is not important. ... At the time I was with the van Oyen family Bep and Herbert, Heb for short, and their two boys, Herbertje and Loetje. In addition there were two other children with us from Buitenzorg—Ank and Meink Bolhuis [their mother was a nurse and their father was also mobilized]. With this group we made the trek through the woods. Thank God Heb was with us, because without him we would not have survived. We were robbed immediately after the invasion—and there was a time when I walked around on bare feet, dressed in a bathing suit and a very muddy dress, with next to me a pale urchin of two, dressed in a sweater and pants, she at least still had her shoes. I was pregnant with Frits then—we walked 12 days through the jungle followed by insurgents who robbed us of our last few pennies.

I have three different sources of information about our terrible two weeks in the jungle trying to evade the Japanese only to be chased and robbed by local *Rampokkers*, or insurgents. Oom Heb van Oyen wrote a report at the end of March 1942, days after we arrived in Buitenzorg. His account of our flight is a draft of a formal complaint, in Dutch a *Proces Verbaal*, addressed to the Dutch authorities. In it, Oom Heb complains that we had not been protected at all by the Dutch colonial forces and that many KNIL military men had deserted their posts immediately following the Japanese invasion. He was especially bitter about the failure of the authorities to anticipate and prepare for an anti-Dutch uprising in the event the Japanese invasion would prove to be successful. Given the occupation of Indonesia and the Netherlands in 1942, it is unlikely that the draft of his complaint was ever received by the Dutch government. A copy of the Proces Verbaal in Dutch can be found in the appendix.

The second account was written much later by Meindert Bolhuis, who was eight years old in March 1942 when he participated in the flight into the jungle. Meink, as he was called, wrote his account decades later from memory. His version of the events of those horrible weeks in the jungle adds color and feeling to the sober facts described by Oom Heb.

The third account of our time in the jungle is a short entry in my baby book, written by Didi in the fall of 1942:

On March 3rd we fled into the jungle.... I am not going to write much about that terrible flight—it doesn't belong in a book such as this. Mercifully, Syts doesn't remember anything about it. It was such a terrible thing for our little one. The first days were all right—she amused herself in the beautiful tent, with all the new impressions.

But after that it began ....When she had to be quiet and didn't understand why Mammie was angry with her while she had not been bad and when she was spanked to keep quiet—she wanted to talk and laugh and have fun. When she had to travel in the night—carried, but still exhausted ..... When she was carried by filthy dirty coolies and didn't want them to and screamed that Mammie had to carry her, and I couldn't, and would just look away, because that would quiet her quickest.... When she thought that we were on our way to Papa Daan and talked about all the things we would do when we were home—Sytske would eat meat and tomatoes; Sytske would drink tea with Papa Daan; Sytske would drink milk .... And then to see her pale little face, so terribly white, marked with red mosquito bites and then—those filthy pants she wore—she wetted her pants often and I could not clean her or give her dry clothes. I was the happiest in the night when she slept in my lap or on top of me to keep warm.

Oom Heb's *Proces Verbaal* is stark. He did not put much emotion into his complaint, but he wrote a gripping tale. He had shepherded the two young women and five small children successfully during the two-week flight through the jungle. He had faced hundreds of angry Rampokkers, many of whom had worked on the plantations and had turned against the Dutch after the Dutch defeat by the Japanese. He had witnessed the destruction of the houses, factories, and administrative buildings of three estates for which he had been responsible. He had lost all of his family's belongings. He had lost his insulin and, at the end of the two weeks, he had surrendered to the Japanese with his small group intact.

We had escaped the violence with no more than the clothes on our backs.

Oom Heb's Account

Of the experiences of H.D. van Oyen. Wife and two sons, 6 and 5 years of age, Mrs. Engelberts and daughter of 2 years, and Meindert and Ankie Bolhuis, respectively 8 and 6 years old during the period from 1 through March 17, of the year 1942...

—Herbert van Oyen, unpublished manuscript, Buitenzorg, March 1942

Oom Heb's account starts on February 28, when the chief administrator at Djasinga left and he was put in charge of the administrative and financial affairs of several plantations. Oom Heb received 15,000 guilders in cash to pay all employee expenses, including two months' advance salaries, as well as to terminate outstanding transactions for the three plantations near Djasinga: Tjigeloeng, Gedeh, and Tjipalar.

Oom Heb, still at Simpang, the plantation he administered, methodically closed the accounts of the estate and distributed the money and rice supplies among the European and local employees of the three plantations. He took the time to determine the value of the harvest in the *goedangs*, warehouses, and gave instructions to supervisors and other remaining personnel to carry on in his absence. In the end, he still had more than 7,000 guilders in his possession, a huge amount of money in those days, which almost cost him and us our lives.

Oom Heb also took time to pack two cars with his family's belongings. By six o'clock in the afternoon of March 1, one car and driver departed for Tjileungsa, where Tante Bep, my mother, and the five children were staying, but by then, the Japanese were rapidly advancing into the interior of the island. Tensions were already mounting, and the defensive forces in the mountains were on high alert. As a result, the driver of the first car was refused passage by the Dutch forces and was told to return to Simpang. Then, at eight o'clock in the evening, Oom Heb received a phone call from the chief administrator advising him that the Japanese had arrived in Tjipanas, not far from Simpang. He ordered Oom Heb to leave immediately for Tjileungsa to join the women and children there.

During the early evening, Oom Heb remained at his house at Simpang to call several other people in an effort to warn them and to obtain more information himself. The messages he received were not encouraging. The local battalion of the army was already in disarray, and according to his informant, various soldiers "had lost their heads," deserted their posts, and fled to the woods. Oom Heb's informant advised him to spend the night in the woods as well because he could not depend any longer on protection from the army.

Soon after that call, the phone lines went dead and communication with the outside world became impossible.

> *The departure from Simpang took place at 12 midnight, on March 1st, 1942 in the pouring rain, which had started earlier that morning. As a result of the rain, the heavily packed cars immediately got stuck in the mud, but with the help of 5 "koelies" [plantation workers] the autos were freed and the trip continued until I arrived at Tjileungsa at five thirty in the morning. That was the morning of March 2, 1942. That day, at twelve noon Djasinga fell into the hands of the Japanese, who had been accompanied by Rampokkers from Bantam.*

The Tent in the Jungle

Immediately upon arrival at Tjileungsa, where the rest of us had been waiting for him, Oom Heb met with the administrator, who had preceded him to Tjileungsa. They agreed that Oom Heb should keep the remaining 7,000 guilders still in his possession for distribution at another time.

The following morning, Oom Heb and Meindert went to the woods to set up a tent in a clearing in the jungle across a small lake, Pintoes Ajer, which had been a beloved vacation spot in earlier times. The tent was put up to offer us a hiding place from the Japanese in the event they got as far as Tjileungsa. Food and supplies that servants had brought earlier to the boathouse at Pintoes Ajer were hidden. Oom Heb and Meink also destroyed most of the canoes kept at Pintoes Ajer for the vacationing Dutch, sinking them to the bottom of the small lake. Only two canoes were saved for our use.

While Oom Heb and Meindert were in the woods, putting up the tent, Tante Bep and my mother, with the four younger children, had remained at the bungalow in Tjileungsa, anxiously awaiting Oom Heb's and Meink's return, but at noon, before Oom Heb and Meinke had returned, some of the workers of the estate came running to the bungalow and warned the two women that a force of 200 Japanese soldiers was no more than two kilometers away from Tjileungsa. Soon after their warning, we could hear "unusual and loud noises" from the factory buildings. Thoroughly frightened, Tante Bep and Didi and the four youngest children fled in a panic to Pintoes Ajer to join Oom Heb and Meindert in the woods. We arrived at Pintoes Ajer at about two in the afternoon and quickly paddled across the pond to the other side. Our flight had begun. We spent the night of March 3 in the tent in the jungle.

Unfortunately, in their hurry to leave Tjileungsa, Tante Bep and Didi had left everything behind, worst of all Oom Heb's insulin, making it necessary for him to go back to retrieve the metal medicine box filled with first aid supplies and his insulin. On March 4, dressed in bathing trunks and carrying his rifle and some ammunition, Oom Heb went back to the house at Tjileungsa while the rest of us waited for his return in our tent in the jungle.

Meindert described our mood while we were waiting for Oom Heb's return: "He stayed away for hours. We listened anxiously to every sound we heard. We wondered if he had found his insulin and whether he would disclose our whereabouts when he returned."

When Oom Heb arrived at the bungalow, he did not find any Japanese troops there but did find a large crowd of locals. He recognized many of them, a large number of whom were employees of the plantations in the area. The crowd of angry men was in the process of looting whatever they could carry and eagerly destroying everything else. The lovely house we had left only twenty-four hours earlier was already utterly demolished by then. When the crowd saw Oom Heb, they ran away and disappeared among the trees. Oom Heb was able to collect his insulin and some of the other medicines that had been scattered by the mob, but he was terribly upset about how little remained of the house and its furnishings.

When Oom Heb returned to us in the tent and reported to Tante Bep and my mother about the dreadful situation at the bungalow in Tjileungsa, the adults realized that we could no longer count on the help of house servants or plantation employees. We had no other option but to go to the house of a neighbor the next morning in the hope of finding shelter there. The woods were quiet on the night of March 4.

On March 5, Oom Heb left the tent early to see whether their neighbor's house was still intact, but the Rampokkers had arrived there before him and were already removing everything of value they could drag out. After he had observed the looting for a while, Oom Heb shot his rifle into the air to scare the mob away. When it was quiet, he gingerly entered the house. Like the bungalow in Tjileungsa, the neighbor's house was in a shambles. Oom Heb was shocked to see that everything that could not be carried off had been destroyed by the mob. Valuable Dutch paintings had been slashed, and antique furniture had been damaged by axes and knives. A valuable stamp collection was scattered outside in the mud. Oom Heb was particularly upset when he found the old and beloved Kokkie of their friend and neighbor trying to gather together whatever she could carry out with her.

The uprising of the native population, the destruction of Dutch property by angry mobs, and the widespread looting that followed came as a great surprise to many Dutch citizens. They had assumed loyalty, compassion, and help from the native population, many of whom had been much-beloved house servants. Instead, they encountered anger and glee over the Dutch defeat.

After Oom Heb had returned to our tent in the clearing, a group of Rampokkers attacked. First, we heard a loud scream from the direction of Pintoes Ajer, and then a shot was fired near the tent, followed by loud yelling and shouting. As had been agreed upon beforehand, the women and the five children fled by sliding into the ravine behind the clearing while Oom Heb ran in the opposite direction, making a lot of noise to attract attention to himself and away from us in the ravine.

While he was running through the woods and shooting his revolver in the air to attract attention, the angry mob followed Oom Heb, who soon got lost in the dense woods. Late in the afternoon, when it was quiet, he arrived at a little kali, a stream, which he followed until it trickled into Pintoes Ajer, near the spot where he had seen the local folks digging for the hidden provisions earlier that afternoon. By then, the men had disappeared and all seemed peaceful, except that the food supplies, the money, and the ammunition that had been hidden there days earlier were gone. Oom Heb later concluded that while he had been preparing to hide from the Japanese, spies among the local employees had observed where he had hidden the money and supplies.

For us women and children, the escape into the ravine had not been without harm. My pregnant mother had ended up sliding down the muddy slope until she was stopped by a log sticking out from the side of the ravine. She had landed violently, straddling the log between her legs. Miraculously, this fall did not start a miscarriage. Didi told me decades later that she believed that the baby was saved because she wore a woolen bathing suit under her dress. The bathing suit had been a tight fit for her, as she had a substantial belly by then, so it had protected her like a corset. Tante Bep, however, obtained nasty wounds that days later became badly infected.

Civilization, "Immensely Far Away"

Although the mob had not found us that afternoon, it was only going to be a matter of time. We had to get out of the woods and find safety. Oom Heb decided to head for Pasir Madang, where he believed a garrison of the army was stationed that, he hoped, would protect us. (Later, we found out that the garrison had deserted and had participated in the looting.) We left the tent at night and traveled by the light of the moon. The bigger children all carried a blanket and some food, the women carried their backpacks, and Oom Heb carried me. Meindert, who was eight years old at the time, later described this trek through the jungle:

> *The moon gave enough light that night so that we could see each other. We walked silently in a row along the dark, slippery paths of the mountain slopes. The only sound came from the noise made of our clothes rubbing against the vegetation as we walked. Every now and then the light of a flashlight helped to determine our route and made sure we were all accounted for. We did not go very fast, the children walked erratically and kept stopping whenever something got their attention. The path curved through the various plantations, which we had to traverse on our way to civilization, which seemed immensely far away.*

Later, we rested on a path in the plantation gardens on *atap*, sheets of woven palm leaves. After all he had been through, Oom Heb still was most concerned about the children. He wrote, "Although there is an immense amount of mosquitoes, the children sleep well for several hours, since we can cover them in their blankets."

Early the next morning, Oom Heb went alone to the small village of Pasir Madang, near the estate where the van Oyens and my parents used to live. He found our house completely empty, but he met several people whom he recognized, among them Sarim and Brani, who had worked for us and were willing to help, but they ran away when a mob of more than 150 Rampokkers approached with guns and knives. Oom Heb was eventually able to calm the threatening crowd by his description of the condition of the young children who were hidden in the jungle.

Things had not gone well for the women and children, however. While Oom Heb had been negotiating with the large mob, a smaller group of Rampokkers had discovered us. Meindert described this attack:

> *All of a sudden the quiet mood in the woods was disturbed. Yelling loudly, a mob of Rampokkers with guns and knives came running up the hill towards us. The moment I saw them I ran for my life. Out of the corner of my eye I saw one of the aunts disappear with some of the children. I had only one goal: to hide somewhere. I found a gully at the edge of the tea plantation and with my heart bouncing in my throat I hid under the sheltering branches of the tea. When the yelling stopped the quiet was deafening. Where was everyone? How can you find your companions in these vast tea gardens? After waiting for a long while I crept out of my hiding place and went back to the clearing in the woods. No one was at the campsite except for my aunt and her little daughter; everyone else was out of sight. Had they just stayed there while the Rampokkers showed up? In any case, they had robbed us of everything. They had even yanked the silver chain with an identity tag from the little girl's neck, leaving a nasty gash.*

That little girl was me. Didi later wrote Oma in 1945:

> *We walked 12 days through the woods, followed by Rampokkers who robbed us of our last few pennies; including also my wedding ring, and my gold bracelet and Sytske's silver necklace with identity tag—they*

took everything. I had sewn Daan's watch in my bathing suit. They tried three times to take that from me as well, and three times I screamed hysterically when they tried—and that made them give up that idea.

The Rampokkers had robbed us of everything we owned: the blankets, the little bit of food that was left, money and jewelry, and, worst of all, Oom Heb's backpack in which he carried his insulin; all we had left were the clothes we were wearing. The only item the Rampokkers had not found was Oom Heb's wallet, containing the bulk of the estate's funds, which he had hidden under some tea bushes before he left that morning.

Upset and frightened, we stayed hidden under the tea for the rest of that day.

Because March is in the middle of the annual monsoon season, we were constantly bothered by torrential rainstorms. Drenched by another downpour that evening, we were too cold and wet and too tired to notice that we had not eaten much that day. Oom Heb had no choice but to go back to the hamlet of Pasir Madang in the pitch dark and look for the house of a factory worker, Kasim, to ask him for shelter, but Kasim refused to take us in because his home was filled with Indonesian soldiers—deserters from KNIL—from Djasinga. Kasim did show some compassion, however, and gave Oom Heb warm food and tea to take back to us, hidden in the sodden woods.

When the rain stopped and the moon had come out from among the clouds, we walked toward the outbuildings of the plantation near Pasir Madang, where we found an open shack. The adults were able to make a fire so that the exhausted children could sleep. Oom Heb and the women stayed awake to keep the fire going. Although the place was dry, it was filthy, the floor covered in feces. Even that sorry place of refuge was not safe, however, for in the middle of the night, a group of seven army deserters showed up to demand money. Surrounded on all sides by angry men, Oom Heb gave them each 100 guilders, the entire visible contents of his wallet.

Early in the morning of March 7, Kasim showed up at the shack and warned us that we were not safe and had to leave, and so we continued on our way. By then, everyone in the surrounding *kampongs*, small settlements for local people, knew where we were. That evening, we received a visit from Pa Laimin, who owned a *warong*, a small shop, in another village near Djasinga. He sounded concerned and helpful and offered to get food for us, but when Oom Heb promised Pa Laimin a reward of 200 guilders if he could arrange a safe shelter for us, Pa Laimin became belligerent. He had heard that we had much more money hidden somewhere, and he wanted it all. From then on, his offers of help and food stopped, and throughout the entire next day, we felt we were being watched.

Protecting the Children in a Cold Bed of Mud

In the evening of March 7, the rains came again. To keep the children warm, the adults slept on the ground in puddles of mud with the children on top of them. Didi cradled me on top of her rounded belly, Tante Bep held her own two sons, and Oom Heb sheltered Meindert and his sister, Anke. The woods were phosphorescent that night, which frightened the older children. Didi remembered that night well. When she felt warm moisture dripping between her legs in the middle of the night, her immediate fear was that her water had broken and that she was miscarrying. Later, she realized that the moisture had come from me peeing in my pants.

On March 8, four men showed up demanding more money from Oom Heb. They were quite well informed about us and knew that Oom Heb had hidden money earlier at Pintoes Ajer. During negotiations with them, Oom Heb told them that we had nothing left, but he did tell the men where the table silver had been hidden near the little pond. The men threatened that they would be back if they did not find anything there. Although Oom Heb's gamble paid off, we were far from safe because he still had several hundred guilders in paper money that had been distributed among the three adults; we had to get rid of it fast. The question was, how? The woods were full of people watching us, so we couldn't throw it away or burn it. In desperation, the adults finally tried to swallow the filthy bills, but there were far too many, and after Didi and Tante Bep began to gag on the stinking pieces of paper, they finally ended up sewing the remainder in the lining of one of our raincoats.

The four men showed up later and agreed to help us get back to the plantation houses at Tjileungsa in the night of March 8. Our bungalow, which we had left only five days earlier, was a sorry sight. Meindert described the scene:

> *We had returned to the plantation, this time by walking rather than by car. We had not been gone for very long but it seemed an eternity. The place was unusually quiet—no noise was heard coming from the factory and there were no human voices—the only sounds we heard were the sounds from the woods. When we turned the corner and saw the famil-*

iar house and its grounds, we stood and looked quietly at the destruction. Every door and window stood wide open as if there had been an explosion. Our belongings were scattered throughout the yard; books had been lying in the rain and had turned into sodden heaps—we entered the humid and deserted house gingerly.

Later Uncle Heb took me to the factory building where the machines had been destroyed. We stood quietly looking at the giant gear of one of the machines that had been removed from its axle. How had they accomplished that? In the repair shop, where nuts and bolts had been neatly stored in wooden boxes, the contents were now lying in a hodgepodge on the floor. With fear we looked around. We felt that we were being watched but were not sure. Down below, the houses of the workers were deserted. We remained in one of them that night, sleeping on piles of rubber sheeting.

Although war is usually filled with mindless destruction, the anger of the local population towards the Dutch may have been caused by several factors: First, Oom Heb had not been able to distribute the funds required to cover the pay of the local workforces when he was preparing to leave for Tjileungsa; second, many of the local workers had fallen under the influence of outside instigators from Bantam; and third, the Indonesian people, under the guidance of Dutch-educated leadership, had been hearing repeated rumors about their work towards independence.

After days in the wilderness, our situation had become hopeless. We desperately needed a doctor to look at the festering wound in Tante Bep's leg, and Oom Heb's condition had seriously deteriorated without the necessary insulin. On March 11, we arrived at Kampong Koening, where we were warmly greeted. Many of the women from the kampong visited with tears in their eyes, but we were not given shelter—Oom Heb assumed that the houses of the local population contained too much of the loot that had been carried away by the Rampokkers.

We finally ended up back at Simpang, the estate that had been managed by the van Oyens. At Simpang, most of the houses were also in ruins. Doors and windows had been removed and smashed to pieces, tile floors were broken, and even porcelain washbasins and toilet bowls had been dragged outside and destroyed. In the factory buildings, everything of value that could be carried off was gone, and the remaining machinery had been demolished. Because we had not much choice, we selected the only house that remained more or less intact. Because

Tante Bep had developed a high fever and everyone needed a rest, we stayed there several nights.

After having run wild for more than a week, the rage of the local people had burned out, and many of them took pity on us and brought us food and drinks. After a while, the many visits from the local people became a serious burden because we needed sleep and were kept awake by them at all times of the day and night.

First Sighting of Japanese Soldiers

On the eleventh day of our trek through the jungle, March 14, all of us suffered from dysentery. We could barely walk anymore after walking barefoot on the wet paths of the jungle. We desperately had to get out of the woods and find our way to Buitenzorg, the town where Meink's and Anke's parents lived. That day, several men helped to carry the youngest children, and as we walked slowly out of the woods along the slippery paths of the *sawahs*, rice paddies, Oom Heb was able to toss his gun into the water before we got to the main road—and then we saw Japanese troops.

Oom Heb described the scene:

> *And then, near Toge we saw several cars with Japanese soldiers. The local people who had been helping us all day stayed behind and we slowly walked towards the Japanese, who checked me thoroughly for weapons. They didn't touch the children and barely checked the women. It was difficult to communicate with the soldiers, but they finally unloaded an opelette which was filled with weapons, and transported us to Doctor Sahit. I was interrogated at length and with great difficulty by the Japanese and in the end I received a travel pass for myself and my seven companions.*

Didi was terribly afraid of the Japanese advance troops we saw that day for the first time as we walked out of the woods with our hands above our heads in surrender. The Japanese were naked except for loincloths. To her, they were a frightening sight because she had heard earlier stories about how the Japanese troops raped young women and children. She knew that the Japanese soldiers could be violent and ruthless.

Actually, the Japanese at Toge started laughing when they saw us. To them, we must have been an amazing sight: a six-foot-tall disheveled Dutchman with a two-week-old beard, two barefoot women, one of whom was quite pregnant, and five muddy children.

A Wild-eyed Woman in the Mirror

For two days, March 15 and 16, we remained in the home of Doctor Sahit and his wife, who gently took care of us. Years later, Didi told me that she saw a woman there in the mirror, dressed in a sarong, with unkempt hair and wild eyes—in her confusion, she had not immediately realized that she was that unrecognizable woman.

Lots of food and sleep were a blessing and restored us enough to continue on our way towards the town of Buitenzorg, where Meindert's parents lived. Meindert described the last day of our trek:

> *We started the final phase of our trip to Buitenzorg. The trip was not as simple as I had anticipated. Almost every bridge had been seriously damaged or had been blown up. Sometimes we crossed the rivers by small, overloaded boats, other times we clambered over the ruins of destroyed bridges. The stream of folks traveling back and forth was huge, consisting of merchants, peddling their wares, travelers with suitcases, and local people on errands. We finally ended up riding the last kilometers in a "Deleman," a horse drawn buggy. Then, at the outskirts of Buitenzorg, we saw our Djongos who had come to look for us near the last bridge we had to cross. It was unbelievable to see Karna standing there among the other people. In his clean and starched white clothes he stood out among the disheveled and moving mass of people. Were they all looking for lost relatives, friends or business partners, or was the tension of the last days broken and were they trying to start their ordinary daily routines? In any case, Karna was there, the man on whom my mother relied in those unsure and frightening days of the beginning of the Japanese occupation. Seeing him again enabled me to relax. His well-known voice and his actions made me forget the rest of the walk home.*

The Aftermath of War

Didi later wrote Oma in Deventer what it was like to see the destruction left behind by the deserting troops and the Rampokkers:

> *Lately I have often thought of* Gone with the Wind—*I too know now what it is like to see everything destroyed around you .... With every house we approached on the way to Buitenzorg we wondered whether we would find it the way it once had been, but everything was always destroyed—over and over again, ruined, filthy—over and over again—all those old, beloved homes—and when Scarlet passed them, her only thought had been: "will Mother still be there—then it won't matter—then I will be able to carry on...." But she did not get that.*

Her mother was no longer there. But my mother is still alive and that means everything to me right now—you, and the children, and everyone together, soon.

This image of abandoned and destroyed houses—windows wide open; doors hanging from their hinges; and furniture, toys, and books lying broken and sodden in the yards—is one that I also carry with me. When I read my mother's words, I recognized the desolation she described and felt the terrible sense of sadness and loss. This is perhaps the reason why I later built tiny villages from sticks and stones under the shrubbery in our gardens. The little worlds I created included houses, roads, gardens, and sawahs with water-supply systems made from hollow papaja stems. I began making these minuscule, peaceful worlds while we still lived in Bandoeng, at the end of 1945, when I was nearly six years old. I made the last one with building blocks in my grandmother's house in Deventer, when I had returned to Holland to attend boarding school at the age of twelve.

Of course, I realize now that I have one more peaceable world here in Millerton: a cozy house with a flower and vegetable garden and, the best part yet, a sweet man to share it with, and five cats who act as if they own the place.

The Relief of Warmth and Shelter

We received a lot of attention and kindness in Buitenzorg from friends and strangers alike. Oom Heb first rested for several days at the home of the Bolhuis family and then ended up in the hospital for further care. Didi and I were given rooms in a small pavilion attached to the house of a neighbor of the Bolhuis family at Tjilendek 39.

In Buitenzorg, we received an outpouring of help from people we didn't know but who had heard of our story. We received food, clothing, shoes, and medicines, and a Mrs. Van der Vecht, who had recently lost her own baby son, gave Didi an entire set of baby clothes. This generous gift included diapers, towels, and baby bottles. Mrs. Van der Vecht also had included a cake of soap which still had the teeth marks of the little boy who had died not long before. Best of all for me, she also had added a white Steiff teddy bear, and because I had lost all my toys, Didi gave the little bear to me. Little "Beary" became a steady playmate, which stayed with me throughout the war years and all the other years of my life. Still dressed in a now faded dress and panties, the small bear sits in front of me on a little chair in my study in Millerton.

Once we were in Buitenzorg, we were quickly restored to good health, but I had changed, according to Didi, who wrote in my baby book:

> *The sweet little baby who tended to go her own independent way without paying much attention to the grown-ups around her was changed into a child that was extremely well aware of her surroundings and everything she did. She was intentionally naughty, she whined and she was very demanding—and if only I had been able to react with a joke it might not have been so bad … but now I was irritable and quick with my anger. The first days she hung onto my skirts and when I did not have time for her (in the past I always had time for her) I put her outside the door to get rid of her—poor little thing.*

At the end of March, when Oom Heb was released from the hospital, he finished his *Proces Verbaal.* He ended his seven-page, densely typed story with the following words:

> *This is the incomplete and unadorned report of our experiences. The writer has only related salient facts with the intent to return to them later for further elaboration and to submit a formal indictment of the authorities who knew so little about the sentiments of the local population and who had taken so few and such feeble defensive measures. It is perhaps useless to complain after the fact, but as a Dutchman I have the right to expect that we would have fought with courage and I believe that if that had been the case, things would have been very different for us. Then the local population would not have gone wild. The Rampokkers had a few leaders and the rest consisted of followers who had had enough after a week and who quickly regretted their actions. Just as we Europeans will be injured by coming events, so will they be affected.*

CHAPTER 4

THE START OF THE JAPANESE OCCUPATION

We have a lot to be thankful for Jan; it could have been so much worse. You learn quickly to sort between what is important and what is not in these times and in the same way you become more knowledgeable about people .... People, from whom you did not expect much, whom you did not even know, gave generously from the little they had. Disappointments occurred too of course, but those were few and in the minority.

—Letter from Didi to Jan, her best friend, March 24, 1942

Rumors were flying in the chaos of those first weeks of the Japanese occupation, with everyone trying to find out where wives, husbands, children, other relatives, and friends were located. Who had survived? Who had died? Who was wounded? For more than a month, Didi did not know where Papa Daan was. He had been garrisoned in Soerabaja when the war began; she had no idea how bad the fighting had been there and, if he had survived, where he was after the capitulation. Finally, on April 16, she learned that Papa Daan had survived the invasion and that he was held by the Japanese as a prisoner of war in Malang.

We have several letters written between Jan and Didi during those first few months, which clearly were not censored. The first letter from Jan was written at Tasikmalaya, less than two weeks after the capitulation. Jan's postcard did not reach us until June 1942.

Tasikmalaya, 20 March, 1942

Dear Didi:
Have you heard from Daan? I suspect not because he is in East Java and communications have not been reestablished. Don't worry about him; I am sure he is safe. How are you and Sytske? Did you stay on in Djasinga? We know so little about what has happened in your area. Although I was on the road to Djasinga, the day before Buitenzorg

fell, all was quiet then. Buis must have been in your area. Have you heard from him? My mother is probably in Bandoengan, while Tiek is in Solo or Semarang. I don't know where Jan [Tiek's husband, Jan Simonsz] is located. I hope very much to hear good news from all of you soon. In my mother's last letter to me she sang Daan's praises. He had been a big help to her in Soerabaja. Later I will thank him myself but for now I thank you. I very much hope that Jan and Tiek are in close proximity to each other, at least they will be able to see each other. They have had so little time together. I don't have the slightest idea when we will be able to go home but I remain an optimist. Please remain an optimist too. Please write soon and keep up your good spirits. Give Sytske greetings from "Oompie." Bye, much love from Jan.

When the Japanese began to take control of the Dutch colony, each civilian received an identity card, had to obey curfews, and lived with various restrictions on life. Starting in early May, the Japanese censored all mail and demanded that everyone write in Malay on postcards so the Indonesian censors could read the messages. This was particularly hard on Oma Borgerhoff, who had arrived in Java relatively recently and did not speak much Malay.

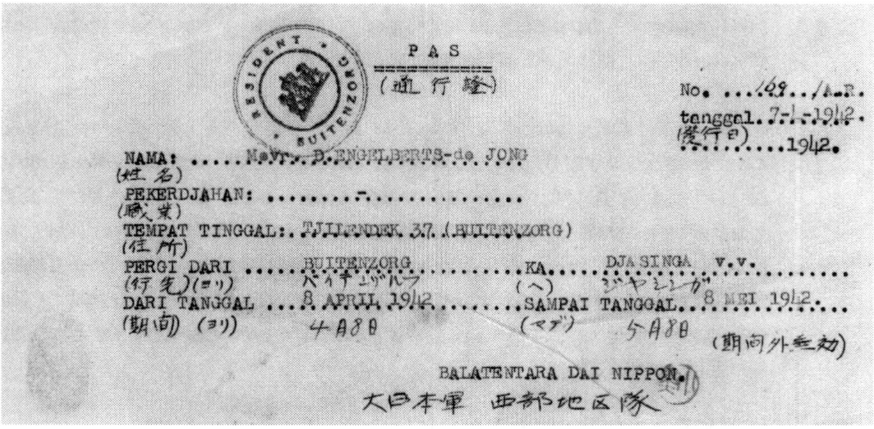
PAS
(通行證)
No. ...169../A.R.
tanggal. 7-1-1942.
(発行日) ....1942.
NAMA: .....Mevr. D. ENGELBERTS-de JONG
(姓名)
PEKERDJAHAN: ....-..............
(職業)
TEMPAT TINGGAL:. TJILENDEK 37 (BUITENZORG)
(住所)
PERGI DARI .....BUITENZORG..........KA........DJASINGA v.v.
(行先)(ヨリ) バイテンゾルフ (へ) ジヤシンガ
DARI TANGGAL ...8 APRIL 1942........SAMPAI TANGGAL...8 MEI 1942...
(期間)(ヨリ) 4月8日 (マデ) 5月8日
(期間外無効)
BALATENTARA DAI NIPPON.
大日本軍 西部地区隊

Didi's indentity card, issued by the Japanese at the onset of the occupation

Of course, the mail was not reliable, with or without censorship, since so many people had been displaced and the addresses of many of the men who had been imprisoned by the Japanese were unknown, but finally, on April 24, Didi received a letter from Oma Borgerhoff, who wrote to tell her where Jan was located. The next day, Didi wrote him a long letter from Buitenzorg:

> *Dear Jan:*
> *Yesterday I received a letter from your mother to my great delight. She had written me a letter earlier to let me know that Daan was safe in Malang but I never received it. Fortunately I already knew but only since April 16. Buis had told me that you were in Tjimahi. Before then I had written Miel to find out if he knew where you were, but he didn't know either. I then wrote to you in Tjimahi but they referred me to the Red Cross. And now you are in Tasik. And how are you now, Jan? You wrote that you are still coughing. Will you be careful Jan? I, old lady that I am, must impress upon you that you must be careful. Bronchitis is not really that bad but the chance is that it will linger and turn into something much worse.*
>
> *You have probably heard about our adventures, so, I will not write too much about that. All of us have survived—it could have been so much worse. Heb van Oyen is the only one who was in a bad way. He has diabetes and needed his injections daily. And he was not getting any during those days. It is a miracle that he did not collapse much earlier. I believe that the knowledge that he had to take care of all of us kept him going, because once he was here, he collapsed completely. He also got dysentery but now all is well with him.*
>
> *I am doing well. Initially it looked as if Frederik Christiaan would arrive early, but that did not happen and now I assume he will be born in the end of May. Syts has become heavy—she is eating very well after those weeks of hunger and she weighs more now than she did during the last weeks in Djasinga. She is perhaps a bit more difficult than she was before, but otherwise not very changed. The first days she only wanted to sit on my lap, not a good sign for Syts who usually does not like to cuddle.*
>
> *Your mother wrote that I can always ask you for help when I need money. Very sweet of you both, Jan, but it is not necessary. I just received my declaration book which states that I get 100 guilders monthly (at least for now—knock on wood!) I am therefore doing better than many. We were supposed to have received three months' salary, but that too has been stolen. But let's not talk about that. There are worse things than that, such as things that belonged to Syts and*

things from home—things without much monetary value… O, there I go again—every now and then it resurfaces, even though I try to fight those feelings.

Dear Jan, I hope I will hear from you soon. I wish you my very best, get better soon and you too don't worry, Jantje! How nice that Tiek still has an income, which must be a relief for your mother. Do you know anything about Piet Tiedeman? I have not heard a thing. Have many of your friends fallen? It is so terrible that in a war such as this one, so many men have died; and then to think about our navy… Bye Jan, much love from your Didi.

On May 7, Didi wrote Jan a postcard in Malay. My translation follows.

Dear Jan:

Thank you so much for your postcard, which I received yesterday. About a week ago I heard from Mr. Sythof and I was very happy with his letter. Mr. Sythof has taken some things to East Java and some letters to Daan, in the care of Mrs. A. v.d. Stadt, Soembing weg 2, Malang. I am very happy to have heard about Daan, now I know he is all right. I am no longer receiving any deposits in my delegation book. In the future I may ask you for some help. At the moment I don't need it—I am o.k.! But if I can save a little money it would be good. I have not heard from Buis and hope that he is well in Soekaboemi. Sytske is doing well—she can be quite naughty. She can now speak Malay like a native! "Stop disini!" [Stop here], this to the driver of a buggy. "Soedah ada tida perloe" [We have that already, we don't need it], this to a door-to-door peddler—quite funny! I am planning to write Semarang tomorrow and hope that you will hear soon from your family there. I am so happy with your letter. Good-bye, Jan—I will write soon again, after the arrival of Frederik Christiaan, expected around the 20th. I will be in the hospital. Good-bye from Didi and Sytske.

By May, regular mail had become unreliable, but private couriers were still traveling between some of the towns on Java. A letter Jan wrote to my mother on May 4 was sent by private courier to her in Buitenzorg. In the letter, Jan writes that he had heard about our weeks in the jungle, and he included 250 guilders to help with the impending birth of Frits.

I heard here that the payments of "delegations" and withdrawals from savings accounts have been stopped as of May 1. Furthermore, you are entitled to a little bit of ease a month before the birth of Frederik Christiaan, and your son will need some clothes ... and that is why I am enclosing 250 guilders. Don't tell me you don't need it because I am sure you can use it and you should not let it bother you but accept it, because I think it completely natural that we help each other. And in case you do not need it now, keep it for the coming weeks or months. Make sure that you, Syts and Frederik get enough and that you remain healthy, so that you will be able to meet Daan hale and hearty in a couple of months, looking like "Holland's Welvaren" [Dutch Prosperity].

Jan then gives my mother several addresses of friends located in different towns in Java who might be able to help her if she ever found herself there. He then continues:

Piet Tiedeman is safe in Bandoeng. He fought like a lion and with success. About my war experience I have little to tell you. At most someone may have bumped his head against the wall of the ship. Other stories about our hasty flight from Tjikembar to Tasik you will hear later. There is so little to be proud of that it is better to remain silent. I do ask myself for what purpose the many men of the navy, the air force and the merchant marine have fallen. But we don't give up and remain optimistic, and who knows, perhaps we will be sitting soon, just like in November, in the Black Cat in Batavia. But I realize that that is not likely since you will have your son by then.

What are your plans, Didi? Are you going to stay in Buitenzorg or are you going to Malang? Even if Daan is not allowed any visitors, Malang is a safer place, where you do not have to expect any surprises from the local population. Indeed, East Java has been rather peaceful. In central Java there was a lot of looting as well, I know that two of our plantations were totally destroyed, and Tiek has also had some experiences like that in Solo.

Thankfully, none of my close friends have fallen, although I slightly knew quite a number of those who died. In our group only one man was lightly wounded during an ambush in Rankas. The mood in our group was terrible. No one had the least interest in fighting; our commander was a coward, who left two airplanes, completely undamaged and ready to fly, behind at the airport in Tjikembar, while he himself and his wife drove by car to Tasikmalaya. I assume that he will have to pay for this at some future time. Among the leaders the mood was "I can't care less." There are lots of people who have not learned anything and believe that things will go on as usual when they are back in civilian life. I hope we move toward communism, Russia has proved that this creates unity.

Frits's Birth on May 22 in the Year 2602

Frederik Christiaan, my little brother Frits, was born on May 22, 1942, while we still lived at Tjilendek 39 in Buitenzorg. By then, the Japanese calendar and Tokyo time were imposed in every country that was occupied by the Japanese. As a result, Frits can boast that he was born in the year 2602. Didi gave birth at the house of a Javanese doctor, Dr. Koesman, and his Dutch wife, who was a nurse, because Europeans were no longer allowed to receive care in the local hospitals. A day later, my mother sent Papa Daan a postcard to tell him of his son's birth. The card was written in Malay, probably with the help of Dr. Koesman, since it is written in a slightly more formal style than I would have expected from Didi.

Dear Daan,
Today I send you good news, our son Frederik Christiaan was born on Friday, 22/5, at ten minutes before three in the afternoon. His weight is 3 kilograms, 370 gram; his length is 53 cm. like Sytske. The children and I are doing well, and I very much hope you are also well. I am fine, Daan, and I only hope that F.C. will be able to see his papa soon. We send you much love and kisses from Didi, Sytske and Chris-Jan.

Prior to Frits's birth, Didi and Daan kept referring to the baby they were expecting as if they already knew that the baby was a boy. They had two names for him: Frederik Christiaan and Chris-Jan. After his birth, my brother was named Frederik Christiaan, after our grandfather Engelberts, but everyone always called him Frits—except for Daan, who kept referring to him as Chris-Jan. The postcard announcing Frits's birth was addressed to Papa Daan in an unnamed camp in Malang. My father received the postcard and carried it with him all through the war years.

When Frits was three weeks old, my mother brought him home in a deleman. She had made his room cozy; his cradle was dressed up with curtains made from white fabric with a small green polka dot, and she had even repainted the dressing table white with green trim—"This way, our little boy makes quite an impression." Herbert and Loetje van Oyen, the two Bolhuis children, and I were delighted with "our baby," who was so small and had a little crunched-up red face and tiny shrimp-like fingers and toes.

In August, my mother received a short letter from Papa Daan, dated July 8, 1942. The letter seems to have been written in haste and in the Dutch language. It did not have an envelope; our address was written in the margin. I assume that a courier, visiting Papa Daan's camp, took it along and then brought it later to my mother. The faded letter is difficult to read, since it is written with very soft pencil on very thin paper. To the best of my ability, I have translated it:

> *Dear Didi, Sytske and Chris Jan,*
> *Quickly a short letter. How are the three of you? Everything OK, of course. Today we are allowed visitors, but I don't expect anyone from West Java. It is now more than five months since we saw each other last, and when you receive this sign of life from me, it will be the first one for you. I did hear from visitors to other people in the camp about Chris-Jan. Did all go well? How are you doing financially? Keep strong, sweetheart.*
>
> *All is well here. I am healthy and miss you terribly. Via third parties, I heard that everything has been ruined at Djasinga and that we have lost everything. Everything will be all right eventually. How are Bep, Heb, and all the others? Give them greetings from me.*
>
> *Also, a belated Happy Birthday—to celebrate your health, I will drink a delicious glass of water. Next year we will be together, dearest. Good-bye, Angel, much love and a thousand kisses from your loving Daan. Much love to Sytske and Chris-Jan.*

Tender Loving Care in Tjimatis

When Frits was three months old, we left Buitenzorg and went to Tjimatis, to *oom en tante in de bergen*, where we stayed several months at the plantation administered by Mr. Claassen in the mountains to the south of Bandoeng. We lived with Mr. and Mrs. Claassen until the Japanese began to assemble the Dutch women and children in internment camps at the end of 1942.

The months in Tjimatis were wonderful for the three of us. We received loving care from the Claassens and had plenty of wholesome food, including fresh milk from the cows and plenty of eggs from the chickens. The best part of the day for me was when I was allowed to help gather the fresh eggs from the henhouse, feed the calves, or splash in the little water-lily pond in front of the house. Didi was physically and mentally much better and had more time for me, and our life together started to resemble what it once had been such an eternity ago.

But Papa Daan remained the center of attention because he was not with us. One afternoon, my mother took me to our old house, where we had celebrated my first birthday nearly two years ago. When we got there and did not find Papa Daan as I had expected we would, Didi burst in tears when I asked her, "Mammie, where is Papa Daan now?" So many memories came back to her, happy memories of a young family in the sunny tropics—memories that were such a contrast with the uncertain days of the present and future.

At Tjimatis, Didi started a baby book for Frits, and since mine had been lost, she started another one for me as well. She maintained the two baby books for a year and a half. The last entry in my book is dated February 1944, and after that, Didi stopped writing in them because the Japanese had forbidden their prisoners to keep diaries or write letters—they confiscated all paper they found. The two baby books did survive the war—they probably were stowed away and hidden deep down in the bottom of our duffel bag.

CHAPTER 5

DAAN AND JAN BECOME PRISONERS OF WAR

Every day trainloads full of men arrive in Batavia—they come from all over. We try to find out where they are coming from and where they are going. Everyone is very upset because some men are being sent away from Java. But don't worry, Didi, because only career military are being sent away.

—Tante Bep van Oyen in a letter to Didi in August 1942

When the war in the Dutch East Indies was lost in March 1942 after a week of tepid fighting, close to 90,000 men were taken prisoner of war. They included 71,000 KNIL men of Dutch, Indonesian, and mixed-blood ancestry; 10,600 British and British Indian men; close to 5,000 Australians; and 900 Americans. Approximately 73,000 of the POWs were located in Java, with the remainder scattered among a large number of other islands in the archipelago.

With the fall of Java, the Japanese had captured a huge area they called The Greater East Asia Co-Prosperity Sphere, which included Japan, Manchuria, a large part of China, and all of Southeast Asia. They proclaimed that they would bring prosperity to all of East Asia and independence to all nations that had been colonized by the British, French, and Dutch. But their victory over this vast area caused a huge problem for the Japanese because they lacked sufficient manpower to control and administer the vast area they occupied. After the Dutch capitulation on March 8, it took the Japanese forces several months to assemble their prisoners of war and find suitable locations for them.

As a result, the initial imprisonment of the prisoners had a distinctly improvised character. In the beginning of their imprisonment, depending on their location and rank, large numbers of POWs were left to their own devices, having to organize their own camps and arrange for their own food and administration. Others, captured near large cities, were quickly housed in camps that had been provisionally created in warehouses, hotels, school buildings, factory buildings, fairgrounds, hospitals and asylums, jails, and private homes.

Daan and Jan Become Prisoners of War

During the early months of the occupation, the treatment of the POWs, and the extent to which they could receive mail or visitors, differed from place to place and depended on factors such as whether the prisoners were ordinary rank-and-file soldiers or officers and whether they were located in large towns or in more rural areas. The initial experiences of Daan and Jan as prisoners of the Japanese were vastly different from each other, as the letters Didi received from them make clear.

Papa Daan was held in Malang in a POW camp, probably a former KNIL military base, with very little freedom and little opportunity to communicate with Didi, who received only two pieces of mail from him. His first message to her in his own handwriting consisted of just one terse sentence:

> *D.L.A. Engelberts is located in Malang and is doing well. He has no complaints. With friendly greetings, until we meet again.*

Jan, in contrast, was imprisoned in a provisional camp at Tasikmalaya in South Central Java with an astonishing amount of freedom. He wrote the following description of his imprisonment in those first weeks of the war to my mother:

> *We are living in a paradise compared to other places. We are allowed to receive mail and visitors, although we expect that the latter will be stopped soon. Food is quite decent and no one is saying that the men in Tasikmalaya are starving.... During the first week we were living in luxury since we were housed in a private home. From there I made some nice new friends, the family Meertens, living in Manondjajaweg 69. If we cannot get any mail one of these days please send me a letter to that address. They will see to it that I will get my mail. I still have my dark locks but tomorrow I will be as bald as a billiard ball. If possible I will send you a portrait of myself in that guise. I think you will love it.*
>
> *We have the advantage that we do not get bored. We work every day at the airport to clear rubble. Four times in the week we go swimming in the afternoon and pretty soon we will be able to play soccer. We shorten the time by writing, playing bridge, and talking. Especially the latter enables us to embellish stories, and every day we have new rumors to dissect, which later turn out to be fantasies. From what I*

have seen thus far I must admit that the Japs have fought fairly and that they act correctly now. They do appear to be rather nonchalant. Every day we have three guards. The day before yesterday, one of them was playing Ping-Pong in the back of the house, while the other two were giving us a Jiu-jitsu demonstration in the front. They had left their fire arms unprotected at the guardhouse.

The Japanese Search for Manpower

While the Japanese authorities were busy gathering and housing their prisoners of war and noncombatant civilians, they were also appointing Indonesians to perform various tasks on behalf of the Japanese military. Several thousand former KNIL members freely joined the Japanese authorities so they would continue to receive a salary during the occupation; others were simply coerced into joining the Japanese military as assistant soldiers. The Japanese called these assistant soldiers *heiho*. They helped the Japanese maintain order in the POW camps, functions they later performed in the camps for women and children and in the separate camps for noncombatant men. The latter category included elderly and sick men who had not fought in the war but who were considered enemy civilians and were also interned for the duration of the war. Oom Heb ended up in an internment camp for disabled, sick, and elderly men on Java.

In addition to the heihos, other Indonesians started performing administrative functions that had formerly been performed by the Dutch. A third group of Javanese men were recruited, or coerced, to work as nonmilitary workers on behalf of the war effort in locations mostly a long distance away from their homes. The Japanese did not like to use the derogatory word *coolie* and called the workers *romusha* instead, which means "economic soldier." These men had been small landowners or farmers, and many of them had been encouraged by their local village officials to work for the Japanese. The farmers were usually ignorant about what was expected of them when they signed up.

Although there are no exact numbers available of the total number of Javanese romusha who were recruited for the Japanese war effort, close to 300,000 men from Java were sent away to work elsewhere in the Greater East Asia Co-Prosperity Sphere. Of the several hundred thousand romushas taken abroad, only about 77,000 survived—a mortality rate of 74.3 percent.

Romushas were recruited on a huge scale throughout Southeast Asia. They were Javanese, Malays, Burmese, Vietnamese, Chinese, Tamils, and Indians, and they were used by the Japanese to perform hard labor, cleaning up harbors, working in mines, and building bridges, railroads, and roads. The workers were admonished by the Japanese authorities to work harder than they were used to on behalf of the Greater East Asia Co-Prosperity Sphere, but although they needed the romushas, the Japanese did not consider the romushas important enough to maintain records of them. Where records once existed, they were destroyed by the Japanese at the end of the war. The total number of romushas within Southeast Asia who survived or who have died working on behalf of the Greater East Asia Co-Prosperity Sphere is unknown.

On the whole, the Japanese military considered the heihos and romushas as even less worthy of consideration than the POWs, and they were treated by the Japanese military hierarchy as lower than the lowest Japanese privates. Although the conquest of Southeast Asia had been advertised as an effort to create prosperity for all East Asia, the Indonesians and other Asians working for the Japanese were little more than slave labor. According to Max Hastings, the Japanese barbarism displayed against their fellow Asians was on a vastly larger scale than against Americans and Europeans. "The knights of bushido made mockery of their lofty ideal of honor by behaving so basely towards the great multitudes who they deemed undeserving of the protection of their code."

The POW Transit Camps in Java

By July 1942, when the Japanese had more manpower to maintain the POW camps, in the form of the recently recruited heihos, all POWs were moved into camps in four locations on Java: Tjimahi, Bandoeng, Batavia, and Soerabaja. From then on, the men were completely isolated from their families and friends. Didi did not receive any messages from either Daan or Jan after July 1942. We don't know where either one of them ended up in that summer of 1942, but because we found a poem about "Jaarmarkt Camp" among Jan's papers, it is probable that he was one of the men who ended up in the large transit camp that was located in Soerabaja.

The word *Jaarmarkt* means "annual fair," and Jaarmarkt Camp occupied the Soerabaja fairgrounds. Before the war, the Soerabaja Fair was famous throughout Java. One could buy wonderful textiles there, such as handmade batik sarongs and silken ikat scarves, delicate Balinese paintings and gorgeous teakwood sculptures. The food at the fair was abundant and tasty, such as satay with peanut sauce, or rice balls wrapped in banana leaves and filled with a flavorful curry. The fragrance of food cooking on charcoal fires permeated the air. There was gambling, and there were shooting galleries for grown-ups and a Ferris wheel for kids. Entering the fairgrounds at night was magical. The entrance gate was decorated with green palm leaves and colorful flowers, and the place sparkled with hundreds of little lights. The sound of gamelan music could be heard throughout the grounds.

Everyone came with their families to the Soerabaja Fair. Dutch planters, traders and businessmen, Chinese bankers and doctors, Arabic shopkeepers and local Indonesians all milled together, enjoying the exciting, festive atmosphere.

With the Japanese invasion, the annual fair was discontinued, and after the Japanese established a POW transit camp there in the summer of 1942, the mood of the fairgrounds changed drastically. The men were housed in the exhibition buildings, the concession stands, and other attractions. When the buildings and stands were all filled to capacity, the remaining men slept in the open lots in between, rain or shine. The camp was used as a short-term transit camp and housed from three to five thousand POWs at any given time. It was closed in the spring of 1943 after most of the POWs had left for faraway destinations.

In contrast to his life at Tasikmalaya, Jan and the other POWs at Jaarmarkt Camp were guarded by angry and cruel guards; they were ordered to stand in formation for the daily appèls and received far too little food. The Jaarmarkt poem mentions that the loss of female companionship was hard on the young men and that boredom was a constant problem. So were the endless rumors and the uncertainty about their future, especially when increasing numbers of their comrades were being shipped off to unknown destinations.

Demeaning Assignments Only

Throughout the occupation, the Japanese treated their prisoners with contempt. The men had lost the war and had permitted themselves to be taken prisoner. The Japanese attitude was that their performance as military men was unacceptable and cowardly and that the prisoners should have fought to the death. Surrender was not in keeping with the Japanese military code of honor, bushido, and consequently, they looked down on their prisoners as unworthy of any consideration.

General Hideki Tojo, who had been a general in the Imperial Japanese Army and was appointed prime minister in 1941, declared that

Japan would only honor the Geneva Conventions "if that was feasible." The Japanese policy was that all prisoners of war would be considered at best as the equals of the lowest ranked troops in the Japanese army, and would be treated as such. All were expected to work, including the officers. The detailed instructions from the Japanese War Ministry declared that the work had to be demeaning and had to be carried out in full view of the local Asian populations, in order to emphasize Japan's superiority relative to the Western powers.

The Hell Ships

To transport so many thousands of POWs and civilian workers, the Japanese loaded the men tightly into cargo ships and shipped them by the thousands away from Java. Regardless of their rank or nationality, the men were almost always transported in the filthy holds of the overcrowded ships, with inadequate space, food, water, sanitation, or fresh air. The POWs quickly called the ships Hell Ships because huge numbers of their comrades died in them from infectious diseases. Some men simply went mad in the overcrowded space in which everyone had to sit with their knees tightly folded against their chests. No man could stand up or stretch out to rest without being in constant contact with his two neighbors to the left and right and the men in front and behind.

The Japanese refused to mark the rusty cargo ships for what they were: people transports. Because the vessels had no insignia that could be seen from the air or by a submarine, large numbers of these ships were bombed by the Allies and thousands of POWs and romusha perished during the sea voyages.

Changi Camp in Singapore

The transit camps on Java and elsewhere were used by the Japanese to assemble their prisoners and then send them to all corners of East Asia: Burma, Siam, Formosa, Manchuria, Japan, and the many islands of the Indonesian archipelago. Of a total of close to 90,000 men who were taken prisoner in the Dutch East Indies in the spring of 1942, no more than 4,500 were still in Java by the end of the war in 1945.

Daan and Jan ended up at a large transit camp on the island of Singapore. Changi Camp was located in two locations on the northern tip of the island: a military base in the small village of Changi and in the Changi jail. There, the prisoners were housed in overcrowded barracks with too little food and medicine. The men had to perform exhausting physical labor and were supervised by brutal guards. Every day, large groups of the prisoners left Changi and no one knew where they were going or for what purpose. Some of the men were loaded in overcrowded railroad boxcars that headed north through Malaya to Siam, while others were put on boats headed for Formosa, Manchuria, and Japan. All soon realized that whatever their destination, the future was very bleak indeed.

Daan was sent to Siam in early 1943 to work building the railroad from Ban Pong in Siam to Thanbyuzayat in Burma, a line that was more than 450 kilometers long. Jan was at Changi in October and arrived in Japan in early December 1942, after a voyage by boat of several weeks. He ended up in Camp Kamioka in the mountains of Western Japan, where the POWs worked in reactivated tin and lead mines.

The Men Who Built the Railroad

The men who built the railroad to Burma were a mixed group consisting of more than 200,000 Asian civilians, the romusha, from Malaya, Siam, Burma, Java, and Singapore, and more than 76,000 POWs from Britain, the Dutch East Indies, Australia, the United States, and New Zealand.

Soekarno had encouraged the Javanese farmers to join the romusha recruitment effort for the greater glory of the promised independence of their country. Of the thousands of Javanese farmers who were transported overseas and put to work as romushas, an estimated 45,000 ended up working on the Thai–Burma railroad.

In Malaya, Burma and Siam, the people had been enticed to work for the Japanese with the promise of decent pay and the ability to bring along their families. Ronald Searle described seeing them walk past his camp through the deep mud of the jungle track: “The Japanese amassed the vast Asian labor force that was necessary for this railway work by offering the incentive of a six-month contract under ideal conditions: splendid food, lots of money—and bring your families. Many did bring them and it was sickening to see women and small children passing through with bewildered-looking groups of Tamils and Chinese, to a miserable death.”

Survival and Death in the Jungle Camps

The conditions in the jungle camps were abominable. The men slept in bamboo huts on platforms that were raised from the ground. The huts were wide open to the weather and were infested with flying and crawling insects. Food supplied by the Japanese was totally inadequate for the men, who worked for long hours in all sorts of weather: fruit and vegetables were nonexistent, and protein in the form of meat, fish, or eggs was rarely available. The main food consisted of third-grade rice cooked in water. A little tea was poured when the work parties set out in the early morning on their way to the site of the railway, sometimes a distance away from the camps, and again when they arrived back at the camp after dark. The local population occasionally came to the perimeters of the camps to barter, and when they were lucky, the prisoners were able to exchange any valuables they still owned for little bits of food.

As a group, the Dutch POWs survived the harsh conditions in the jungle camps slightly better than the men of other nationalities. One explanation is that the Dutch POWs, who had been civilians in Indonesia before the war, had lived in the tropics for years and were thoroughly familiar with the food and climate. The prisoners from other countries consisted mostly of recently recruited young men from England, Australia, New Zealand, and the United States. They were completely unprepared for life in a tropical jungle and could not stomach the local food.

Perhaps most important, the Dutch were familiar with the vegetation of the jungle and used various plants for many purposes. The doctors among them were familiar with the bark of trees that could treat malaria and were inventive enough to harvest the sharp hollow thorns of certain plants to use as intravenous drips. They treated patients with festering deep tropical ulcers with the leeches that lived in the river. The leeches would eat away the dead flesh, cleaning wounds that could not be adequately cleaned otherwise. The Dutch also knew that the hot red peppers they were sometimes able to buy from local people were rich in vitamin C and were therefore an important addition to their diet. As a result, the Dutch were better able to withstand the tropical diseases that afflicted the men in the camps than the unprepared and very young Allied soldiers.

The romushas were segregated from the POWs and lived in their own camps. Their situation was completely hopeless. They did not speak a common language, as they had come from all over Asia, and most of them had been simple farmers and did not have the wherewithal to organize themselves or to develop some kind of indigenous leadership. There were no doctors or nurses among them, and when cholera broke out, which the Japanese feared more than anything else, they were left to their own devices in their isolated jungle camps and simply perished by the thousands. Lacking as the romushas were in any understanding of how cholera was transmitted or the importance of clean water, outbreaks of the disease were devastating among the romushas.

Seventy-five percent of the romusha who worked on the railroad died. Among the Allied POWs, the percentage of deaths among the various nationalities ranged from a low of fifteen percent (among the Dutch) to a high of twenty-three percent (among the British). The Greater East Asia Co-Prosperity Sphere had perhaps been an attractive slogan at the start of the war for colonized Asia, but very soon after the Japanese occupation, it became clear to most Asians that the promised prosperity was a phantom of Japanese military imagination. The term was just empty words without meaning. No Asian people, including the Japanese people themselves, benefitted from the planned co-prosperity. Instead of prosperity, it brought death to the Southeast Asians, some five million of whom died during the Japanese occupation.

Burials in the Jungle

Most of the Allied dead were initially buried in cemeteries that were located near the labor camps in the jungle. After the war, their remains were moved to Kanchanaburi, where the vast cemetery in town now houses the remains of more than 7,000 Allied POWs who had perished. Another cemetery on the outskirts of Kanchanaburi houses the remains of another 2,000 Allied POWs.

There is no cemetery in Thailand, or anywhere else, that contains the graves of the romushas who died unknown in the service of the Greater East Asia Co-Prosperity Sphere. They perished by the thousands without ceremony and without leaving any records of their presence in the camps. Only a handful of official and academic papers have been written about these forgotten dead, and not a single book records their fate.

After Indonesia gained its independence, Soekarno was haunted by his role in the romusha tragedy. In one of his speeches, he said the following.

> *They died in foreign lands. Often they were treated as inhumanly as the prisoners of war with whom they were shackled side by side to build the notorious Burma Road .... Yes, yes, yes, I knew they'd travel in airless box-cars packed in thousands at a time. I knew they were down to skin and bone. And I couldn't help them. In fact it was I—Soekarno—who sent them to work.... I shipped them to their deaths. Yes, yes, yes, yes, I am the one.... It was horrible. Hopeless. And it was I who gave them to the Japanese. Sounds terrible, doesn't it? ... Nobody likes the ugly truth.*

Labor Camps in Japan

The Japanese established a total of eighty-five camps in Japan that housed 37,000 POWs, among whom were about 8,000 Dutchmen. The conditions of the camps in Japan were harsh, although there were significant differences among the camps.

Jan was among an estimated one thousand Dutchmen who in November 1942 were loaded onto the *Kamakura Maru* in Singapore harbor. The ship had been a luxurious Japanese passenger liner before the war, sailing between Japan and San Francisco. The POWs were ordered to remain on deck rather than occupy the fancy passenger cabins below. At the beginning of their voyage, the men found it rather pleasant being on deck because they could breathe fresh sea air and move around; sitting in the fresh air on the deck was certainly to be preferred over the crowded holds of the Hell Ships they had been on before.

Jan and his fellow prisoners did not know their destination when they set sail from Singapore, but when the ship turned north, the men, still dressed in their tropical uniforms, began to suffer from the cold and the November rain. North of Formosa, now Taiwan, the rain changed into sleet and snow, and they began to wonder whether anyone would survive this journey.

Just before they arrived in Japan in early December, the shivering men were given secondhand British uniforms that had seen service in North African battles. Although they were threadbare and filthy, the uniforms added some warmth and protection from the elements. On December 7, exactly one year after the bombing of Pearl Harbor, the *Kamakura Maru*, with its load of cold and wet Dutchmen, arrived in Nagasaki during a snowstorm.

Three hundred of the miserable prisoners, Jan among them, were sent by train to central Japan. The next day, December 8, 1942, they arrived at Kamioka, a camp that had been established as Osaka Kamioka Branch Camp. In so-called branch camps, POWs were handed over to private industries to perform labor that was essential for the war effort. In branch camps, the Imperial Japanese Army supplied the POWs with housing, food, and clothing, but the privately owned company was in charge of production, work schedules, supervision, and safety for its workers.

At Kamioka, the POWs had to work in the dilapidated zinc and lead mines of Mitsui Kozan. The men worked twelve-to-fourteen-hour shifts with a day off every two weeks. The unlucky men who worked the daytime shift in the dark mineshafts hardly ever saw any sunlight during the short days of winter.

Osaka Kamioka Branch Camp was located at Kamioka-cho, Hida City, Gifu Prefecture, which today is surrounded by several national parks. The area is now famous for Alpine skiing in Japan's snowy winters.

The Tin and Lead Mines of Camp Kamioka

Jan, "War Criminal 6," in front of the barracks in Kamioka, October 1944

Life at Kamioka was extremely hard, especially for the men who had to go down into the mines for the twelve-to-fourteen-hour shifts, supervised by sadistic guards. It was a debilitating schedule, and because of the antiquated conditions in the mines, there were many accidents, in which the exhausted men were seriously injured and sometimes killed.

After returning to their barracks, the men received a meager meal consisting of a bowl of rice, a cup of miso soup, and some pickles. Some days, the prisoners received a small, clammy loaf of grey bread that tasted mostly of sawdust. The men were housed in drafty wooden barracks divided into small rooms. About a dozen men lived together in each room, sleeping next to and above each other in cramped quarters. Each bed was made of hard wooden boards covered with a thin *tatami* mat. The only heat in a room was provided by a tiny coal-burning stove located in the center. The Japanese gave the men cheap cotton blankets resembling thin felt, which did little to protect against the bitter cold.

Twenty percent of the Dutch POWs died at Kamioka. As a consequence of inadequate clothing, poor bedding, and little heat, they mostly died of exposure and pneumonia. In addition to suffering from the horrible cold during the winters, the men also suffered from such typical camp diseases as dysentery, malaria, beriberi, and hepatitis. When a POW was too ill to work, his food ration was cut in half; as a result, starvation and malnutrition were common.

The Power of Friendship

In most camps, wherever they were located during World War II in East Asia, the POWs soon formed small groups to help each other in times of need, so-called *Kongsis*. A Kongsi, similar to a fraternity, would usually consist of six or eight men who watched out for each other and helped each other to survive. They would take care of each other by performing extra labor on behalf of a sick friend. They would share whatever they were able to barter along the edges of the camp, and they saved food and other necessities for those who had not yet returned from their work on the railroad or in the mines.

Kongsis were the key to survival in the camps.

CHAPTER 6

OUR INTERNMENT IN CAMP TJIHAPIT, BANDOENG

From December 22nd, 1942, we were interned in Bandoeng where we remained until November 1944. There we lived in houses and we were fine, especially in the beginning when I had a lovely room, alone with the children. Later we had to share a room with two other people, a mother and daughter.

—Didi's first letter to her mother, November 12, 1945

Late in the fall of 1942, after the Japanese had assembled all their prisoners of war and had sent them away from Java, they began to assemble an estimated 100,000 Dutch women and children in internment camps located in so-called protected areas, residential neighborhoods in various cities. And so, days before Christmas, Didi, Frits, and I were ordered by the Japanese authorities to leave the safety and comfort of Tjimatis and the wonderful care we received from Mr. and Mrs. Claassen. We were transported by train. The first stop on our journey was Tjiandjoer, where we were housed for three days in a school building. We stayed in one classroom together with thirteen other women, eleven children, and three dogs. From there, we were transported in overcrowded trains to Bandoeng, where we were interned in camp Tjihapit until November 1944.

The House of Many Aunts

During the first months of our stay in Tjihapit, we lived in the Seringen Laan no. 7, in the so-called flower quarter in Bandoeng, with its tree-lined streets and comfortable one-family homes previously occupied by Dutch families, with gardens that had been carefully planted and maintained. The living conditions in Tjihapit in the early days were not bad at all. The three of us lived in a pleasant house together with several other women and children. We had a room of our own furnished with beds, a table, and chairs that had been left behind by the original occupants of the house.

Everyone used the covered patio in the back of the house as a common living and dining area where we ate our meals and where the children played games or listened to one of the mothers telling stories. The house had regular bathroom facilities with fresh water and a flush toilet. We could buy our food and other things at the passar, the local market, and the women pooled their funds, shared household tasks, and took care of each other's kids. The women all became *tantes*, aunts, to the many children living under one roof.

Best of all for me and the other little kids was the little school, organized by the younger women in the camp. There I learned to make drawings on the pages of the monthly accountings everyone apparently had to submit to the camp leadership—accountings that seemed to focus primarily on the use of electricity and water and shoe repair. We also learned to sing songs in school. A popular one was about a little train leaving its station, complete with sound effects at the end:

Op een klein stationnetje, 's Morgens in de vroegte, Staan de kleine wagentjes Netjes op een rijtje, En de machinisten Draaien aan een wieletje ... *Hakke, hakke, puf, puf* Weg zyn wij!	At a little station, Early in the morning, Stand the little wagons Neatly in a row, As the engineers Turn a little wheel ... *Hakke, hakke, puf, puf* Away we go!

Our little family in Tjihapit, spring 1943—the photo was made so that Papa Daan would have an image of his cute son as a little baby when he came back from the war.

During the time we lived in the Seringen Laan, we were able to visit Tante Bep van Oyen, interned in another camp in Bandoeng, and we even met Oom Heb once, to my very great pleasure. According to Didi, I turned beet red when I saw him, and then ran into his arms and hid my little face against his chest.

When Frits was about nine months old, in the spring of 1943, Didi and Tante Bep had photographs of themselves taken with their children for Papa Daan and Oom Heb, for the time when they would be back with us. Didi was glad that she would be able to show

Papa Daan how adorable his little son had been as a little baby, a son he had never yet held in his arms.

We celebrated Frits's first birthday in style with presents and a birthday cake with a candle on May 22, 1943. Frits must have relished the attention—he was a cheerful little boy that first year of his life, even though he often looked with a serious expression at the people and activities around him. For his birthday, one tante gave Frits a piggy bank on which was written, "Admiral Frits Engelberts, 22/5/2603." Frits was called "little admiral" because he had such an imperious little face. This same aunt had first told my mother that Frits had the face of a little bureaucrat, but when Didi protested, the little bureaucrat was transformed into an admiral, which was a much more acceptable profession at the time.

A Fence of Bamboo and Razor Wire, Our Instant Prison

The relative comfort of the early months in Tjihapit was short-lived. In July 1943, the Japanese started to clamp down on the limited freedom of the women and children in the protected areas. The passar was closed down, our meals had to be fetched from a central kitchen, and the school for the little children was discontinued. From that time on, each neighborhood was completely surrounded by a fence of *gedèk*, woven bamboo sheets, topped with barbed wire. The Japanese protected area we had lived in until then had become a hermetically sealed internment camp: a prison we could not leave at will—a prison that made it impossible to visit with Tante Bep and the boys or Oom Heb.

We never saw them again.

Several months later, the three of us were moved within Camp Tjihapit from the Seringen Laan to the Barendsz Straat, a few blocks away. There, too, we lived in a relatively nice house, in a room comfortable enough for the three of us. But when increasing numbers of women and children were moved into the camps we had to share our room with another mother and her daughter, most likely Tante Mimi Koning and her daughter Edje, who was slightly older than I.

A Very Sick Baby Brother

Within weeks of our move to the Barendsz Straat, fifteen-month-old Frits became very sick with diarrhea and vomiting. He was unable to eat or drink for days on end and became seriously dehydrated. Fortunately, there was a Dutch pediatrician, Dr. Cramer, also interned in camp Tjihapit. She ordered Frits hospitalized so he could get the best food and liquids the camp had to offer. During the several months that little Frits was in and out of the camp hospital, he became a small, sad little boy who kept losing weight, cried a lot, and lacked the energy to sit up or smile. Didi described one of her visits to Frits in the hospital in November 1943:

> *When I visited last week he looked at me with a hopeless expression on his little face and sat on my lap during the entire visiting hour, leaning into my arms—no smile lit up his little face. One of the sisters had said with very little tact: "a sweet little guy, Mevrouw, but he probably always was a delicate little child ..." She spoke with such resignation in her voice as if she wanted to say: "We shall do our best to make him stronger, but he will never be a sturdy child." ... I cannot imagine that I will ever have him back or that he will be like his old self again.... If only we could give him what he needs—Dr. Cramer said a few days ago: "If you could take him to the mountains now, he would be better in no time." But when will that be..?*

Dr. Cramer was initially unsuccessful in her efforts to treat Frits, but eventually, it was found that Frits suffered from giardia, a bacterial disease. Although medicines were extremely scarce, the Catholic sisters who worked as nurses in the hospital still had a small supply of Stovarsol, used in the treatment of giardia as well as other diseases. Frits received a total of two tablets which had to last six days; the small dose of one-third of one tablet daily did the trick, and he started to get better—but he was a frail little boy when he came home in December. He had lost a huge amount of weight and was barely able to stand alone. He didn't learn to walk until he was nearly two years old, but thanks to Dr. Cramer, he had survived.

Fortunately, the food was still relatively decent in Tjihapit, and the central kitchen was able to cook a special kind of thick soup, called *nassi-tim*, for the littlest children. Nassi-tim consists of rice and vegetables cooked in salted water and then strained through a sieve. The youngest children also got porridge made from sago, a starch extracted from sago palm stems. While he was recuperating, Frits received watered-down buttermilk and, if available, bananas or orange juice, but fruit was not often available in the camp.

At the house in the Barendsz Straat, we celebrated three major holidays. First, we celebrated the Dutch feast of the birthday of Sinterklaas, the bishop Saint Nicholas, on the fifth of December, when Frits was still in the hospital. Didi played the piano on the back porch and taught the kids various Sinterklaas songs: "Sinterklaas Kapoentje" and "O, kom er eens kijken wat ik in myn schoentje vind." On the big day itself, a real Sinterklaas visited our house, dressed in a bishop's mantle and accompanied by real Black Peters, the saint's assistants, and he brought presents for all the children. Didi did not describe how the women in the camp had managed to create such a feast in those days of scarcity.

The Miracle of Christmas

Not long after the feast of Sinterklaas and shortly after Frits had come home from the hospital, we celebrated Christmas in our room, together with Tante Mimi and her daughter Edje. Didi and Tante Mimi had decorated the table with green fir boughs, probably from a tjamara tree, and red paper ribbons, along with real candles. They also had been able to get some candies for the five of us. According to my mother, it was primitive but, for the children, no less beautiful. Frits sat on Didi's lap, rocking back and forth with glee, and I sat next to them at the foot of my bed. Tante Mimi and Edje sat on my mother's bed, and the beautifully decorated table stood between us. We all had a most wonderful time; the mothers loved seeing the light of the candles reflected in our shining eyes, filled with wonder. All five of us loved singing the old songs. We sang "Silent Night" and other Christmas songs. Little Frits, who loved singing, "sang" along loudly, while Edje and I looked with huge eyes at the beauty of the decorated table with its candles and candies. Afterwards, when I was put to bed, I hugged my mother tightly and whispered, "Those candles were so beautiful!"

A Tiny Skirt Made of Kitchen Towels

On January 31, 1944, we celebrated my fourth birthday. It too was a huge success with yet more presents. Didi had made a skirt for me out of two blue checked kitchen towels, and a tante had made a little apron from various tiny squares of fabric, in the manner of a quilt. When I had dressed up in this finery, nobody could question which one of the children had a birthday that day.

Shortly after my fourth birthday, I started developing memories of my own. I can still recreate the layout of the house in the Barendsz Straat and point out where our room was located. Next to our room was a small room that was occupied by a tante who once gave Didi a light blue evening dress with a matching bolero jacket. It was the last thing my mother needed just then, but it was no doubt the one thing of beauty Didi owned. She carried this dress with her throughout the war as a token of the good times of the past and in the hope that those good times would come again. After the war, when we were in Deventer, Didi had the dress shortened and wore it on special occasions as a party dress. Ordinarily, she wore shorts and a blouse throughout the war years, keeping the few dresses she owned in our duffel bag, to save for "later."

Becoming a Camp Child

Edje had become my special friend. We used to take baths together in the back yard in a zinc laundry tub that had stood in the sun for hours, warming the water. Playing with the water in the tub was the best part of the day for Edje and me. Sometimes, Edje got to take a bath by herself, which made me green with envy, especially because her bath water was sometimes colored yellow. Was it infused with mercurochrome, I wonder, and if so, why?

I also remember going to a large field at the end of the Barendsz Straat with some of the older children, who would try to scare me about the bad smell under some shrubs, telling me there were dead dogs underneath there. This was very disturbing, because I remembered stories about Datiko, our dog. Poor Datiko and the dog of the van Oyens had initially been left at the plantation when we ran in a panic to the woods on March 3, 1942, but it wasn't long before the two dogs had found us in the woods. Given the need to be as quiet and invisible as possible, we needed to get rid of them. Shooting them was not an option, because that would have alerted the Rampokkers to our whereabouts. Uncle Heb tried to poison the dogs, but that didn't work. Didi told me much later that the two dogs were tied up in the woods and left behind, but Datiko continued to live in the stories Didi told us at night.

One day, I became very sick with dysentery while we lived in the Barendsz Straat. I had used the common bathroom, unbeknownst to my mother, and had not washed my hands afterwards. Living in close quarters with small children was difficult for everyone, because the kids easily infected each other and it was almost impossible to keep us all apart. If one child got sick, all children got sick.

Early in 1944, a major measles epidemic broke out in our camp, paired with smallpox and whooping cough. Dr. Cramer told my mother to keep Frits and me "at home" in our room, because if little Frits were to be exposed, it would be a calamity.

Because all of us children were surrounded by playmates of all ages all day long, we learned good as well as bad habits from each other.

Our mothers and tantes would try to keep the children from using bad language and curse words, but it was a thankless task, apparently. In a letter home to Holland, my mother wrote:

> *Frits just walked in with Mareo's chick, which Mareo constantly carries with him—the poor little beast won't last another week. Now Frits has it and it has disappeared under the bed. Frits ran around to try and catch it unsuccessfully and he became increasingly more hot and angry, until finally a hearty "Godverdomme" [Goddamn] resounded throughout the room. I heard the shock of my neighbors: "He curses like a stevedore!"*

The children played with each other but also fought over scarce toys or any other thing that belonged to one of the others. I would even become enraged when my friend Edje would hug Frits a little too much—after all, he was *my* little brother! On the other hand, with so many children of all ages together, there were also wonderful play times, when the little kids and the big girls would stage plays or "weddings," which were very popular with Edje and me.

We also learned to be generous with each other. On one occasion, my mother found me sitting on the floor with a circle of friends surrounding me while I distributed precious morsels of *dendeng*, dried meat, to everyone.

Remembering Our Fathers, and Other Children's Games

One of the most popular of the children's pastimes was boasting about our absent fathers. I participated in these boasts, although I had no idea what a father actually was—I just had Papa Daan and Mammie. When Didi asked me where I thought my father was, I answered nonchalantly, "My father is with my mother."

For me, after all that time, Papa Daan had become a story character, quite similar to Datiko, and not unlike the four girl elephants my mother had invented and would tell Frits and me about. The little elephants were dressed in beautiful dresses—a pink one, a blue one, a yellow one, and a green one—and they had all sorts of scary adventures, but they always ended up safe at home, where they belonged. Didi also told us stories about Papa Daan to keep Papa Daan alive in our minds, but those tales never ended quite so peacefully—he never came home. Every night, after my mother had tied small bags on my little hands to keep me from sucking my thumb and had told me that night's story about the four little elephant girls, I said a prayer to Onze Lieve Heertje, asking him if he please would send Papa Daan home soon.

For me and the other little kids in the Barendsz Straat, the fathers, whom we could barely remember, had acquired mythical qualities—not the least of which was their unfailingly unconditional love for us. Didi described my usual reaction to her attempts to discipline me in my baby book: "Whenever I try to reprimand Syts or tell her not to do something, she always responds by saying confidently: 'Papa Daantje zegt: Sytsje mag wel!' [Papa Daan says that Sytske *may* do that!]."

The absent fathers were kind and sweet in the memories of the children, in contrast to the other men we saw in the camp, the Japanese guards and their Indonesian assistants, who were frightening. Even though the Japanese were not a very great presence in the camps in Bandoeng, we were still exposed to their unpredictable cruelty. My friend Edje had trouble sleeping at night and would frequently wake up with a scream and then stare with big frightened eyes toward one corner of the room. When Tante Mimi asked her what the matter was, she never answered. About me, my mother commented in my baby book that I had developed a great fear of the Japanese ever since I had seen them beating a woman in the street.

On February 26, 1944, Didi ended up in the camp hospital with bacillary dysentery, a condition she would suffer from throughout the remaining camp years. Although she hated leaving Frits and me in the care of Tante Mimi, she was glad to be away from us, since she was so terribly afraid of infecting us. To make her feel better, I gave Didi my little bear so she would not be all alone in the hospital. On my last visit to her in the hospital, she told me that she would be coming home in two nights' time. I counted the two nights on the fingers of my right hand and kept my little hand behind my back for the remainder of my visit, with two little fingers up in the air, so as not to forget. This account was the last entry Didi made in my baby book.

A Card from Papa Daan from Far Away

In the fall of 1944, we received a sign of life from Papa Daan. This postcard, the only mail Didi received from Papa Daan while we were in internment camps, is the one I have here in Millerton. It was mailed from Camp 2, POW Camp, Thailand, dated January 23, 1944. The card has prepared multiple-choice texts that had to be filled in or crossed out by the sender; there was no accommodation for a personal message. The card was provided by the Imperial Japanese Army and

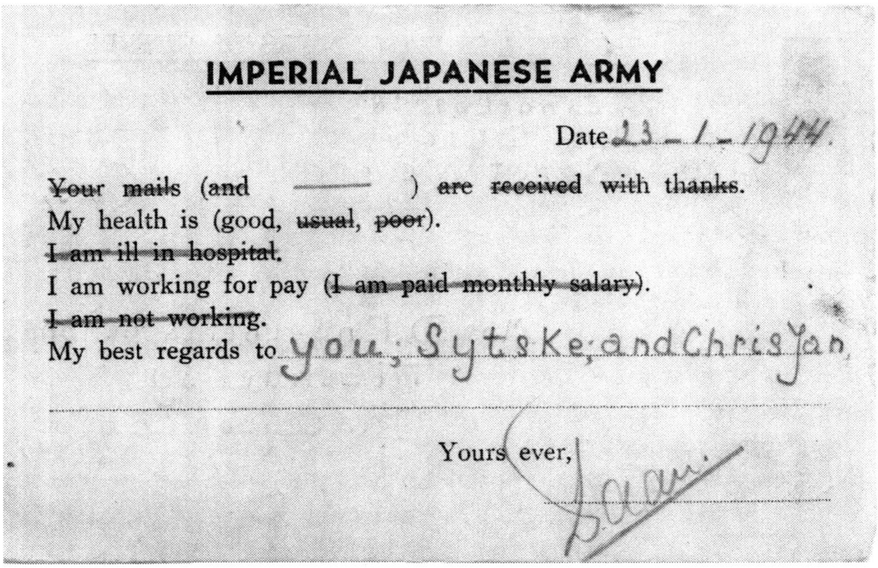

IMPERIAL JAPANESE ARMY

Date 23 - 1 - 1944.

~~Your mails~~ (~~and~~) ~~are received~~ with thanks.
My health is (good, ~~usual~~, ~~poor~~).
~~I am ill in hospital.~~
I am working for pay (~~I am paid monthly salary~~).
~~I am not working.~~
My best regards to you; Sytske; and Chris Jan.

Yours ever,
Daan.

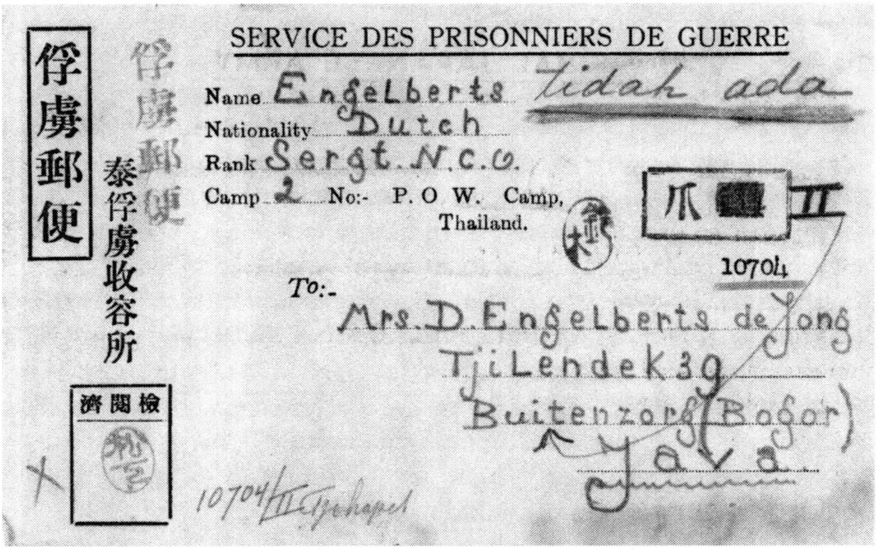

俘虜郵便

泰俘虜收容所

SERVICE DES PRISONNIERS DE GUERRE

Name Engelberts tidak ada
Nationality Dutch
Rank Sergt. N.C.O.
Camp 2 No:- P. O W. Camp, Thailand.

爪 II

10704

To:- Mrs. D. Engelberts de Jong
Tjilendek 39
Buitenzorg (Bogor)
Java.

檢閱濟

10704/II Tjihapit

Front and back of the postcard we received in Tjihapit, signed by Papa Daan, January 1944 mailed through the efforts of the Service Des Prisonniers de Guerre. From the postcard we learned at least that Papa Daan was still alive in January 1944. Because it had taken about eight months for the postcard to reach us, there was no way of knowing if he was still alive at the time we received it.

An entry on a small scrap of paper written by my mother describes my reaction:

> *Finally a postcard from Papa Daan—Syts asks: does Papa Daan write that my Oma is dead? No, sweetheart. Ha—then, my Oma is still alive. I try to explain to her that Papa Daan is not in Holland. No, says Syts, but he does go there for visits and Oma also goes to our house to drink tea [our house is where Papa Daan is]. Oma is far away and Papa Daan is far away—therefore they have to be together.*

For the 100,000 women and children living in Japanese camps after two and a half years of the Japanese occupation, the war became an endless string of days and nights of boredom and worrying, as they were unable to find out what was happening in the world outside the fences of the camps and not knowing where their husbands and fathers were or what was happening "at home" in Europe.

We had not learned that the Japanese were beginning to realize that they were losing the war. On October 26, 1943, Emperor Hirohito stated that his country's situation "is now truly grave."—but of course the women in their isolated camps had no way of learning of Hirohito's words. Then, in September 1944, while we were still in Tjihapit, pamphlets signed by the commander of the Dutch forces, Lieutenant General L.H. van Oyen, Oom Heb's older brother, were dropped from Allied planes flying high over Java into the camps below. The pamphlets announced that the Allies were advancing on all fronts in Europe and in East Asia, and that Japan was losing the war. The flyers stated that the hour of our freedom was near. But it would take another twelve months before the POWs and internees would celebrate peace.

For the women and children in the camps, the worst was yet to come.

CHAPTER 7

INTERNMENT IN AMBARAWA AND BANJOEBIROE

I am no longer an old lady, like I was a half a year ago. I was very old then—I now know exactly what it is like when your legs cannot carry you, everything aches and you have to stop after four steps to catch your breath and to make sure you don't fall.

—Letter from Didi to Oma in Deventer, December 1945

In the fall of 1944, Japan began to prepare for the possibility of losing the war, and the lives of the civilian internees deteriorated dramatically when the Japanese started to concentrate the thousands of women and children within two primary locations in Java: Batavia in West Java, and Semarang and its environs in Central Java. The Japanese also decided that from then on, children over the age of ten were to be considered either men or women, and as a result, boys who were ten years of age or older were ordered to leave the women's camps and move to men's camps. Some of the frightened little boys climbed into the trucks that would transport them away from their mothers with their favorite stuffed animals in the bottoms of their small backpacks. No one knew where the boys were going.

In November, more than eight hundred women and children—Didi, Frits, and I among them—were transported by train during a three-day period from camp Tjihapit in Bandoeng to the provincial town of Ambarawa in Central Java, about forty-five kilometers from Semarang. Dr. Cramer, Frits's pediatrician in camp Tjihapit, was terribly worried when she heard that we were leaving the camp where she had been able to treat Frits successfully. With a somber heart, she saw us off for an unknown destination.

I don't remember the train ride at all, but it doesn't take much imagination to speculate about the fear the mothers had during the many nighttime hours the train spent traveling slowly to its endpoint, stopping frequently at dark stations or just somewhere along the track, our destination entirely unknown to everyone. We were all packed closely together in the darkened train while Didi and the other worried mothers tried to keep us children comfortable and quiet.

Our destination turned out to be Ambarawa 9, a former boarding school for local girls, where we lived in a big dormitory, packed together with 134 other women and their small children and babies. Didi wrote later to Oma that "one gets used to everything—even that—but much worse was that we did not have enough water there and I could not digest the food. In Bandoeng we always had had access to buttermilk and special milk for Frits—in Ambarawa we had none of that."

When we first arrived in Ambarawa, we looked for a corner space or a location next to a wall to have some privacy in the large, overcrowded hall, but it did not take long before we stayed as far away as we could from the corners and the walls, because of the bedbug infestation. The bugs hid during the day in the cracks of the walls and came out at night to feed. We had no mosquito netting, and in addition to the bedbugs and the mosquitoes, we shared the space with ants, flies, cockroaches, lice, and rats. In some camps, women and children were ordered to collect the flies, and if their catch was substantial enough, their reward was a small increase in their daily rations.

With so many people packed together without adequate water, it was inevitable that infectious diseases would crop up everywhere, and many women and children began to suffer from chronic amoebic or bacillary dysentery. The communal latrines had long lines of people waiting for their turn at the holes in the ground with two footrests that were slippery and wet from excrement that could not be flushed away. There was no toilet paper and too little water to clean oneself. The poor hygiene, lack of medicines, and poor nutrition contributed to an increase of illness and death during this last year of our imprisonment.

A Very Old Woman of Twenty-nine

Didi was one of the women who got desperately ill. She suffered primarily from chronic dysentery and lost a huge amount of weight. I remember the many nights when she sat on a chamber pot between the rows of women and children, unable to go to the latrines that were a distance from our barracks, while someone tried to give her some privacy by holding a sheet around her. In one of her letters home to Oma, Didi wrote how much she was looking forward to the privacy of a Western toilet, one she could use all by herself, without anyone else sitting to either side of her.

During the last months of the war, twenty-nine-year-old Didi was so weak that she could barely walk across the campgrounds. One day when I was with her, she tripped and fell down, hitting her forehead hard on a rock. The wound bled profusely, and I watched with fear and horror as other women took her away to the camp hospital. In time, the wound healed, but Didi had an indentation in the middle of her forehead for the rest of her life.

Banjoebiroe Prison, Our Last Wartime Home

Our stay in Ambarawa was short. On May 3, 1945, we were moved again, together with 250 other women and children, to Banjoebiroe. Didi and Frits were transported by truck together with the other sick and disabled women and children, while those of us who were able had to walk. I remember this five-kilometer walk in the middle of the night quite well. We walked to the next camp in silence, shuffling along in the dark and listening to the night sounds of the country: the noisy jangkriks, crickets, the rustling of leaves at the sides of the road, and the eerie song of the night bird that whistled Pieeet van Vlieeet—Pieeet van Vlieeet … endlessly. The silhouettes of banana and coconut trees were sharply outlined against the sky, and then, at some point, we saw a shooting star streaking along the horizon. For a moment, our thoughts turned away from the problems of the present and everyone made a wish for our survival and a life of well-being in the future. I wished for a doll.

Though I must have been upset to have been separated from my mother and Frits, I don't remember my feelings of that night and guess that I, like everyone else, just did what was demanded. Even the smallest children in the Japanese camps had learned at a very early age to be stoic and not to be "difficult" in the presence of the Japanese and Korean guards. In any case, by daybreak, we arrived in Banjoebiroe, where I found my mother and Frits again. Didi wrote Oma about this move in her first letter home after we had been liberated:

> *In May of this year we were moved to Banjoebiroe, the old Javanese prison, behind high walls and with iron bars in the windows. I have been terribly ill there with malaria, hepatitis, and my horrible belly which continues to act up. A doctor finally almost cured me by insisting I eat raw vegetables—slices of a large sort of radish and cabbage stalks. But then I got beriberi, which I had feared most of all, having seen, while I was hospitalized, what it can do to a person.*

Banjoebiroe Prison, built like a fort, was surrounded by a high stone wall with, at one side, a big gate with doors that were usually shut. A number of the barracks, our living quarters, surrounded a center field, a dusty open space with a few tall kenari trees that offered some shade in the heat of the day. The dusty space turned to mud with the downpours of the monsoon season.

The barracks were sparingly furnished with rows of *baléh-baléh*, wooden platforms, where each person had no more than a foot and a half of space to call her own. Laundry lines overhead were covered in clothes, and some of the women who still owned sheets arranged them on the clotheslines like curtains to create private spaces for themselves and their children. Of course we had lost everything right at the beginning of the war, so we had nothing to make a private space on our corner of the baléh-baléh.

One somber day during the rainy season, when the world could not stop crying, I was sitting all alone on the steps outside of our barracks, looking at the rain splattering in the puddles in front of me. The light was grey and gloomy, and I was cold, sitting there alone on those steps. The desolation I felt then comes back every once in a while, when the clouds are low and the rain slants down without interruption. This emotional flashback comes unexpectedly anywhere, even when I have not been thinking about the war and I am right here in Millerton.

Camp Children's Games

My memories are not all of desolation. During the day, we children played on top or below the platforms while we secretly listened to our mothers' conversations and arguments with the other women. A favorite game was playing with the round little balls of goat turds we gathered at the goat field in the corner of the camp, which were excellent substitutes for marbles. We had a particularly good time on the rare days when we received hard-boiled eggs, one half egg per person; we would pierce tiny holes in the eggshells and snake a piece of thread through the holes. In that way, we created miniscule, and extremely fragile, buckets with which we tried to scoop water out of the well in the corner of the camp. This effort could occupy us for hours, until we lost the eggshell-bucket in the deep water. Later, when food in tin cans was distributed, we made holes in the sides of the empty cans and strung rope through them, allowing us to walk on top of the cans. On our improvised stilts, we would teeter in the dust of the center field.

Paying Homage to the Emperor of Japan

One of the rules the Japanese imposed during the war consisted of daily appèls, in which all imprisoned men, women, and children had to stand in formation outside their barracks to pay homage to the emperor and to be counted. As we were being counted, we had to bow our heads in the direction of Japan to honor the emperor. Appèls started when the guards would scream, "Kiotsuke!" (attention), and we would close ranks; then the order was "keirei," bow; and then they counted us in multiples of ten "ichi, ni, san, shi, go, roku, shichi, hachi, ku, ju."

Appèls could take hours under the hot sun or in the pouring rain, because the uneducated guards had trouble counting the large numbers of women and children—after losing count, they would start all over again. Women would faint if these sessions lasted too long, and those of us still standing had to leave them lying in the dust. Nobody was allowed to come to their rescue until the Japanese were satisfied that all were accounted for and we were allowed to rest: "Yasumi!" These appèls were regularly used as punishment and could take hours, even in the middle of the night.

Dr. Bekkering, a Dutch therapist quoted in *Indisch Kampkind, een eigen gezicht?* by Wil Dekker-Belgraver, noted that "standing at attention, and not understanding it, but knowing that there was danger, but not knowing from where to expect it, yet knowing that you had to behave, gives young children a sense of threat that required them to pay attention to the rules, even though the rules no longer made sense." Even the littlest kids learned to stand like statues while the Japanese and Korean guards shouted and raged in front of us.

One morning, Didi was too weak to stand outside at *appèl* and remained on our sleeping platform—a daring thing to do, as the Japanese did not take kindly to sick people; they saw illness as a form of sabotage. An elderly woman had stayed behind, as well. Didi told me later that she had tried to look defiant and unafraid when the Japanese guard had come to check our barracks and found her lying there; with fear in her heart, she had stared him down with her big blue eyes and the man had walked past her, acting as if he did not see her. A little further on, the man had come across the elderly woman, who had started whimpering when he came near—he beat the old woman mercilessly. Fortunately, Frits and I had stood outside with Tante Ruth, who took us under her wings when our mother had a bad day. We did not witness the man's cruelty.

Tante Ruth, Our Guardian Angel

Tante Ruth Kersten, our guardian angel, who had promised to take Frits and me to Holland if Didi died in the camp. The picture was taken in Holland after the war.

Most mothers in the camps relied on someone else to stand in for them when they got sick. In Banjoebiroe, we had a guardian angel in the form of Tante Ruth Kersten, who was a member of the Hernhutters, a religious group called the Moravian Brethren in the United States. Tante Ruth took care of my mother, Frits, and me and promised Didi that if she did not survive the camps, Tante Ruth would see to it that we would end up in Holland with Oma de Jong in Deventer. Later, I learned that Tante Ruth was a mother herself, with a daughter in Holland. Neither Tante Ruth nor her daughter knew where the other was during the war and whether she was still alive. Tante Ruth and her daughter were reunited after the war and ended up together in Zeist, living in a substantial community of Hernhutters.

When Didi and Frits both were in the hospital, Tante Ruth took care of me. She was strong and efficient, unlike my mother, who was weak and often very ill. Although Tante Ruth was not in the habit of being demonstratively warm and loving, I admired her and wanted to be like her. One thing in particular still stands out in my mind: Tante Ruth had narrow, pursed lips and a determined expression on her face, which was so different from my mother's or my face—we both have *tuut*, protruding lips. Tante Ruth's "stiff upper lip" was the thing to have!

Medical Care in Banjoebiroe

The camp hospital in Banjoebiroe consisted of barracks with separate cots for the patients, who were cared for by nuns, still dressed in their habits. The nuns received some deference from the Japanese camp commander, but medical care in the camps was extremely limited. Yet, the hospital environment was cleaner and quiet, and the food was slightly better and more plentiful. Quite a few patients did get somewhat better there.

The boxes filled with medicines sent by the Red Cross and intended for the women and children never ended up in the camp hospitals but were hoarded instead by our Japanese guards. After the war, stores of medicines sent by the Red Cross and intended for the women and children in their internment camps and for the men in their POW camps were found all over Southeast Asia. They had never been distributed to the camp hospitals to treat desperately ill people and had been barely used by the Japanese themselves.

Like Didi, Frits was frequently in and out of the hospital. He remained a frail little boy with severe anemia and little resistance to infectious diseases. Out of desperation, the camp doctor, also a European prisoner of the Japanese, finally ordered blood injections for him in an effort to inoculate him. For lack of anything else, unsterilized blood, donated by several of the healthiest women in the camp, was injected into his little behind.

On May 22, 1945, we celebrated Frits's third birthday with Tante Ruth while Didi was in the hospital. Didi had managed to save some of her special food for him, and on his big day, he was allowed to visit her and received two magnificent birthday presents: one hardboiled egg and a djeroek, a small orange. Didi always remembered this day fondly and liked to tell us how Frits happily wobbled out of her hospital room on his unsteady legs, carefully carrying these amazing treasures, one in each hand, to show Tante Ruth and me.

Wallpaper Paste and Snail Soup

While we were in Ambarawa and Banjoebiroe, the bulk of our diet consisted of watery sago porridge, similar to the sort of substance one can starch clothes with or use as wallpaper paste. The grey, glutinous porridge occasionally included a few tiny pieces of greens or meat. Sometimes the gluey porridge was augmented with cattle corn that was hard and difficult to digest, and sometimes we had small loaves of grey, clammy bread. It all tasted awful, and it was far too meager to keep our hunger away.

The nutritional value of daily rations in the last year of the war for the internees wherever they were located was generally estimated at 1,250 calories per person, having steadily declined throughout the war years. One in eight of the civilian internees in the camps died during the three years of their internment.

The lack of protein in our rations became a source of great distress for the mothers, and to add a little protein to our diet, everyone, especially the children, started collecting snails that lived on the moss-covered walls of our prison. When we had gathered a large enough supply of snails, they were boiled in water, which made for a relatively tasty, and presumably nutritious, soup.

For the women in the camp, one unintended benefit of starvation diets was that they stopped menstruating, which was a huge blessing for them under the circumstances, yet that, too, was a cause for worry because they wondered whether they would be able to have children once the war was over. The men in their camps were equally worried about their inability to have erections. The mothers also worried a great deal about the lack of protein in the diet of the young children and wondered whether they should give the children their portion of eggs or tiny crumbs of meat in the soup, or whether it was better to eat these sporadic little bits of protein themselves. But the doctors in the camps advised the mothers to eat their own shares of protein, as the children could survive only if their mothers did. I remember fishing some of the little meat pieces out of my bowl to give to my mother whenever I could find any.

Widespread Famine among the People

For the ordinary people in Java who were not in camps, the effects of the war were perhaps even more deadly. With the widespread recruitment of the men as romushas, the few remaining workers in the agrarian areas of Java could not adequately work the rice paddies or harvest any substantial foods. Furthermore, the Japanese authorities had insisted on agricultural practices that were not readily applicable in Java and were misunderstood by the farmers, and in addition, the Japanese had insisted that rice fields be turned into fields to grow hemp. Finally, to make matters worse, Indonesia experienced a widespread drought in 1944. Battle had not devastated Java or any other island in 1944 or 1945, but four years of war had emaciated its people.

All over Java in the last year of the war, people were starving. Famine was everywhere because even rice, a common food crop in the Indies, had become scarce. Hunger, disease, lack of medical attention, merciless use of romushas, and executions had produced, at an outer estimate, three million dead in Java alone. Historians estimate that about five million Southeast Asians died as a result of the Japanese invasion and occupation.

Drafting Messages to Papa Daan

The Japanese had forbidden the women and children to have paper, but I have a small book that my mother carried with her throughout the war years: *The Man Nobody Knows, a Discovery of the Real Jesus,* by Barton Pocket

Books, 5th Edition, 1941. Didi did not remember how it was that she had this little book—it is not the sort of book she would have selected under ordinary circumstances, but during the war, it was valuable, nonetheless, because it offered her access to scarce paper. Didi penciled drafts of messages to Papa Daan in its margins, messages she prepared for the Red Cross and that could immediately be mailed to him the moment she got word that the Red Cross had located him.

The little messages had to be in either Malay or English, and Didi drafted the same message in both languages in the margins of the book:

> *Disini semoea baik. Sytske dan Fritsje soedah besar. Moekaraja Syts seperti poenja saja. Fritsje seperti poenja Daan. Doea doea manis betoel dan pienter.*
>
> *Here all is well. Sytske and Fritsje are already big. Sytske looks just like me. Fritsje looks like Daan. The two of them are very sweet and intelligent.*

The Man Nobody Knows also contains endless numbers of recipes for tasty meals, scrawled in its margins by Didi: Norwegian fish pudding, ajam koening, chicken curry, tongue in wine sauce, German goulash, applesauce cake, and pickled sardines, to name just a few. Didi had initially refused to participate in the exchange of recipes that was widely popular in the camps, but she too succumbed to its seduction as food became increasingly scarce, was unpalatable, and had no nutritious value at all. Sitting on their baléh-baléhs in the evening, someone might call out, "Hungarian goulash," and everyone would get into the game by shouting out the necessary ingredients and writing the assembled recipe into the margins of books or on scraps of paper.

But there was one thing everyone agreed was even more important than imaginary cooking lessons: having drawings made of their small children for later, in lieu of photographs, when the war would be over and they would be reunited with their husbands and families. Even though food was so scarce, Didi once gave some of the rare loaves of clammy bread we had received to one of the artists in the camp, someone who still had paper and pencils and who made portrait drawings of Frits and me.

Surviving Illness through Willpower

An estimated 15,800 internees lived in the overcrowded internment camps of Ambarawa and Banjoebiroe during the last months of the war. The conditions in the camps varied, but in all camps, the internees suffered from severe overcrowding and a lack of food, clean water, and medicines. It was impossible to maintain a semblance of hygiene, especially with the overflowing, snake-infested, stinking latrines covered in flies. Large numbers of women and children, who no longer had any resistance to diseases, were sick, and the funeral cart was busy almost every day in the summer of 1945. Those of us still more or less healthy would silently watch the cart, pulled by an emaciated old horse, as it carried its load out of the prison gate to the camp cemetery.

Sometime during that summer of 1945, twenty-nine-year-old Didi was so weak and had so little faith in her survival that she wished she could go to sleep and never wake up again. She later told me that this moment was a turning point for her, because she realized that she simply could not give up—she had to fight hard to stay alive to make sure that Frits and I would survive. In a letter to Oma in 1945, she wrote the following about Oom Heb and his inability to fight for his life:

> *Heb's diabetes has become secondary to "general weakness." But for him the worst is that he has been in a camp of 122 men, of which only 42 are still alive. He cannot forget that and as long as he cannot, he will not get better. I know this—I have seen it with other people—if you don't want to survive with all your might, then you are finished.*

In the summer of 1945, Didi willed herself to stay alive.

Worries and Dreams

As I got older and Didi was seriously ill, I would stand in line to get our meals at the central kitchen, together with the other women and children. I started doing this when I was only five years old, on days when Didi was feeling particularly weak. At about the same time, I started to worry how Didi, Frits, and I would get away from the camp. I knew that somehow we had to get ourselves to Oma in Deventer, which was, according to my mother, the only safe place in the whole world for us.

Didi talked often about her home and Oma, and how wonderful it would be when we were there, a place where we would be safe and where Oma would take care of us and where we would have enough to eat. But Oma's house in Deventer was a place that I could not imagine, no matter how hard I tried. I could not believe that in Deventer, one family lived in an entire house all by themselves, without any other people crowded in, that it was a place where everyone slept in a separate bed of her own, a place where people sat on chairs at a table when they were eating—I found this particularly funny! In the camp, we lived in overcrowded barracks, slept side by side with dozens of other women and children, and sat on our platform when we ate, with our enamel bowls on our laps. But though I had no idea what Deventer was or where it was, I knew that we had to get there somehow.

My sense of responsibility for the safety and well-being of my family remained throughout my childhood. I vividly remember many sleepless nights, years later, when we lived in Makassar, Singapore, and Semarang, and our parents were away from home for an evening out at the Dutch Club or visiting with friends. During those long hours, I worried how I could get Frits; our baby brother, Jan; and myself back to Holland, where we would be safe, if something were to happen to our parents. Lying wide awake in my bed, I would stay alert until I could see the lights of my parents' car turning into our driveway. One very late evening when my parents had not come back home by the time I had expected them; I went outside and hid under the tall cana plants alongside the driveway of our house. It was a place to hide from danger under the protection of large leaves, the way I had done as a small child in the jungle.

CHAPTER 8

THE END OF THE WAR—FREE BUT NOT SAFE

The last few days we have been awakened by the thunder of gun shots and a few days ago some people threw bombs near here. One hardly notices it any more. It is a good thing that the other side doesn't own an air force, because then it would look a lot worse for us here. But please don't worry; they are completely on top of the situation here. The only thing is that it is time to stop the kidnappings and things like that. The Dutch are now putting together a special corps to counter the kidnappings which will use so called "blitz buggies."

—Didi's third letter to Oma in Deventer, December 3, 1945

All during the early summer of 1945 in Banjoebiroe, we had seen airplanes with the colors of Allied flags on their tails flying high in the sky above us; they were probably reconnaissance planes taking photographs of the locations of the many internment camps in Java. Then, in August, rumors were beginning to fly, hinting that the end of the war was now really in sight and our suffering would soon be over. But few people dared to believe that peace was around the corner—there had been so very many rumors throughout the years that had been proven false later that the idea of the end of the war was especially hard to believe.

Of course, in our isolated camps, we had not heard that the Americans had dropped the atom bombs on Japan, and not until almost a week after the fact did we learn that Emperor Hirohito had publicly announced the Japanese surrender on August 15.

The Long War Is Over

Finally, on August 21, everyone assembled in the middle of Camp Banjoebiroe's center field to sing "Het Wilhelmus," the Dutch national anthem, while one of the women ceremoniously lowered the flag with the rising sun and replaced it with the Dutch red, white, and blue flag that someone had saved throughout the war at great peril to herself. I stood among the crowd of women and children, and the celebration made a huge impression on me, but I did not understand why so many women were crying or what the fuss was really about. I am not sure if my mother or Frits was present—Didi was so very weak at the time and had so little energy. Peace had come at last, and none too soon; Didi later told me that if the war had lasted two more months, she probably would not have survived. I am not sure that Frits would have survived, either.

The next day, the old gate in the thick walls of our prison was opened and we were free to leave, but few of us did. We had no place to go to, and there was no way we could take care of ourselves. We probably had not learned that Indonesia, under Soekarno's leadership, had declared its independence from the Netherlands a few days earlier, on August 17. Most Dutch assumed that they would soon be in charge of their colony again and that their ordinary prewar colonial lives would be restarted. The only thing we learned quickly was that it was unsafe outside the walls of our prison.

The Bersiap Period

The Indonesian fight for independence from colonial rule had started when the Japanese had invaded the islands. Immediately after the declaration of surrender by the emperor of Japan, Soekarno formally declared Indonesia's independence with a short proclamation:

> We the people of Indonesia hereby declare the independence of Indonesia. Matters which concern the transfer of power and other things will be executed by careful means and in the shortest period of time.

The proclamation was dated "Djakarta, 17 August 1945" and was signed by Soekarno and Hatta, who would become Indonesia's first prime minister in 1949, in the name of the people of Indonesia.

Immediately after Soekarno's statement, young revolutionaries, eager to fight for their country's freedom and independence, started to attack Dutch men, women, and children who were beginning to leave the camps. This period is referred to as the bersiap period. *Bersiap* means "be prepared," and it was the battle cry of the revolutionaries. The most turbulent time was in the months of October and November 1945, when bands of young men started roaming around indiscriminately robbing, kidnapping, and killing *orang blanda*—white people—as well as large numbers of local Indonesians who were suspected of having sided with the Dutch during the Japanese occupation.

Protected by Our Former Jailers

During the bersiap period, we could not leave the relative safety of the camp. Didi, Frits, and I continued waiting for our freedom behind the walls of Banjoebiroe. We had no choice but to stay under the protection of our former Japanese guards, who had received orders to treat the Dutch women and children decently, to provide for our safety, and to supply better food. Part of the declaration of surrender signed by the Japanese and Allied representatives stated:

> We hereby command the Japanese imperial government and the Japanese imperial general headquarters at once to liberate all Allied prisoners of war and civilian internees now under Japanese control and to provide for their protection, care, maintenance and immediate transportation as directed.

Miraculously, the Japanese camp commanders in Banjoebiroe were able to provide the internees in the camps with more and a better quality of food almost immediately, and within weeks, we started to gain weight. By the end of the war, Didi had lost about one-fifth of her normal weight, but she gained it back very quickly when better food was made available. She wrote Oma a few months after the liberation:

> *Thankfully, the war ended then and things got much better. Especially the young people got better fast. Within 3 weeks I gained 12 kilograms. At the moment I look pretty much like I did in the past—perhaps a little bloated—but that will go away by itself.*

Soon after the day of liberation, we saw airplanes flying low over the trees of the center field, dropping boxes down into the camp. The cardboard boxes usually broke apart on impact, and out would roll dark green cans filled with things I had never seen: chocolate, butter, cheese, milk powder, Spam, and cigarettes for the women—manna from heaven falling among the starved women and children. For us children, the wrappers that were left after the butter and cheese had been eaten were a special treat. We found them discarded in the center field and would sniff at the wonderful, unusual odors that clung to them.

Trucks Filled with Fathers

Another big event occurred in September that will remain with me forever. Near Banjoebiroe was a men's camp, and some of the men who had been interned there and who had wives or children in Banjoebiroe were allowed to visit our camp. I remember the day when I stood inside the gate of the old walled prison, waiting for the trucks that would bring husbands and fathers to some of the women and children who had lived in our camp. Didi must have told me that Papa Daan would not be among the men who would come to our camp that day, because our last postcard from him had been sent from Siam, but I went looking for him nonetheless, together with all the other children who were hoping their fathers would come for them. As I stood among the other kids, looking at the faces of the men in the trucks, I wondered which one was coming for me. After the last man had come down from the truck and had joined his family, I and most of the other children were left standing with no one to take our hands.

Recovery of Allied Prisoners of War and Internees

We had to wait two months, until late October, before we were finally evacuated from Banjoebiroe by British Ghurka troops, who transported us in convoys of heavily armed trucks to Magelang, a camp in Central Java that could better be defended against the roving bands of young armed Indonesian men.

Magelang was operated by an organization called Recovery of Allied Prisoners of War and Internees (RAPWI), which had been established by the British who had been assigned the task of finding, safeguarding, and helping to repatriate the former Dutch POWs and internees in Indonesia and most of Southeast Asia. RAPWI had established a rehabilitation center at the military hospital in Magelang, a place that was miraculously equipped with real beds, one for each one of us, with clean sheets and fresh *klamboes*, mosquito netting—unforgettable luxury after so many years of squalor.

Papa Daan's Death

It was in Magelang that Didi received a letter from their old friend Buis Hofstee, who wrote while he was still in Tamarkan, Siam. Buis wrote Didi about Papa Daan's death in November 1944 and his last relatively good months in the hospital camp on the banks of the River Kwai Noi. Sadly, Didi lost this letter when we were being evacuated from Magelang days later. What follows is part of a letter Didi wrote home to Oma, quoting Buis about Papa Daan's death:

> *After many detours and marches through the jungles of Thailand he ended up in Tamarkan, in pretty decent health. He suffered lightly*

from beriberi, but so did everyone else. The allied forces then bombed the bridge next to Tamarkan. Four bombs fell on the camp, primarily on top of the British barracks. Seventeen men died—16 Brits and Daan, who was visiting a British friend....

It happened last year, on November 29th, at 8 o'clock Nippon time in the evening, that is at 6:30 our time. There were quite a few old Deventer people in the camp and Daan had just organized a get-together; a clear sign that he was quite healthy, considering all. The worst is that he never will see the children. Sytske, who is already such a big girl, and little Frits, whom he has never seen at all, not even as a baby.

I don't believe that the news of Papa Daan's death was a complete surprise for Didi. Somehow, she had known that we would never see Papa Daan again. In a letter home, she wrote about her longing for the time she would be at home with Oma: "I have so often imagined myself with the children in Holland with you, but without Daan. I don't know how, but I have known that he was not coming back."

For a few days, we were able to relax in Magelang, but very soon, heavy fighting broke out between the local revolutionaries and the British Ghurka troops. Because we were located smack in the middle of the line of fire, we again ended up lying *under* our beds, seeking shelter from the bullets, instead of on top of them. I remember our shock and fear, and my high, piercing scream of terror when a hand grenade exploded in the corner of our room while we were lying there, hiding under our beds.

Within days, we were loaded into heavily armed trucks, protected by mattresses hung from the sides, and were driven in a convoy past the villages and towns of Central Java to the relative safety of camp Halmaheira, in Semarang.

Another Heartbreaking Loss

I remember the truck ride at night to Semarang and still see us sitting at the back of the truck, among other women and children and piles of baggage. Didi always kept her shoulder bag on a strap around her neck and back, but had removed it to get some water for Frits and me. In the crowded space, the bag was set aside for a moment, and when the truck rumbled over a pothole, the bag tumbled from the moving truck and disappeared under the wheels of the next one. My mother wrote Oma about this awful night:

I first wrote you from Magelang, the day after I received the news from Buis that Daan is no longer alive. I have lost that letter and everything else that was most dear to me; everything that I carried with me in my bag, and had with me all the time; it fell out of the truck we were on—gone. The letter from Buis in which he wrote about Daan; Daan's watch—the last thing that I had that belonged to him; Daan's old wallet which I found in an old safe in Tjimatis, in August after the invasion, and which I cherished, because it contained the letters you and Father had written Daan on the day I left for the East Indies; a few photos of the children; and a pair of beautiful drawings of them which someone made for me in the camp—I paid for them with a small loaf of bread during the worst hunger period—it was therefore particularly valuable—it is all gone.

But, we don't depend on our possessions any longer here, we have learned not to, but that loss was very difficult. At the time we were being transported by Ghurka army trucks—and I could hardly ask them to turn around—it was not a pleasure ride—and I noticed it too late.

By November 12, 1945, we were in Camp Halmaheira in Semarang, which was initially built in the 1920s as a neighborhood of modest homes for railroad workers of the Nederlandsch-Indische Spoorwegen, the Dutch-East Indies Railway. These one-family homes ended up housing about seventy persons per house in the last months of 1945; the compound of fifty houses was home to nearly 3,800 people. Because of the overcrowded little houses, uncertain sewer drains, and sporadic freshwater supplies, Halmaheira was known as one of the worst camps at the time. The overcrowded camp stank of sewage.

Didi's First Letter Home

On November 12, 1945, Didi wrote her first letter home to Oma in Deventer.

Camp Halmaheira, Nov. 12, 1945

My Dearest Darlings,
Today we expect the arrival of the airplane from Holland and I hope so very much that there will be a letter for me, so that I will know exactly how you all are and who I will see again. I heard by way of Francine, from Bram Lammers (Mam, who is that?) that you are

well, Mam, but that Father has died. Is that true? I cannot yet believe it—it is such a terrible thing, because there was so much I needed to set right .... Kuk is married to Cor van Nieuwland and then, Francine writes: "Your brother is doing well," forgetting that I have two brothers ..... Oh, the terrible uncertainty ....

From here I have good and bad news. The good news is that I have a son—Frederik Christiaan—Fritsje, now already 3½ years old, and a real sweetheart. He was born in Buitenzorg on May 22nd, 1942. Sytske is doing very well. But our dear Daan is gone. I received the news only two weeks ago—Buis Hofstee wrote me about it. And if it is true about Pops, that too is the worst. He would have enjoyed the children so much.

I will come home as soon as possible—the New Amsterdam *is leaving for Holland this coming Friday and I hope to be on board—if that doesn't work out, then the next boat. Imagine that I might be home by Christmas...! Gosh, Mam, imagine that! It will be a very different home-coming than we had hoped it would be, but still—going home!*

From then on, Didi could not stop dreaming about going home to Holland so she could leave the horror of the past four years behind and return to the safety and comfort of her family to start a new life with the help of Oma and her sister, Kuk, and two brothers, Gerrit and Piet.

We did not have to stay very long in Camp Halmaheira. One day soon after our arrival, one of the Dutch leaders of the camp showed up at our house, saying, "Mevrouw Engelberts, if you can get ready and packed in half an hour, you can be on the next plane headed for Batavia this afternoon." This was *no problem!* Didi ordered Frits and me to stand in the corner of the room and dress ourselves with the clothes she tossed us. In the meantime, she threw everything else we owned into the canvas duffel bag, and within minutes, we were ready to go. Going to Batavia meant that we were that much closer to RAPWI offices and a boat that would get us back home to Holland.

From Batavia, we were transported by RAPWI to Bandoeng, to wait there for our passage back to Holland. We lived in Bandoeng for several weeks, in Riouw Straat 47. This was a private house where several Dutch families were staying, awaiting repatriation to Holland. Our room was a sunroom, entirely enclosed in glass. Although we had at least a room of our own, we were separated from the next room by nothing more than a *tikar*, a thin mat of woven bamboo strips. There was no privacy, since we could hear our neighbors' conversations word for word (and they ours), and everyone could see us.

Ghurkas and Blitz Buggies

Bandoeng was a dangerous place in the fall of 1945. The bersiap period was in full swing, and roving bands of armed, angry young men roamed the street, kidnapping or killing any Europeans they saw. Every house on the Riouw Straat that was occupied by Dutch women and children was protected by Ghurka troops lying on their bellies among the bushes in the gardens, guns at the ready to shoot the bands of young men looking for Europeans. "Our" Ghurkas sometimes had a helper in the form of three-and-a-half year old Frits, who would lie right next to the men with a stick in his arms, ready to defend the property. Of course, Frits and I were under strict orders not to leave our yard.

The Ghurkas were not alone in trying to protect the Dutch women and children. When former POWs returned to Java, they were soon involved in bringing some normalcy and peace into the towns that had been occupied by the Japanese and that were now a battleground for Indonesian revolutionaries. Miel de Mos, one of Didi's friends from the voyage on *The Marnix of St. Aldegonde*, was now back in a Dutch uniform, driving around Bandoeng in a Blitz Buggy, a jeep, safeguarding the women and children in the residential neighborhoods in town.

Some of the houses near us in the Riouw Straat had recently been abandoned, and though it was incredibly dangerous, Didi and the other women would regularly go into empty homes nearby to look for anything useful that had been left behind by its previous occupants. She once came back from such a scavenger trip with a sack of sugar and an old rag doll that had been left behind. These were treasures, especially the sugar, which would be added to a few spoons of strong coffee and then beaten until it turned into coffee foam, called *koffieklop*, an unbelievable delicacy in those days. Whenever a mother or tante made koffieklop, all children in the house would gather to watch the foamy substance grow with every beat of the fork until it filled the whole bowl. We could not wait to taste the airy, sweet substance and dreamed about it when we had none.

Children's Fears of Abandonment and Death

The years of deprivation, uncertainty, and fear had left their marks on Frits and me; we had become frightened children. We were terrified that we might lose Didi. We had seen so much violence and disease and had heard far too much about death, so that when Didi was not around, we spent our day filled with watchful waiting, scared to death and in tears, convinced that she would not come back. In a letter home to Oma, Didi wrote:

> *A few days ago, when I had left them to get a pail of water and returned to our room, I found them both in tears—sobbing—and I heard Syts say: Frits, shall I go look on the street? Mammie is probably walking on the street again. . . ! They don't let me out of their sights and when I leave for a few minutes they are in tears. Once, in Semarang [Halmaheira], I had stayed away longer than I had told them and everyone in the house got involved to calm them down—Syts said: I thought that you too were dead... She is still completely upset. It is time that they get a normal childhood.*
>
> *This afternoon I was talking with someone in another room and apparently they had been looking for me. When I returned, Syts said: I thought that you were on the street again and did you know that the kidnappers have "tjientjanged" a lady [hacked a lady to pieces]?*

Frits, who was only three and a half years old at the end of 1945, once asked Didi in his baby-Dutch about life in Deventer: "Are there kijzeberen in Holland and are there boerekazen who will kill the kijzeberen?" By *boerekazen* he meant Ghurkas, and I assume that the word *kijzeberen* was his garbled way of referring to kidnappers.

News from Oom Heb and Tante Bep

At the end of November, Didi received letters from Tante Bep and Oom Heb, who had survived the war but were not well. Both of them were hospitalized in Carolus Hospital in Batavia, while their sons, Herbert and Loetje, were living in Bandoeng. Tante Bep wrote that she suffered from a severe case of edema and was "blown up like a gas-filled balloon." Oom Heb was very weak after his ordeal in the camp and continued to be "skin over bones, weighing 47.5 kilos." The letters Tante Bep and Oom Heb wrote were mailed to Magelang and were forwarded by RAPWI to Didi in Bandoeng.

> *Dear Didi,*
> *It is so awful that you are so far away; it would have been so wonderful if you had been here in these days, because then we would be able to do all we can to help you get passage to Holland.*

It is so horrible the way East Java is suffering under the gangs of Rampokkers. It is a little less bad in West Java; every now and then there are demonstrations and some gun fire. It has been particularly bad in Buitenzorg—Kedoeng Malang has again become a "protected area" there.

Mr. Fermin [the top administrator of the plantations near Djasinga] and Eric [his fourteen-year-old son, the brother of little Robert Fermin] are missing and we must assume that they have been killed. They had been dragged from the train they were on by the revolutionaries. It is so unbelievable that you can survive the entire camp period and then, at the very end, lose your life this way.

I so much hope that you will be strong and courageous to deal with your loss.

We believe that it would be best for you to return to Batavia as soon as possible; we are doing everything we can to get you passage on the same boat we will be on. The rumors are that the New Amsterdam *will leave the 22nd, but RAPWI still doesn't know—so, we will have to wait—Love from Bep.*

Oom Heb also wrote Didi on the fourteenth of November:

Dear Didi,
We received your postcard with the sad news the day before yesterday. We had been afraid all along because it took so long to get any news. It is especially sad that Daan had to die because of a friendly bomb. Zusje Lief *[dear little sister], you are now one of the many who have lost so much, but Daan continues to live in your sweet children, and remember that they will need you now more than ever; stay courageous and strong, the way we have gotten to know each other in March 1942.*

Because we are most likely leaving on the Oranje *we are trying to get you passage as well, I don't dare to hope for that, but it would be lovely.*

Don't worry too much about the family in Holland; the losses there are not nearly as bad, and God won't take everything from you. In any case, you have to leave here and get away from the interior of Java. Try to get here, dear, and remain calm and strong. We'll see each other soon, much love, Hep.

Oom Heb and Tante Bep and their two boys sailed home together on one of the very first boats out of Java in the fall of 1945. The voyage on the *Nieuw Amsterdam* was designated to carry the sickest survivors of the war back to the Netherlands. Sadly, Oom Heb did not survive that voyage; he died a few days before the boat was to arrive in Holland. In the presence of Tante Bep and their two boys, Herbert and Loetje, he was buried at sea in the Bay of Biscay. It was the last day of December in the year 1945.

The Many Faces of Truth

Tante Beb told Didi after the war that Oom Heb's burial at sea had been a sober and solemn ceremony, with the crew standing at attention and a respectful speech by the Captain of the *Nieuw Amsterdam*, Captain Dekema, the father of Harold Dekema, the husband of Oom Cor's sister, Mies. Tante Bep praised the efforts of the captain and crew to make the burial dignified and memorable. Little Herbert, on the other hand, who was about ten years old when his father was buried at sea, remains bitter. His memory of Oom Heb's burial at sea is that "They threw my father overboard."

CHAPTER 9

PAPA DAAN'S DEATH IN CAMP TAMARKAN

It is terrible that Old Frits [our Grandfather Engelberts] didn't live to see the liberation, the war was so terrible there and he missed the contact with the East Indies—I am glad that he has not known that Daan has died. But it is too bad that he never knew that there is a little Frits Engelberts, because he would have been extremely happy with that news.

—Oma's first letter to Didi, October 18, 1945

After Papa Daan had left Changi, his journey by railroad from Singapore to Nom Pladuk in Siam took five days. He and the other POWs were loaded tightly into boxcars that turned into baking ovens in the hot tropical sun. There was no sanitation in the cars, and the only way the men could relieve themselves was when the train made a short stop and they could climb down from the train and squat in the jungle next to the track. Because almost everyone had dysentery by then, the boxcars became filthy and stank in the heat of the noonday sun.

Daan was one of close to 18,000 Dutch POWs who were transported to Siam to work on the railroad that the Japanese Army was building from Siam to Burma. In the 1930s, British engineers had considered building a railroad along that route but had rejected the idea as impossible. The track would have had to be laid through virgin jungle, vast tracts of swamp, and through tunnels made in limestone bluffs.

The Japanese military command, on the other hand, needed an overland connection between Burma and Siam to support their forces in Burma, which they had seized from the British in 1942. The sea route to Burma was too long and was vulnerable to attack by Allied submarines. The Japanese military authorities, far away in Tokyo, ordered the railway to be built, notwithstanding the difficult terrain. Started in 1942, when the Japanese had plenty of manpower in the form of the huge number of POWs and romushas they had captured with the fall of Southeast Asia, the railroad was finished in less than two years.

Especially during the infamous Speedo Period of 1943, the Japanese forced their slave laborers to work hard, constantly yelling, "Lekas, lekas," faster, faster. In the spring and summer of 1943, the prisoners worked side by side with the romushas for long days in the drenching monsoon rains that made the dense jungle a mosquito-ridden swamp. By early 1944, the railroad was completed—an unbelievable feat, but one that was accomplished at great cost and a huge loss of human lives. The railroad became known as the Death Railroad.

Of course, soon after the line was finished, the Allies started to bomb the line. During the last year and a half of the war, work parties, as the groups of POWs were called, had to go back into the jungle to repair the line and the bridges, over and over again. After the war, the rail line was abandoned, and today, only a small piece of it is being used by the Thai Railway.

Most of the old railroad track is again covered in dense jungle.

A Letter from A.L.Th. Heil

I never knew much at all about Papa Daan's wartime experiences, other than that he had died in a bombing raid by the Allies in November 1944 and that he was buried in the large War Cemetery in Kanchanaburi in Thailand. But in October 2009, when Frits came to visit us in Millerton, he brought me a letter that gave me information I had never seen about Pappa Daan's death. The letter was written in May 1946 by someone whose name I had not heard before: A.L.Th. Heil. The letter was in response to an inquiry written by Jan, who was still in Batavia and who had asked Heil whether he had any information about the circumstances of Papa Daan's death. Heil wrote Jan back while he was still in Bangkok, editing the *Dutch Daily* for Dutch former prisoners who were still in Siam waiting to be evacuated to the Netherlands.

Heil wrote that he and Papa Daan had been study friends in Deventer and had been in Malang in 1942 when they were first imprisoned by the Japanese. They had remained together during the war, and both of them had worked on the infamous railroad the Japanese were building between Siam and Burma. He wrote that they had been together in Camp Number Two of the cluster of four Kinsayok camps in the jungles of Siam during 1943 and part of 1944 and that they both had been sick at Kinsayok and had been sent to Tamarkan for rehabilitation sometime in 1944 after the railroad had been finished.

They were both at Tamarkan, the rehabilitation camp on the River Kwai Noi, on the night that the Allies bombed the bridge over the river—the night when some bombs missed their mark and fell on the camp, killing Papa Daan and fifteen young British prisoners of war. Heil's letter to Jan has been translated by me and reproduced in its entirety:

> *Bangkok, May 4, 1946*
>
> *Dear Sir:*
> *I received your letter this morning and I am glad that you have contacted me, because I was concerned about Daan's possessions.*
>
> *I don't know whether you or Daan's wife are familiar with the circumstances of Daan's death. I will attempt to tell you about it objectively.*
>
> *On November 29, 1944, Daan and I had made a date with other old Deventer men to get together after the evening appèl. During the evening appèl, 21 bombers with their engines turned off unexpectedly glided over the nearby situated railway bridge and our camp, Tamarkan. Four bombs fell in the corner of our camp, where the hospital latrines were located, next to the military police barracks. Somewhat farther back were the hospital barracks.*
>
> *It had been Daan's habit to go the latrines during the evening appèl; he was still a hospital patient and therefore did not need to participate in the appèls. He did so that evening as well.*
>
> *Initially we had no idea what happened to Daan; we only heard that 13 or 15 men had been buried in sand in the M.P. barracks. Later that evening, Daan's neighbor from the hospital came to see me to find out if I had seen Daan. The next morning at the appèl, we were told again that Daan was missing. Soon afterwards, they found Daan on the podium of the theatre, behind the curtain. We heard later that some Aussies had found his body at the latrines and had carried him to the theatre. Because of the rescue efforts to free the buried POWs first, Daan had been forgotten by the Aussies. According to the doctor who examined Daan, he did not suffer much at all. His death was attributed to the immense air pressure that had hit him; he had few wounds.*
>
> *The same day, I talked with Lieutenant van Esch to ask for Daan's belongings, especially because I knew that a lot was always stolen*

immediately after the death of any patient in the hospital. It is very likely that I came too late to prevent theft, which can be established by the following:

Daan and I shared everything and had done so at Kinsayok, from where we had been transported. At Kinsayok, we were part of a Kongsi with a group of men who worked in the Japanese kitchen. Whenever a pig had been slaughtered for the Japanese, the group received the head to take home. Because Daan and I had stayed in our quarters because of illness, we did all housework for the Kongsi, especially also because the group did not come home until the late evening hours. Because of the rendering of the fat of the pig, our Kongsi had saved a considerable amount of lard. When Daan and I were put on a transport to Tamarkan, we received each a large bottle of lard by way of thanks for all we had done for the men.

Because I started working very soon upon our arrival at Tamarkan and started to earn money, I visited Daan every day and would bring him a fried egg or some other food. He did need the additional nutrition because he suffered from a light case of beriberi. I had given Daan my bottle of fat for safekeeping because I saw him regularly. Lieutenant van Esch had all of Daan's possessions. When I did not see the two bottles containing the lard, I knew immediately that they must have been stolen.

When I lived in the barracks in Malang with Daan, I knew for certain that he wore a signet ring and I believe also his wedding ring. I also remember that he told me later he had sold a gold ring in exchange for extra food. I really cannot remember whether he had any rings left when the camp was bombed. I have carefully checked Daan's belongings but I did not find the signet ring, or a little gold chain with an aquamarine stone.

As was common, I had to give Daan's clothes and utensils to those who had survived the bombings but had lost their own possessions. I will give you an inventory of items I am keeping to give to his wife: a saffron leather billfold, which contained his driver's license, a postcard from his wife, dated May 25, 2602, undersigned with Didi, Sytske and Chris-Jan [this must be the postcard to announce Frits's birth]. A postcard from his wife dated May 23. [Heil described several photographs that had been included and a program for a small party, written in French and illustrated by Daan]. In addition, there were

Two drawings of Didi and Sytske, copied by Francken from the photo made in Soerabaja in 1942 on the eve of Sytske's second birthday

several letters in the billfold from Mrs. Engelberts to Daan. Since the Japanese confiscated all letters of more than 25 words and because the content of the letters was rather intimate, I reluctantly decided to burn them before the Japanese could get ahold of them. I did not want to give those Japanese who could read Dutch the pleasure of having fun with these letters. In addition, I have in my possession Daan's wallet, which I continue to use. I have deposited the little bit of money I found into the food fund for the hospital. Finally, I have a bamboo tube that contains two drawings made in Malang by the artist Francken. This is all that I have in my possession.

I plan to leave Bangkok with one of the last evacuation ships. Unfortunately, I cannot go earlier because I cannot leave my work as editor of the Dutch Daily *until the last evacuees have left.*

I don't think it is wise to ask me to mail Daan's possession since the mail is unreliable and parcels frequently are lost. Because I plan to go to Holland one of these days, I prefer to take Daan's belongings myself and to bring them to Mrs. Engelberts in Deventer.

Would you be so kind as to inform Mrs. Engelberts about the contents of this letter? I will very much appreciate your help in this.

I don't know whether you are an old Deventer man, but you probably know very well how close our friendships are. This was also the case between Daan and me.

I am including my business card with the request to send it on to Mrs. Engelberts as an introduction and to ensure that she knows exactly where she can reach me in Bangkok.

With the expectation to hear from you soon, I remain yours,
A.L.Th. Heil

The business card Heil had mailed to Jan did end up among Didi's papers, where I found it when I was sorting her possessions after she had died. From the card, I finally learned Heil's first name, Arnaud, and that he worked for Netherlands Public Relations in Bangkok and lived in Room 1A at the Oriental Hotel.

A Name in a Notebook

When Jon and I were in Kanchanaburi in 2004, we met Rod Beattie, the director of the Thailand-Burma Centre, who told us a great deal about the jungle camps. He had walked the entire length of the old railroad track and had found many items that once had been lost by the POWs. This collection is now located in the museum he built with his own funds. Rod gave us two days of his time in 2004 when he learned that I was the daughter of a POW.

Rod told us that Papa Daan initially was buried in the camp cemetery of Tamarkan, about one kilometer from the camp, together with the fifteen young British men who had died during the bombing raid. An Australian priest, Padre Mathieson, had presided over the burial ceremony. The padre had maintained relatively detailed records while he was at Tamarkan, and after the burial of the sixteen young men, he wrote their names, with their ranks and serial numbers, in a small notebook. For Papa Daan's entry, the section for known next of kin was left blank.

Padre Mathieson's notebook is now part of the collection of the Imperial War Museum in London. Not long before we met him, Rod had been in London and had made photocopies of the notebook's pages. We found Papa Daan's name scrawled among those of the others who had died on November 29, 1944. At age thirty-three, Papa Daan had been one of the older men who had died during the bombing raid.

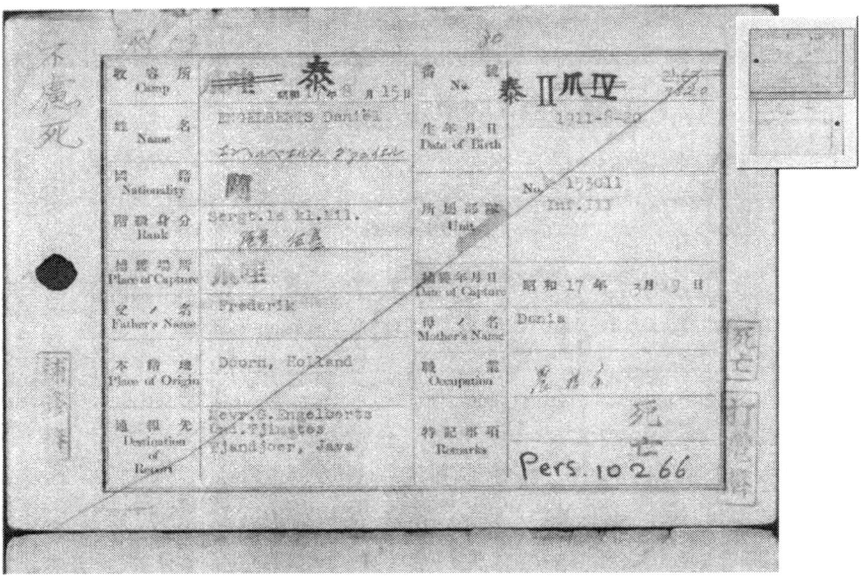

Camp: 泰 — 昭和 年 月 15日 | No.: 泰 II 爪 IV
Name: ENGELBERTS Daniel | Date of Birth: 1911-6-20
Nationality | No. 153011 Inf.III
Rank: Sergt.le kl.Mil. | Unit
Place of Capture | Date of Capture: 昭和 17年 3月 9日
Father's Name: Frederik | Mother's Name: Donia
Place of Origin: Doorn, Holland | Occupation
Destination of Report: Mevr.G.Engelberts, Tjandjoer, Java | Remarks: 死亡
Pers. 10266

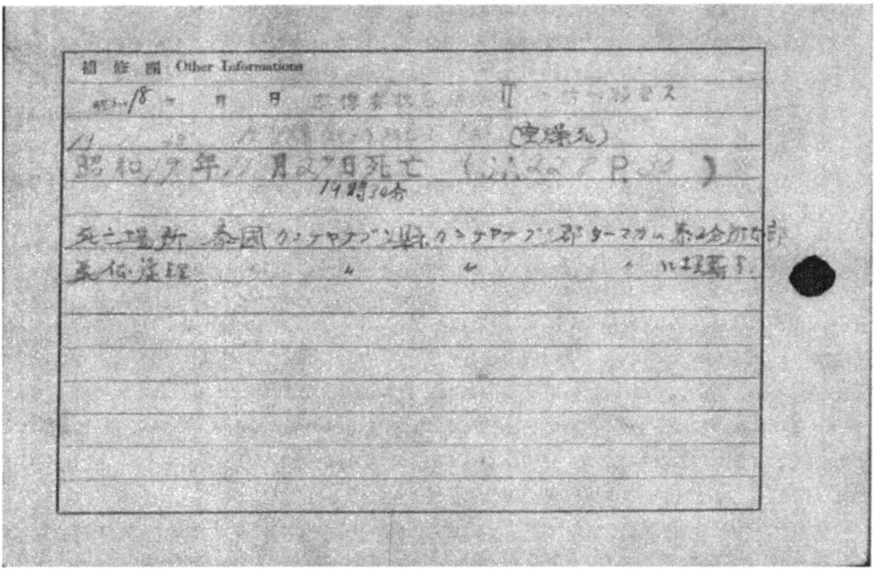

Other Informations

死亡

Papa Daan's registration card and record of his death,
in Japanese with partial Dutch translations

Rod also showed us large copies of aerial photographs of Tamarkan, probably made toward the end of the war. Between the huts and barracks of the camp, we saw small figures of the men who were imprisoned there, tiny shadows falling away from them—was one of these small figures Papa Daan?

Recently, I was told by Frits that I could find more information about Papa Daan at www.gahetna.nl/collectie/inventaris. This website of *Het National Archief* in the Netherlands has compiled the camp registrations of 48,000 Dutch prisoners of war in Japanese camps. From the website, I found copies of Papa Daan's registration card and the notice of his death.

Connecting with Our Engelberts Family

Although we always heard that Papa Daan was a nice person, Frits and I had very little other information about him. We knew that he was the youngest child of my grandparents, Frederik Christiaan Engelberts and Dania Lena Anna Engelberts-Hakkert and that he had a sister, Tante Willy, and two brothers, Oom Gerard and Oom Frits. We knew that his birthday was August 20 and that he had married our mother in Malang in 1936. We had some photographs of Papa Daan, taken before the war, but we had no photographs of him as a child, had heard no stories about his childhood, and had very little contact with our Engelberts relatives after our arrival in Holland in 1946.

Our grandfather Engelberts had been a *notaris*, a lawyer in Hazerswoude, near the city of Leiden, with expertise in real estate, family, and corporate law. He had died from a massive heart attack in April 1945, days before the liberation. Our grandmother, who had survived the war but had been very ill, died days before we arrived in Holland in 1946.

Frits and I never met Papa Daan's sister, Tante Wilhelmina, or Willy, or his brother Gerard, or any of their children after we arrived in Holland. The only relatives we saw sporadically were Oom Frits and his wife, Tante Tinie, and our cousins Dania and little Fritsje. Although my mother and Oma told us that Papa Daan was a wonderful person and that he had been much loved by the family in Deventer, he remained a remote figure for me. I never learned what he really had been like. No one told us family stories about particular incidents that he had been involved in, or any idiosyncratic details about him that could shed some light on Papa Daan, the man.

Later, while I lived at the boarding school of Louisa State, in Holland, I never displayed Papa Daan's photograph with other family pictures and knickknacks on the shelf above my bed. I understand now that I had been eager to embrace the new father I got when Didi and Jan married. In time, the love for my new father turned into embarrassment over the absence of the first father who had left me so abruptly. Finally, the embarrassment had turned into feelings of hurt and anger.

Slowly, the puzzle, the fragmentary connection to Papa Daan and the Engelberts family, is coming together. Through our cousin Dania Engelberts, Frits and I are now in contact with other cousins, Gerard and Annelei Engelberts, and their spouses. Gerard and Annelei are the children of Willem Reinier Engelberts, Papa Daan's cousin. We have become friends and enjoy each other's company as much as if we had a family relationship all along.

We also now have photographs of our great-grandparents and grandparents that Frits was able to have printed from old glass plate negatives. Best of all, there is a family photograph of our grandparents with their children, Wilhelmina, Gerard, Frits, and three-year-old Daan, who stands at his mother's knee, looking straight at the camera.

Papa Daan and his family, 1915. From left to right, standing in the back row: Daan's sister, Wilhelmina, and our grandfather, Frits Engelberts. Sitting in the front row on the far left is our grandmother, Dania, with little Daan standing next to her. Sitting on the steps in the front row is Daan's brother, Oom Frits, and on the stool on the right sits Oom Gerard.

CHAPTER 10

JAN'S SURVIVAL AND RETURN TO JAVA

Gosh, Jantje, it is such a blessing that all four of us are still alive and it is so wonderful that we can start anew again, something so many others, who are no longer, would have wanted to do but will not be able to. And then, all the others, who are still alive, and will not be able to because things will have changed for them.

—Tante Tiek's first letter to Jan in Manila, November 1945

The adults around us never talked about the war in our presence, and we had no idea how Jan, our second father, had survived the camps. There was only one story he told us about that time, a story Frits and I loved to hear over and over again. The story was about the amount of snow he had seen in the winters in Japan. Jan told us that he and his friends sometimes had to climb out of an upstairs window to dig shoulder-high tunnels through meters of snow to free their own front door. To us, living in the tropics, this sounded too good to be true. Imagine the snowman you could make and the snow castles! You could have huge snowball fights with your friends—nothing could be more fun.

Of course, we never asked what Jan had been doing in Japan, because we knew perfectly well that he had been in a prison camp there just as we had been in camps for women and children in Java and just as Papa Daan had been in a camp in Siam. What was there to talk about?

Camp Kamioka, December 1942

When Jan arrived in Kamioka with the other prisoners of war on December 8, 1942, the camp was covered in deep snow and it was very cold. The men did not know at the time that they would have to work in old tin and lead mines to support Japan's war efforts. Three days after their arrival, they were called together to meet Colonel Mirata, the camp commander, who welcomed the men to the camp. His speech was translated on the spot by the camp translator, Ikada, who spoke English because he had spent many years on the West Coast of the United States.

Mirata's speech is printed in the addendum to *The Nacht van de Ryzende Zon*, by Johannes Wormser, who was at Kamioka together with Jan from December 1942 through September 1945.

Fair and Impartial Treatment

To all prisoners of war!

Recently most prisoners are working conscientiously, but there are still some whose attitude is not what it should be. It seems to me that you are forgetting where you are standing.

You fought to protect your colors for which I honor you as a soldier. But at the same time our people will not forget that you shot at our brothers and sons, killed some of them and wounded others. To this fact you must pay your toll very heavily.

You fought well, but lost and were taken captives. It would be all natural and possible that you would be standing before a firing squad before long. However, by the August Virtues and Grace of His Majesty the Emperor and also benevolence of our Military Authorities you are still sound and alive, having necessary quarters to live in, with clothing and food properly supplied. Moreover, you are allowed to communicate with your loved ones. Did this fact ever occur in your mind? If not, just stop and think it over.

If there is anyone who does not live up to our expectation in every respect, those are the ones who forget the above facts. We are doing our utmost to make your life comfortable under the circumstances. Our treatment is fair and impartial in regard with our Military Laws as well as the International Treaties. This fact should be appreciated, although we are not insisting on it.

When you work hard you may think that you are helping the enemy, and by slacking down on your work and disobeying orders, you may think that you are doing your country justice. It may be true, but it is not doing justice to your selves. Because we are watching over all prisoners of war individually and keeping daily records in every respect, so that when the time comes for your return to your country, we will give first preferences to the best ones and those who dare not to do their best will probably never get their chance to join their loved ones.

So it is only natural that you should do your task conscientiously to acquire your freedom and to join your loved ones at the earliest dates.... To conclude this statement, I should like to say: to acquire freedom, there are always hardships and sacrifices. Without those hardships and sacrifices, freedom can never be acquired. Bear this in mind, never to forget and you would know how to behave in the future.

The Family Borgerhoff before the War

Jan was born in Amersfoort on August 6, 1911. He was the son of Jan Marie Johan Borgerhoff Mulder and Maria Frederika Geertruida Rincker. His sister, Tine – tante Tiek or Tikoes, as I called her, was two years older, and as young children, Tiek and Jan grew up financially secure in a luxurious home in Amersfoort. The family even employed a nanny when the children were very young, which is not common in the Netherlands. Sadly, our grandfather Borgerhoff Mulder committed suicide in December 1926—most likely a reaction to huge financial losses he had suffered in that year—and after that, the comfortable lifestyle of the Borgerhoff family was gone forever.

Jan was only fifteen years old when he lost his father, and although he never talked about that loss with us and we don't know how the terrible circumstances of his father's death affected him, he became, overnight, the "man in the household," on whom his mother and sister depended completely. Tiek and Jan and their mother became financially dependent on their extended family and probably received support from them for several years until Tiek and Jan got jobs and were able to support the three of them.

Jan had wanted to study medicine after finishing high school but had to abandon that idea after they ended up in such reduced circumstances. He served in the Dutch Air Force instead and ended up with the rank of lieutenant after a few years. He then enrolled in business school in Amsterdam. After graduation, he was hired by the Amsterdam-based firm Mirandolle Voûte, an import/export company with offices in the East Indies.

In July 1936, Jan left Holland on the *Marnix of St. Aldegonde* to start his first job in the firm's Batavia office. He met Didi on board of the ship, and after he had settled into his job and she had married Daan, the three of them became close friends. Jan's sister, Tiek, followed him to the East Indies in 1937, and their mother joined her children in Java a year later, in 1938.

Establishing a Home in the Indies

The prewar years in the East Indies were good for the Borgerhoff family. Tiek married Jan Simonsz, and their mother, called "Mamp" by her children and their friends, became a surrogate mother to all of their friends. Mamp Borgerhoff Mulder was one of few middle-aged women living in the Dutch colony, and their home became a beloved second home for many young people, including Daan and Didi. Their home was known as *The Vergulde Bor*, the Gilded Bor, probably a reference to the name Borgerhoff, although it may also have referred to the borrels, drinks that were enjoyed by the young people who came to visit.

January 1, 1939—from left to right: Bruno Tiedeman? Buis Hofstee, Mamp, Didi, Tiek, Mieke Hofstee, Jan. Daan and Datiko are in the foreground.

On New Year's Eve 1938, the Borgerhoff family hosted a party for their friends. Mamp had made sure that it was a wonderful feast, and the party was a great success, yet the mood seems to have been wistful, judging from the small poem of thanks that Didi and Daan wrote in the guestbook of the Borgerhoff family when they were ready to leave for Donowarie:

New Year's Eve!—A strange evening
Much cheer and yet, so quiet ...
Looking back and looking forward,
What will this year bring?
Around us sit dear people
And for all of us it is the same
Yet, everyone has different thoughts
But no one is indifferent.
The clock chimed twelve
The New Year has begun ...
Best wishes for everyone,
May all of them be fulfilled.

Just before the Second World War became a reality in the Indies, Mamp and Jan were living in Soerabaja, but when Jan was mobilized and had left town, Mamp joined her daughter, Tiek, in Semarang at the urging of Papa Daan, who had become concerned when she became increasingly more frightened in those prewar days and after the first bombing of the city in early 1942.

Tante Tiek and Mamp Interned in Camp Lampersari

When all Dutch women were rounded up by the Japanese and moved into camps at the end of 1942, Tante Tiek and Mamp ended up in Camp Lampersari in Semarang, a so-called "model kampong." The little houses of the kampong were made of wood and *bilik*, mats of woven bamboo strips, and had been built for local low-income employees of the Dutch East Indies Railroad Company. Five women lived in the house for a year and a half. Together, they composed the little poem below.

In this small luxurious house
We are all very much at home
We have a bedroom nice and neat
And when it rains we can swim on our sheets
We have a dining room with four chairs
And a patio covered in swarms of ants
And a storage room with a door that locks
And a door-less kitchen without much food
We have a cat with mangy ears
Caused by the moisture, as they say
And, as "piece de resistance"
We have a bathroom and toilet "à la Turque"
The whole is surrounded by a flowerless yard,
Covered in mud, where the mosquitoes hum
We live here in peace and quiet
And often think 'je maintiendrai.'

Je maintiendrai is the motto of the Netherlands, meaning "I will persevere."

By the time Tante Tiek and Mamp had moved to Lampersari, we now know, Jan was already in Japan. Of course, Tante Tiek and Mamp did not know where he was until years later, after the war was over.

Jan's Treasures in an Old Cigar Box

In 2007, I spent two weeks helping to clean out Didi's old apartment when she had moved to an assisted-living facility, only to find some of the questions about my second father's experiences in Japan during World War II were suddenly, unexpectedly answered.

One evening, while I sat on the floor of my mother's bedroom in her empty apartment, I sorted through the many old shoe boxes in her linen closet that were filled with old letters and photographs, and I found an old cigar box that I had never noticed before. I gasped when I opened it—the box was filled with old pieces of thin rice paper, curled around the edges—papers so fragile that I was afraid to touch them. I immediately recognized Jan's robust but almost illegible handwriting. In the bottom of the box, wrapped in thicker paper, were two sets of drawings depicting life in a POW camp.

The papers contained copies of ditties and humorous songs that had been written during the war years in Japan, undoubtedly for the entertainment and encouragement of the POWs there. I imagine that the poems and drawings must have given Jan and his fellow prisoners a great deal of amusement, as well as coded information under the grimmest of circumstances. These must have been very precious to him. The poems were written in Dutch, but some of them had Japanese titles, such as "Nantomonai" and "Kamioka ABC."

Finding My Father's Name on My Computer

When I was preparing to fly back to the States, after cleaning my mother's apartment, my brother Jan agreed that I should take the cigar box and its contents to Millerton so I could make copies of the texts and drawings and to find out more about Nantomonai and Kamioka. One evening, sitting in my study at home, I Googled "WWII Japanese POW Camps," and within seconds, I found www.mansell.com. The site offered a long list of eighty-five POW camps that had housed Allied prisoners of war in Japan, and I was able to compare the list of camps to the titles of the poems, "Nantomonai" and "Kamioka."

Sure enough, there it was: Kamioka was a hit! There *had* been a camp in the mountains of central Japan by that name, and within seconds, I found Jan's name among those of the 300 Dutch POWs who had been imprisoned there for close to three long years. The site also recommended a book written by a Dutchman, Johannes Wormser, who had been at Kamioka together with Jan. The book, written in the 1990s, mentions Jan on pages 155 and 156. The contents of the old cigar box unexpectedly offered a picture of Jan's experiences as one of the 8,000 Dutch POWs who spent three long years in Japan during WWII.

Japan's Plans to Hide War Crimes

When the Japanese began to realize in 1944 that they were going to lose the war, the authorities in Tokyo began to consider how their treatment of their prisoners needed to be kept hidden from the world's view in the event they lost the war.

Some of the POWs were convinced in the last months of their imprisonment that the Japanese had developed plans to murder all internees, civilians as well as POWs, if the Allies were to invade the occupied territories. Evidence developed during the war crimes trials held in Tokyo after the war showed this to be the case.

To what extent the men at Kamioka had heard the rumor, we don't know. Wormser doesn't mention it, but it is possible that they knew about it because they still managed to gain access to information from the outside. For almost three years, through the help of some Korean prisoners, who also worked in the mines, the men smuggled Japanese newspapers into the camp. The newspapers were hidden between the men's thighs when they left the mines at the end of their shift, so the Japanese would not easily find them. One of the Dutch POWs at Kamioka had learned to decipher the Japanese texts and was able to inform the officers about the news from the outside world.

Soccer Scores and Tasty Soup

Jan, who was one of three Dutch officers in Kamioka, had been complicit in this very dangerous undertaking, and it was Jan who told the other prisoners that the information from the outside was encouraging. One memorable evening, he visited each room in the barracks, closing the door behind him after having put a POW outside to guard the entrance. He told the men that one of them had been smuggling local newspapers into the camp at great peril to them all. The Japanese newspapers contained maps of the European theatre, and from the detailed maps, it had become crystal clear that Germany was losing the war.

In addition to the maps, one of the prisoners had received a tiny dictionary from an "old Methodist" he had met in the mines. The ancient dictionary was in three languages: Japanese, English, and eighteenth-century Dutch. One of the young reserve officers, a language expert, was in the process of painstakingly translating the newspaper articles as they were smuggled in. Jan told the men that it appeared that their long imprisonment would soon come to a close when the Allies would turn their attention to the Asian theatre, but he warned the men that they had to be extremely careful and should never ask, "Is there any more news?" They all agreed that they would ask coded questions instead, such as what the soccer scores were that day, or whether the soup was tasty.

Nantomonai! Germany Has Lost the War

Lieutenant Semmelink, another officer at Kamioka, wrote the poem "Nantomonai" in April 1945 to celebrate Germany's impending defeat and the imminent end of the war in the Far East. Written in Dutch in rather graphic language and recited by Semmelink to the assembled prisoners of Kamioka on April 30, 1945, the poem "Nantomonai" consists of seven stanzas each followed by a chorus, sung by the audience of POWs to the melody of "Y a de la joie," a popular Charles Trenet song at the time. The word *nantomonai* means "never mind" or "whatever," while the word *Mof* is a middle-Dutch word that means "foreigner." During WWII, the word was widely used as a curse word for the German occupying forces.

Friend Goebbels shouted through the radio again
About Germany's strong defenses and other non-sense
But the scoundrel will soon face the law
And be given his death sentence.
When Goebbels doesn't speak, Himmler will
And with him too the game is the same.
Number two of this awful twosome has
Also reserved a place in the hotspot of Hell

Nantomonai: the matter is coming to an end
Nantomonai: The "Mof's" knees are finally bent
Nantomonai: Here too we know the story's end
The focus will now be on Java's land.

When you reflect on how the "Mof" has fared
Then you can count on the fingers on one hand
That it will soon be finished for this yellow land
Cause the Yanks are aiming straight for the main island.
Those "slant-eyes" with their "crooked legs"

Soon will be the underdog and understand full well
That I, if I were to gamble, would not place one bet
On the chance they could prevent a landing yet.

Nantomonai: the matter is coming to an end
Nantomonai: The "Mof's" knees are finally bent
Nantomonai: Here too we know the story's end
The focus will now be on Java's land.

The camp commander will be upset to hear
That the daily paper was delivered here at home
For almost three years the guards checked us out
And thought that they could deny us the truth
May the camp staff be damned!
The worst punishment will not be enough.
And for the next ten years or so I hope
That I won't see another "slant eye" again.

Courage and Fear

What it was like for Jan and the other officers in the camp to receive the smuggled newspapers, have them translated, and then give everyone the information that was gained, we shall never know. The officers knew full well that their Japanese guards would be outraged if they found out and would mete out the cruelest punishments to everyone involved. Where did they get the courage to receive the smuggled information and make sure that it would not fall in the guards' hands? How did they decide to take the dangerous step of informing all the other men?

I assume that the decision to do so was made to boost everyone's morale. The men had already spent more than two and a half years at Kamioka by April 1945 and had buried one-fifth of their comrades. They needed the secret information they received to keep going and to help them withstand the awful deprivations and the uncertainties they were living under for those long years.

According to my brother Jan, our father suffered from a nervous breakdown sometime in the last year of his imprisonment. Perhaps he had been aware of the orders to kill all prisoners of war if the Allies were victorious; perhaps he was terribly worried that their ability to get outside information was going to be detected; perhaps he was, like so many others, at the end of his ability to cope.

The End of the War—Americans to the Rescue

The men who lived at Kamioka, near the west coast of Japan, had not heard about the American atomic bombs or the terrible loss of life in the large cities on the Japanese east coast. Neither did they know about the surrender by the emperor on August 15, 1945. They had, however, noticed in September that there was a change in the attitudes of their Japanese guards.

Jan later told Didi about the day the first Americans arrived at Camp Kamioka in September 1945. The first American they saw after their close-to-three-year-long imprisonment there seemed so very young—he was about twenty-five years old, and he looked so healthy, with his clean-shaven face, his crisp uniform, and his broad shoulders. The American officer asked the POWs what it was they needed most, and their answer was simple: "We have got to get out of here fast." The officer promised that he would be back soon to get them out. No one believed he could do that.

But sure enough, the Americans were back within days, loaded everyone into trucks, and drove them to the nearest railway station at Gifu, where a train was waiting to take them to Yokohama harbor. Jan never forgot the long train ride to Japan's east coast, where they finally saw the devastated towns and villages of Japan.

Hold That Tiger; California, Here I Come

Jan also remembered vividly what it was like when they pulled into Yokohama railway station, when he and the other emaciated and exhausted men from Kamioka struggled to get off the train in their threadbare, filthy clothes and an American military jazz band, its brasses polished to a brilliant shine, started up with "Hold that Tiger" and "California, Here I Come."

While the band was playing, the disheveled and unwashed men from Kamioka were met by young members of the American Women's Army Corps (WAC), who served the liberated men their first sandwiches, coffee, and soft drinks after years of miso soup and sawdust bread. The girls were pretty, healthy, and very young, and the newly liberated men, who had not seen a Western girl for years, were not sure what they liked best—the lovely girls in their spiffy uniforms, the abundant and tasty food, or the band playing upbeat prewar tunes.

After they had showered and had been deloused, everyone received a clean set of American uniforms. Afterwards, they were examined by a doctor. Jan could not praise the Americans enough—they were so efficient, so generous, and so fast. They were excellent examples of the "can-do" spirit the Americans were known for during the Second World War.

Going Home to the Future

Jan in Manila, October 1945, exhausted but free

The men who survived the backbreaking labor in the mines, unsafe conditions in the old mineshafts, extreme brutality of the guards, starvation rations, debilitating diseases and lack of medicines, unsanitary conditions and filth, and exposure to extreme cold were first sent to the Philippines for rehabilitation. From there, the Dutch POWs among them were sent back home to Java or Holland.

A photograph of my thirty-four-year-old father made in Manila in 1945 and still in the envelope, in which he received it, shows a very thin man dressed in an American uniform. He looks straight at the camera, black circles under his tired eyes. The envelope advises that the photo was taken at the Smile Art Studio at 123 Escolta, Manila.

Tante Tiek's First Letter to Jan

Dear Jantje,
We regularly receive your letters, but the first time I learned that you were still alive was when I discovered your name, as one of the first ones on the list from Yokohama, written as J. Mulder Burgerhof. After all that waiting that was the most important.

The tension of the last few weeks of waiting and searching was unbearable. I had the exact same feeling that you describe when you saw Mamp's first letter to you. It was like that when I received Jan's [Tiek's husband's] first letter. Because of my nerves and my trembling hands I couldn't read it the first two minutes and then I began to sweat, like an idiot.

I am looking forward so much to seeing you again, Jantje. Do you know yet when you might be able to join us here? A few days ago I read in a British newsletter from the South East Asia Command (SEAC) that you might get shipped out sometime later this month. It would be so wonderful if we could be together at New Year's, but I have little faith and because of that I am not looking forward to the holidays, because for so many years we could not be together and now, while it is actually possible, we still may not be together. If only we had the Americans here instead of the British.

I have not heard from Jan [Tiek's husband] in ten days. Perhaps it is his fault, now he knows I am alive and well he writes long letters, but they are infrequent. We had good contact with each other immediately and that was so wonderful. That was something I had been so afraid of. By the way, I have not heard anything from him about his experiences during the war. I don't even know where he had been imprisoned. He apparently does not want to speak about that.

Tiek's remark that she wished the Americans, rather than the British, were in Java refers to a common complaint among the non-British POWs and internees after the war. The reason was that when the British were given the task of rehabilitating Southeast Asia and established RAPWI, they moved their own nationals back home very quickly but were very slow in repatriating all the others. Some Dutch POWs were not repatriated from Asia until the fall of 1946. As a result, RAPWI was frequently referred to by the Dutch as Retain All Prisoners of War Indefinitely instead of Recovery of Allied Prisoners of War and Internees.

In all fairness, the infrastructure in Holland and the Indies had been completely destroyed during the war. The return of so many sick former POWs and civilian internees required a monumental effort on the part of all parties. Ships had to be refitted to transport sick people, and the most ordinary necessities of food, clothing, and shelter were scarce everywhere. RAPWI had a formidable mandate.

When he became a little stronger, Jan started to volunteer with RAPWI, and by the middle of December 1945, he was in Batavia, working hard to locate former prisoners and internees, to forward mail to them, and to get them passage to Holland as soon as was feasible. In Batavia, he also found out that Didi, Frits, and I had survived and were living in Bandoeng.

CHAPTER 11

MOVING HEAVEN AND EARTH TO GO HOME

There is a rumor that the Johan van Oldenbarneveldt *is expected to leave the 28th from Tandjong Priok. That would be wonderful. In a bit I am going to the office to find out. I am going everywhere in the hope that they will not forget about us. One has to be vigilant like the dickens.*

—Didi's third letter to Oma in Deventer, December 1945

While we lived in Bandoeng, waiting to be repatriated, RAPWI personnel worked around the clock to locate the people who had left the camps and to forward mail between them and their relatives in Holland or elsewhere in Java or Asia. The mail from Holland would first be sent to the Red Cross in Australia, and from there, it would be forwarded to Batavia, where RAPWI volunteers would sift through the chaotic jumble of wartime addresses of former prisoners and internees. RAPWI personnel must have spent hours going through handwritten lists of thousands of people and many camps to find us.

Messages of Survival and Loss

On October 19, 1945, a Red Cross telegram arrived at the Brinkpoortstraat in Deventer, Oma's home, informing her that Didi had survived the war and was hoping to come to Holland soon. Oma wrote Didi back the same day, but that first letter from Oma never reached us. It was first mailed to Australia. From there, it was sent on to Central Information and Post Office in Batavia. By the time RAPWI had tracked us down in Bandoeng, we were no longer there but had left on the *Johan van Oldenbarneveldt*, sailing to Holland. The letter was returned to Oma and is now lying here in Millerton, together with all the other letters.

Deventer, October 19, 1945
My sweet, dear Dietje,
This morning we received the telegram from Indië and now we finally know that you have been liberated and that your horrible imprisonment has ended. My sweetest, we are so terribly happy now that we

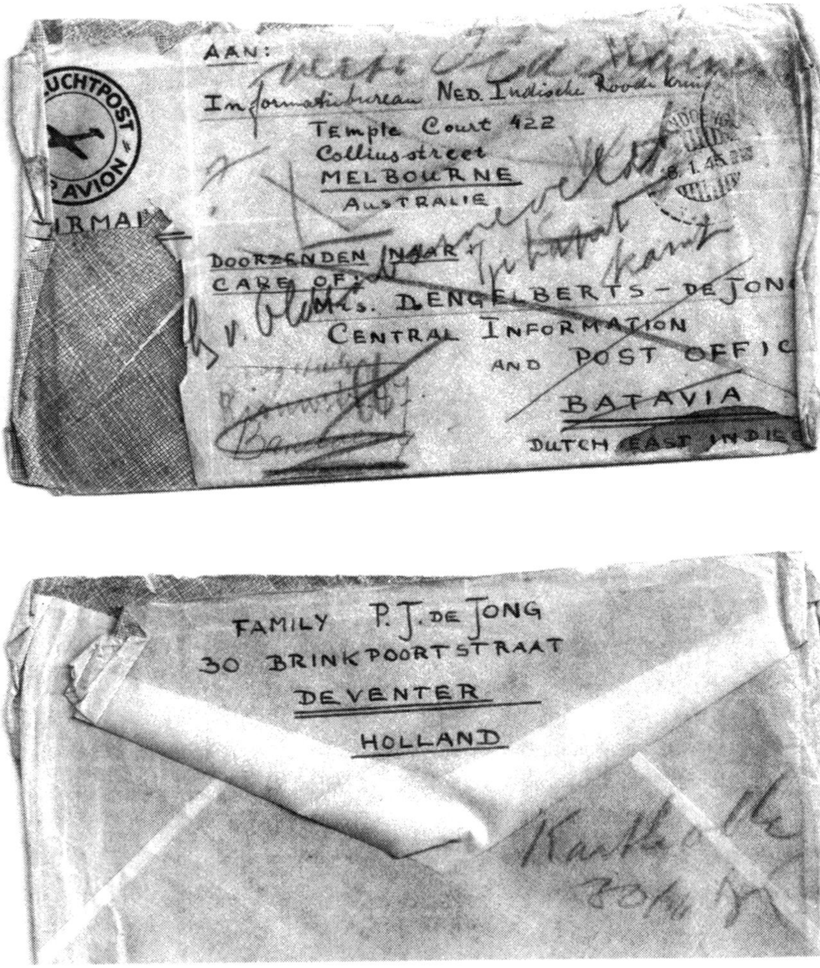

Front and back of the envelope of Oma's first letter to Didi with forwarding addresses, written by RAPWI. Te letter never reached us and was returned to Deventer.

know! Kukje came to my room upstairs and we both cried with relief and gratitude. We have been so very scared for you, especially the last few months with all the unrest in Java. Finally we know now that for you the worst is over and we wait with great longing for a letter from you, my dear heart.

Tuesday, three weeks ago we received the terrible news that dear Daan has died in Siam during a bombardment. Since then all of us had only one thought: how is our sweetheart and how is she dealing with this terrible ordeal? We wanted so badly to help you and there wasn't a thing we could do for you and we wondered whether you were still alive, and how you were managing and how terribly difficult your circumstances were. And we, who wanted to help so badly and give comfort, could not do a thing, nothing.

These were terrible thoughts that constantly assaulted us; in the morning you woke up with them and you took them to bed with you at night. But now we know that you have survived the horror, my dearest, we are looking forward to the time that you will be back with us and we can help you and do everything in our power to make your life whole again.

Oma then went on to describe the situation in Deventer:

A lot has happened in Deventer, dear; forty percent of the houses are not habitable at the moment and whole sections of our town are destroyed, among them the New Market and the old Gymnasium. A lot of people have been killed which is the worst, and we have all suffered badly.

Our own neighborhood is pretty much intact, except that all our windows were shattered during several bombardments, they have not yet been repaired and that may still take a while. The windows are now sealed with wood or cardboard in which we have placed small glass panes from the greenhouse in the garden, and we are managing quite well this way.

We have not suffered from hunger because we had our own garden planted with vegetables and potatoes, rye and wheat, and we also have not suffered from cold since we had plenty of old wood from the orchards. But in the province of Holland it was terrible. The people came on foot or bicycle to Overijssel, Drente, Groningen and Friesland to get some food [a trip of 100 to 200 kilometers one way]. Gerard Engelberts [Papa Daan's brother] has been here twice to get food, the first time by bicycle; the second time he came on foot with a handcart. It really was so horrible. This happened in the winter, in the beginning of 1945. Deventer looked awfully sad then with its destroyed houses, empty shops and so many homeless people walking on the roads. Many farmers have helped wonderfully but many others were terrible leeches, demanding huge sums for food.

On November 25, Oma finally received Didi's first letter, and she wrote back immediately:

> *We received your letter yesterday morning and you don't know how happy we are. Kukje got it from the mailbox and brought it to me in the kitchen. You don't know what it meant to me to see your letter with the familiar handwriting after four long years. I had so much looked forward to it and had dreaded it at the same time, not knowing how you would be. Sweetheart, you have been so courageous and strong with all the sadness, horror and hardship.*
>
> *We are so very happy with the great news that you will come with two little sweethearts, instead of one! I long for that moment and so do the others. I wished you could have seen us yesterday—we were so happy.*
>
> *Tante Kuk en Oom Piet are already planning to make toys, and the little table with two chairs will come back in the dining room, then two little kids will be playing there again, and I will be able to read to them on the divan, with a sweet little thing on either side of me, and I will sing to them at night. Do you remember I used to do that for you, dearest?*
>
> *Thank God that you will be here soon and we will be able to help you and comfort you and we will be able to talk about all of it and tell each other everything, so that those four long years without contact will disappear. Actually, they already have disappeared because when I got your letter it felt as if everything was wiped away and that we restarted where we had left off only yesterday.*

Finally, a Letter from Jan

On December 19, when Didi received Jan's first letter to her, she was so happy to hear from him that she wrote him back within minutes after she had received it.

> *Bandoeng, December 19, 1945*
>
> *Dear Jan,*
> *I received your letter about five minutes ago and you cannot know how happy I was. It was so wonderful to see your "gorgeous handwriting" again, Jan! If only I had known that you were already in Batavia when we arrived there! I hope so very much that I will be able to see*

you and speak with you before I leave for Holland. If you could find us a place to live, I will make every effort to come to Batavia. An old-fashioned chat with you would be wonderful.

Days later, Didi wrote Oma:

Jan is trying to get us to Batavia because he believes that it is far easier to get passage to Holland from there than from here. I hope that he will be successful. He has written me that we always can count on him wherever I will be—he will always be there for us, whether I want him to or not. Jan has always been a true friend.

Buis Hofstee also wrote me a lovely letter. We have made really great friends here in the Indies and I will always have good memories of our time together here.

Jan wrote that he thought about us a lot while he was in the camp and that he often had a feeling that Daan was with him because he felt that he was a good example to hold on to—how two friends help each other through difficult times!

I will be so glad once I am on board ship. The passage will not be a pleasure trip—it is very crowded and you must do everything for yourself, but it sails in the right direction and to that end almost anything is acceptable.

Although Jan was not able to move us to Batavia, he was still working hard on getting us passage on the *Johan van Oldenbarneveldt*, which was expected to leave for Holland in January. While Jan was doing his part in Batavia, Didi was hard at work herself, attempting to get us on the necessary list for departures:

I have been to the office again and they told me there that the Johan van Oldenbarneveldt *is expected to arrive on the 28th at Tandjong Priok and that it will leave with widows and orphans. They are working on lists and we can expect more confirmation in a few days. If that is true, then we may celebrate Syts' sixth birthday with you—can you imagine that, Mam?—And soon thereafter your birthday as well. How utterly wonderful!*

At the end of December, we heard a rumor that the departure of the *Johan van Oldenbarneveldt* had been delayed to January 25.

> *I think they want to wait so that we arrive in the spring—they are having trouble getting enough warm clothes. I was told that the people who left on the first few boats received blankets to wear as clothes—pretty horrible. It is awful if it is true, but it may be better this way for the children, the change would be awfully big. Still, I hope it is not true.*

Making Plans for the Future

The biggest thing on Didi's mind was our passage back home to Holland. In each letter home, she expressed the hope that we would be able to leave on the next boat out. But while she was waiting, Didi also began the tedious and mostly unsuccessful process of trying to obtain outstanding salary payments from Harrison and Crosfield, along with other financial support that was due her as the widow of a former sergeant in the Dutch East Indies forces. She wrote Gerrit, her brother:

> *It is good that you are in contact with Harrison and Crosfield. I have also tried from here. Mr. Korte has received power of attorney from me to manage my interests in the fullest sense of the word. He has been very friendly. Harrison and Crosfield will have to pony up one of these days. Before the war started the entire Batavia office of Harrison and Crosfield got themselves to Australia. Prior to the Japanese invasion I did receive the equivalent of three months' salary—that was taken by the Rampokkers, and since then I have not seen a penny. When our manager Fermin offered to help me I asked for money and received 25 guilders, I had to share that with someone else. My reaction at the time was "You can drop dead before I will ask for anything else." Perhaps that was stupid, but I still have Friesian blood in my veins—quite a bit, apparently.*

Didi never received any compensation from Harrison and Crosfield, nor did she get any insurance payment from the life insurance policy Papa Daan had established before the war, or payment for his participation in the Dutch colonial army.

Didi also started to plan for guardianship for Frits and me and asked her brother Gerrit if he would mind being our standby guardian:

A short while ago I had an interview with someone from the Department of Orphans. I have given your name as the guardian for the children—I hope that that is all right. I'd rather appoint you than one of the Engelberts family.

Christmas 1945: Wonderful and Lonely Days

Didi, Frits, and I celebrated Christmas in our glass-enclosed room in Bandoeng, still waiting for the notice that we were listed to leave on the *Johan van Oldenbarneveldt.* After she had put us to bed, Didi wrote Oma a long letter on Christmas Eve.

Dearest Mam,
Christmas has come and we are still so far away from each other. I wanted so badly to be with all of you—I would have liked to sit close to you when you read the Christmas story. I am with you in my thoughts and together with you I miss our Pops who will never again celebrate Christmas with us, and Daan who will never smell pine needles from the kitchen.

I am sitting here alone in front of the wide open doors; in front of me is the dark garden. Earlier it rained a little bit and it is cold. My little treasures are in bed. I had made a little Christmas tree from pine branches and there were ten candles underneath the tree, one for each year I was not with you in these wonderful but loneliest days. They thought it was beautiful and the little lights sparkled in their eyes. I have told them the Christmas story which they easily understood: "They asked everywhere, at all houses, if there was a room available, but the people always said: no, our house is filled up, we don't have room for you." They also can imagine the warm stable and that it was wonderful there. But I did have to reassure Frits that the big cows would not harm the little baby.

Afterwards we sang songs—"Silent Night" and others—and we each had a piece of the gorgeous Christmas cake I had made earlier this morning. The lovely mood ended when they were allowed to blow out the candles—there was a lot of laughter, blowing and spitting and excitement so that I had to rescue the Christmas tree which was about to tumble to the ground. The feast ended for Syts in tears—I don't think she knows herself why. I guess it was from the excitement and the emotions—little sweetheart. Frits' reaction was "Oh, poor sad Syts." Sometimes he tries to be sweet to her and will say to her: "Mammie is bad, Syts."

They are singing Christmas songs in the room next to me—in harmony—it is so lovely that I can barely stand it. I wished I could fall asleep and wake up in Holland. It is taking so long and I am sometimes afraid that something will happen before we arrive. Please promise me that you will not get sick, Mam, I need you. I depend completely on you, dearest. The children are different, they need me—but I need you—exactly in the same way.

December 26, to continue

Sweethearts, today I received my notice—we are definitely leaving on the Johan van Oldenbarneveldt! *Our heavy luggage had to be sent away today, but I don't have any. We received another message that we would have to be ready to leave within 24-hour notice. How is that? I still don't know the date of our departure. I have heard that it might be the 29th—others say it won't be until the 10th of January. Whatever—we are coming!—They are working on it! The trip by boat will be slightly different from the previous one! We will sleep in hammocks and we have been told that we must bring a pillow to be able to sit on deck since there are no deckchairs. No matter—we will be sailing in the right direction.*

Sweethearts, I will write soon again. I am going to bed now, there will be a lot to do tomorrow. Bye my dearest. Big kiss from your Dietje, Sytske and Fritsje.

As our departure got closer, Didi began to think more about what it would mean to leave Java forever behind with all of its good memories and horrible experiences. She wrote Oma:

You know what is truly amazing is the fact that, notwithstanding my longing to leave, that as time is getting closer, there is a small part in me that is sad to leave this gorgeous country where I have enjoyed so many wonderful years, at least those before December 1942, prior to our internment in the camps. I shall always hold Indië dear, not the people, but the land. It is such a permanent end of these ten years of my life.

But I am going to go on with pleasure, Mam. I am still young enough to be able to start all over again and there is still so much that is good and I will be able to find that.

CHAPTER 12

GOING HOME TO HOLLAND, LAND OF FAIRY TALES

We are leaving with the Johan van Oldenbarneveldt. *This is it. I have so much looked forward to this moment and am of course very happy, but there is still a small part of me which regrets leaving. It is now definite—such a big fat period after these nine and a half years during many of which I have been very happy. I can see that I may be one of those people who long for Holland when they are in the Indies and even more so in the reverse. I am sure you understand me. And who knows what will happen—perhaps I will be back some day—when Indië is Indië again and no longer the witches' cauldron it is now.*

—Didi's letter to Jan, December 26, 1945

On January 13, 1946, the *Johan van Oldenbarneveldt* slowly moved away from the quay at Tandjong Priok, Batavia's harbor. After having said good-bye to Oom Cor van Nieuwland, Tante Kuk's new husband, and Oom Jan, who had brought us to the boat, the three of us stood on the deck among the countless other women and children who were finally going home to Holland. As the boat slowly turned its bow away from the shore, Didi stood looking with mixed emotions at the country she was leaving—a place she had called home for ten years, a place that had given her so many good times and so many awful memories, and she was not sure she would ever be back. Frits and I were leaving the only country we had ever known and going to a home that was very far away and as unbelievable as a fairy tale.

Jan stood on the quay, waving the boat off, together with all the others who were hoping their turn to leave would come soon. He was saying good-bye to Didi, the woman he loved and who had fallen into his arms just twenty-four hours earlier. His thoughts must also have turned to the wonderful voyage on the *Marnix of St. Aldegonde* ten years before, when he had met Didi. He remembered the many other cheerful times before the war when he had brought departing friends to the harbor to see them off for their furlough in Holland. This leave-taking was so very different: there was no band playing popular tunes, there had not been a party onboard ship before the announcement was made that guests had to leave, and there were no serpentine tapes in the colors of the rainbow, linking the hands of the passengers onboard with the friends who remained ashore as the boat slowly moved away from the quay.

Our Elegant Troop Ship

The *Johan van Oldenbarneveldt* was roughly of the same vintage as the *Marnix van St. Aldegonde*. It had been an elegant ocean liner sailing back and forth between Amsterdam and Tandjong Priok before the war. During the war, the ship had been converted into a troop carrier for use by the British and had been stripped of all its luxurious amenities. In January 1946, the ship's passengers, consisting primarily of widows and orphans, were not housed in the elegant cabins that once had been such a wonderful comfort in times gone by. On this voyage, our living quarters were down in the hold, where the troops had been quartered only months earlier. Instead of beds made with pressed sheets, we slept in hammocks strung between the beams in the ceiling. Below us were platforms on which we could sit during the day.

The hold was airless and hot and resembled the cramped quarters of the Japanese internment camps far more than the opulence of a passenger liner—but no matter; as Didi had often said, we were sailing in the right direction, and we children found the hammocks a great deal of fun, especially in the evening, when we were put to bed and all of us would kick our feet against the ceiling beams to keep the hammocks swinging wildly.

The first morning, after a full night in our hammocks, the hold was chaotic with mothers and children getting ready for the day. Long lines formed in front of the small washroom we had to share; our belongings were piled on the platforms below; and children played between the aisles while the empty hammocks hung limply from the beams.

While we were trying to wash up and get dressed, a young sharp-looking marine officer arrived, who looked with a horrified expression at the disorder before him. In a loud, no-nonsense voice, he announced to one and all that passengers were expected to obey the rules onboard ship. First, the sleeping quarters were to be kept tidy at all times; second, all our belongings had to be put away neatly; and finally, and most important, the hammocks had to be removed and rolled up to be placed under the platforms first thing each morning.

Stunned silence followed this announcement until one formidable mother raised herself to her full height and in a loud voice answered, "Young man, I have seven children with me, and all of us have survived the camps—for more than three years, I have obeyed Japanese rules that never made any sense, and I am damned if I will take eight hammocks down every morning and then string them up again at night. That is just not going to happen."

After a moment of silence, the officer took a deep breath and turned away, never to be seen again. The hold remained chaotic for the duration of our voyage.

Rough Weather and the Measles

During the next days, the boat sailed through rough weather and many people became seasick, but a much bigger problem soon required everyone's attention: Many of the children on board came down with the measles, including Frits and me. Outbreaks of infectious diseases were greatly feared because none of the passengers had adequate resistance to them. In a letter to Jan, my mother wrote:

> *All children who have not had the measles are getting a blood injection. I cannot give it to them unfortunately since I have had Malaria, but they will get blood from someone else. I hope so fervently that this will not happen, because all sick persons who are in the hospital have to leave ship in Colombo. The same in Port Said; they go to a Dutch hospital with Dutch doctors, specially created for the evacuees. It would be awful if we had to stay there. Please keep your fingers crossed for us. They are particularly careful, because so many children have died on the* Nieuw Amsterdam, *as a result of the measles or its complications. Rumor has it that there have been about 40 [that died]. It is so terrible, it is hard to believe. One has to be especially careful not to catch a cold with the measles and that is almost impossible on a voyage such as this one.*

For more than a week, Frits and I stayed in our hammocks. We were too sick to eat much or to go outside, and Didi spent much of that time in the airless hold taking care of us while she desperately longed to be out on the sloop deck, taking in the warmth of the sun and enjoying the fresh ocean air. When she was able to leave us for short moments, she hurried to a quiet spot at the railing to remember the heavenly weeks on the *Marnix van St. Aldegonde* in July of 1936, when she and her friends were having such a wonderful time on the voyage out. But mostly, she thought about Jan, the best friend she had ever had, the friend she had been able to confide in about anything that bothered her, including the difficulties of her marriage with Daan. When she was alone for even a few minutes, Didi dreamt of the wonderful new life ahead of her, together with Jan.

Didi and Jan had found each other in Batavia, days prior to our departure from the Indies. On January 12, while Jan was helping us to get settled in the hold of the *Johan van Oldenbarneveldt*, they had fallen into each other's arms in the stuffy space of the washroom. They had hoped to have a short moment of privacy, but in the overcrowded ship, they had not found a corner where they could be together unseen.

One day, when Frits and I were allowed outside again with scarves tied around our ears and dressed in the warmest clothes we owned, I surprised my mother with the following question, which she reported in a letter to Jan:

> *"Mam, why were you so happy when the uncle with the big nose was here? Yes, I saw you. Are you going to get married?" At which point she burst out laughing. Have you ever seen such a nutty child? She talked so loud that I looked around me to see if the others had heard as well. Fortunately the air ducts were making such a noise that I don't think the others heard anything. Enfant Terrible! It is perfectly possible that she will say something like that to Oma—some introduction to Oom Jan. She is such a monkey! And then to think that she waited fourteen days before saying something like that. I thought that they had not noticed a thing—but sure enough: "I saw you there near the washbasins"!*

A Ration of Winter Clothes

While the ship was sailing north, the temperature became increasingly chilly. Just before we arrived at the Gulf of Suez, an announcement was made over the ship's intercom announcing that we were nearing the place where we would get our packets of winter clothes. Soon after the announcement, the ship docked close to the harbor of Adabiya. From there, the evacuees were transported by small boats to the quay and then traveled in a little train to a British military desert camp near Ataka, where a distribution center had been established to give us the necessary winter clothes. The ship's doctor had advised my mother that Frits and I should remain onboard ship while she was to go ashore to get the clothes she was entitled to for the three of us; he was still afraid that we were not well enough. My mother wrote eloquently about this wonderful day to Jan:

> *You cannot imagine how amazing our reception in Suez has been and what lovely clothes we have received. They had decorated everything with flags and there was a band. A heartfelt speech welcomed us and after that we could sit in a large hangar, beautifully decorated, with on one side a play area for the children and at the other side a cold buffet (from the British troops in Egypt) from which we could eat and take with us as much as we wanted; very hot coffee and ice cream! O, Jan—this is how I had imagined peace. After we had had our fill we went to the shops, where I received a handbag and a winter coat and a dress and two sets of underwear, two pairs of stockings, shoes, gloves and a hat. It was unbelievable! And we were allowed to make our own selection. I have a dark grey coat, black shoes and a light green dress, lovely! The children had not come along, they are better but the doctor was afraid they would catch a cold. It was the right decision, it took us 3 quarters of an hour on the small boats to come ashore and it was frightfully cold.*

The next day, Frits and I received parcels with clothes for us that had been selected at Ataka based on our ages, but mistakes had been made and I received a winter coat that could fit a girl of sixteen. Fortunately, a few days later, we were able to exchange clothes that didn't fit us for ones that did, and all three of us were ready for winter weather when we entered the Suez Canal. Once we were in the Mediterranean Sea, it became too cold to go outside and we had to spend most of our time in the hold, nursing colds and fighting pneumonia and bronchitis. During that time, I made a variety of outfits for my little bear, which had to be dressed just as we were, in warm clothing. I made a coat and a scarf from the faded old clothes we had used in the camps. The scarf was to be wound around Beary's head so she would not get an earache from the cold.

Golden Dunes and Dipping Gulls

Finally, on a cold day in February, the *Johan van Oldenbarneveldt* sailed slowly past the coast of Holland, following the minesweepers ahead of us while most of the passengers stood at the railing, watching the Dutch coast slide by with its golden dunes and broad beaches. This was a moment Didi had been looking forward to for close to ten years, and although her return home was so different from the way she had expected it to be when she had left, it was far more joyous. All her senses were on alert: The air smelled like frost on a clear day, massive clouds sailed along the low horizon, seagulls screeched and dipped alongside the boat, and memories came back of summer vacations at the beach in Ameland, with her father and mother and Gerrit, Kuk, and Piet, the baby. "Oh, yes, this is how it was…."

And then we were at IJmuiden, the gateway to the canal that leads to the harbor of Amsterdam. The boat sounded its whistle three times to announce our homecoming, and everyone who was able stood on the decks in the cold air, tears streaming down the cheeks of the adults. We thin, tawny-skinned children stood perplexed at the railing, looking at the white people with their red cheeks on the roads alongside the canal who were cheering and waving as we slowly sailed past them. I marveled at the rows of small, neat houses, their red roof tiles shining in the grey sunlight: "Mam, look at those cute doll houses they have in Holland; they are so clean!" One amazing sight followed the other. We could not believe our eyes when we saw the vast green fields that stretched to the horizon without any mountain ranges impeding the view: "Look at the sawahs they have here in Holland; they are so very green!" Everything was new and marvelous and unfamiliar. When we saw some women dressed in their native North Holland dress, aprons covering long voluminous skirts, lace caps on their heads, we wanted to know if they were *Dutch Baboes*, Dutch house servants.

Pealing Bells, Amsterdam's Welcome

Late in the afternoon, the boat entered *het IJ*, the wide harbor of Amsterdam, filled with boats of all sizes. At the south end of *het IJ*, the city of Amsterdam stood, showing itself proudly as it had to all arriving sailors and travelers throughout the centuries. Piers, barracks, and warehouses stood at the water's edge. Behind them, we could see houses and the tall towers of the many churches that receded far into the distance. Bells were pealing, and once again, the boat's whistle sounded its greeting as we made our way to the quay. We were home in Holland!

The next day, we disembarked in our strange new clothes, our meager belongings stuffed in the old duffel bag. The first hours were spent going through customs. When all the paperwork was finished, we were treated to a real Dutch lunch, consisting of cups of pea soup, buttered buns with cheese or sausage, hot coffee for the adults, hot chocolate and milk for the children, and an apple for each one of us.

Soon, the lucky passengers who had homes to go to were put on buses that would drive them to their destinations in the other provinces; others, who had no relatives waiting for them, were bused to centers and shelters in Amsterdam to wait for more permanent housing. We were among the luckiest ones; we had a home to go to, and our bus, bound for the province of Overijssel, was soon filled. It was early in the afternoon when we began the last part of our journey, to meet the family that had been waiting for us for so many years. Deventer, where Oma's house was, was one of the first stops on the way.

In the bus, Frits and I sat looking out at this new, water-soaked country that was so very different from the one we had left. Unrecognizable animals stood in the fields, the sky with its big clouds touched the low horizon, and little collections of houses, clustered around church spires, could be seen in the far distances, like toys scattered in the countryside. Oh, and we were so very cold ... even though we were wearing our new clothes and the gloves and knit caps we had received in Ataka. Every now and then, the driver slowed down when the road was flooded. Sometimes we had to ride through high water, but on we went that afternoon to go to Oma's house.

After we passed the town of Apeldoorn, we noticed that our mother became tense, knowing that Deventer would come into view at any moment, but just as she expected to see Deventer's round-domed church tower appear on the horizon, the bus came to an abrupt halt. The dikes of the River IJssel had been so badly damaged during the war that high water covering the road appeared too deep to drive through. We saw a car stalled in the high water with a man standing on its fenders, waiting to be rescued.

Didi's moment of panic must have lasted a long time for her while the bus driver contemplated making a detour and not going straight to Deventer after all, but just then, a guide came to our aid and helped the driver maneuver the bus safely through the high water and we were able to cross the bridge over the IJssel to enter Deventer. In a letter to Jan, my mother described our homecoming:

> *And then we entered Deventer: the gas factory, the "Knutteldorp," the "Handelskade," the "Gedempte Gracht" and then the "Brinkpoortstraat." We stopped in front of no. 30 and Kuk jumped up in the front room and then I saw my mother in the street. Oh, God, Jan I am beginning to cry again—Mammie, my own Mammie, she looked just like my Oma now. I don't see that anymore; that was my first impression—now she looks like she always has, except for more*

lines in her face that had not been there before and her hair, nearly completely white, but otherwise exactly as she always had been.

While Didi and Oma stood there crying and hugging each other, Frits and I sat on the front stoop of the house, hoping they would stop soon so we could go in and see the toys that had been promised us. I finally took matters in my own hands and walked up to Tante Kuk. "Tante Kuk, where is my doll?" Tante Kuk got the message and took us inside to the front room, where the stove burned red to keep us warm and where the toys stood waiting for us—toys that had belonged to my mother, to Tante Kuk, Oom Gerrit, and Oom Piet and that had been carefully saved all these years, as if it had been foreseen that one day, two little children who had no toys would come to the Brinkpoortstraat to live.

Brinkpoortstraat 30, Deventer—Oma's house and our new home

For me, there was a doll carriage, complete with all the trimmings, and in it was a porcelain doll with curly blond hair, eyes that could go to sleep, and joints, like round marbles, in her arms and legs that moved just like a real person. Her name was Elsje, and she had been Kuk's favorite doll. Elsje wore a beautiful dress, a coat, and shoes, and she had far more clothes than I; the doll was like a little princess in my eyes. Kuk later told me that Oom Piet, when he was a little boy, had also loved that doll and liked to shake it so he could see its eyes jiggle between its long eyelashes.

In addition to the carriage and Elsje, there was doll house furniture made by Oom Piet, and lots of games, carefully saved in their intact boxes. Frits got building blocks and cars and a mechanical toy monkey you could wind up—

the monkey did gymnastics if you turned a small key in its back. Frits also got, like me, many games that had been stored away decades earlier. And there were lots of children's books with beautiful pictures in them for both of us.

Our Oma, Richer than the Queen

Oma's house, with its comfortable, solid furniture, was even more wondrous then Didi had told us way back in the camps. There were enough chairs to sit on for everyone! And Oma had rugs on the floors, and she even had rugs on the tables. Downstairs were the living and dining rooms, and near the big glass doors that led to the verandah overlooking the walled-in garden stood a small table with two chairs, just the perfect size for Frits and me. In Oma's house, there were beautiful pictures on the walls and mirrors in gold frames above the mantelpieces, and everywhere things gleamed in the light of the lamps.

Oma had something else, too: a cupboard full of beautiful china, crystal glasses, and silver. When I saw the shelves packed with things that I could never have imagined, I said to Didi, "Oma is so rich, she must be even richer than the queen!" I had never seen such splendor, and so much of it. I was absolutely sure that no one could be richer than our Oma—it was simply not possible.

Instead of drinking out of our beat-up enamel mugs we had used in the camp, we drank tea out of lovely cups with flowers painted on their sides. The cups came with their own saucers, and there were small silver teaspoons you could use to stir the sugar in your tea. And there was one other thing … in the dining room stood the upright piano, a thing of wonder to us children, something we could not remember ever having seen before. Of course, we had only heard sporadic singing in the camps and could not remember ever having heard an instrument that could make such beautiful sounds. When Oom Piet played his beloved Chopin waltzes or nocturnes on the piano, I would listen dreamily, mesmerized by the unfamiliar sounds that were played on this unusual piece of furniture.

In the evening, we had dinner at the dining room table in the back room, near the large wood-burning stove, and there was an abundance of delicious food. We had meat and potatoes and vegetables and more milk for us and pudding for dessert. The whole family—Oma; the three of us; Tante Kuk and two uncles, Oom Gerrit and Oom Piet—gathered together around the table. The large shaded lamp hanging over its center embraced us all in its soft golden light, leaving the corners of the room in shadows.

Later, we washed in the kitchen, where a petroleum heater kept the room hot and where we could comfortably get into our pajamas before climbing the steep stairs to our bedroom, where our beds were piled with blankets. Hot water bottles, covered in old socks so we would not burn our feet, had been placed deep inside.

Everything was new and strange. We had never slept in a bed with blankets, but we quickly understood that the important thing was to stay under the covers and only stick our noses out to catch some air. The room had no heat source, and we could see our breath in clouds coming out of our mouths. Oma, Tante Kuk, and our mother kissed us goodnight in this big wonderful house that was now our home.

Frits, Oma, Didi, and Sytske sitting on the floor in front of the bookcase in the living room in the house in Deventer, February, 1946—Sytske's doll, Elsje, sits on her lap

The next morning, we got up and explored the whole house from top to bottom. In the basement, which my grandmother called the "sousterrain" or "het onderhuis," we noticed a large wooden cage with a locked door. Along the sides of the cage were many shelves that were now bare. Frits and I were afraid of this cage which looked like a prison for people who needed to be punished. Even when we were told that it really was to store food supplies, we always kept a wary eye on the cage when we were downstairs in the cellar. On the second floor of the house, at the top of the steep winding stairs, were four bedrooms and one floor higher was the attic, where the apples from Oma's farm were stored – their aroma filled the air. But I was afraid of dark corners and didn't like to go there by myself. The best place to be was always downstairs in the rooms where the stoves were burning and it was cozy and warm.

Safe at Last in Oma's House

In Deventer, at Oma's house, time moved along in predictable measure, exactly as it had when Didi had been a little girl. There we found the life my mother had been longing for and had told us about during the years in the camps. Instead of uncertainty, daily bouts of fear and boredom, and constant hunger in the overcrowded and squalid barracks of the camps, we found a loving grandmother and an aunt and two uncles. We found more toys than we could play with and three square meals a day that we ate at the dining room table, always spread with a tablecloth, with each of us having a plate and cutlery and full glasses of cold milk.

In the morning we had porridge, over which Tante Kuk would dribble our initials in brown syrup, or we had slices of bread and butter covered in chocolate sprinkles or peanut butter. After breakfast, the table was cleared. In the middle of the morning, when the adults would have their coffee, we would have hot chocolate, and everyone had a cookie. Then, at noon, the table was once again set with the tablecloth, napkins in their own napkin rings, and place settings for everyone, and we had lunch—more bread with cheese and sausage, an apple, more milk. After lunch, the table was cleared again and we could play or go into town with Oma or Tante Kuk to shop for the evening's dinner.

Frits and I liked these trips into town and loved looking at the shop windows that to us were filled with marvelous wares. We loved to point out things that were really special to us and would exclaim loudly in partial Malay and Dutch: "Adoeh—look at that!" We particularly liked to go into the shops because we got a lot of attention from the shop owners where Oma had been a steady customer. The news that we had come home from the camps was known by every one of them. All of the merchants where Oma had been shopping for decades were delighted to see us. We especially liked to visit the butcher, whose white-tiled store was shiny and where you could buy sausages and other meats that were unfamiliar to us. Sometimes, if the butcher was in a jovial mood, we each got a slice of liverwurst.

And then, one morning, Frits and I saw the most wonderful thing yet during one of our walks in Deventer: a man in uniform! Beside himself with joy, Frits shouted that here in wonderful Holland, they even had Ghurkas! "Adoeh—look there, a Ghurka…!"

Later, in the afternoon, tea was served, and then, in the early evening, the table was set once again and we had dinner. If there was soup, we did not get dessert, but on good days, we ended the meal with a deep plate of *Pietjepap*, custard, or *griesmeel pudding met stroop*, farina pudding with syrup. The only dessert we didn't like was buttered rice with sugar. After all, as far as we remembered, rice was supposed to be eaten with meat or vegetables. To us, eating rice with sugar didn't make any sense at all.

After dinner, Frits and I were allowed to dance around the table for a little while, skipping and jumping while Didi or Oom Piet played the piano and the other adults sat and talked. And then it was time for us to go to bed. In the winter, we washed in the warm, steamy kitchen, a big production that required the efforts of both our mother and Tante Kuk to get us cleaned up and settled in our beds upstairs.

Going to sleep upstairs was not easy for us. For one thing, the rooms were so cold. When we arrived at the top of the stairs to be put into our beds, we ran over the icy floor and with the biggest leaps we could muster, we jumped into bed to quickly warm ourselves on the hot water bottles that were always waiting for us.

Also, aside from the cold, we were not used to being alone in the dark, as we had been used to sleeping in crowded barracks among dozens of children and their mothers. Several times during the evening, one of us would be sure to call Didi, Oma, or Tante Kuk with trivial requests that the adults downstairs tried to ignore, but one windy night, I screamed so loudly and with such terror that my mother ran upstairs to find me sitting in bed, shaking, and looking with frightened eyes at the wallpaper that was moving ever so slightly. Hugging me, my mother explained that houses in Holland were made out of brick and that between the brick and the wallpaper was a small space. When it was very windy outside, drafts in the space made the wallpaper jiggle slightly—it was nothing to be afraid of.

And then there was another huge surprise. One morning soon after our arrival, we woke up to find a white backyard. A few inches of snow had fallen in the night, and the garden in the back of the house had been transformed into a dream landscape. Every small branch of the old apple tree was covered in white, and each one of the steps from the verandah down into the yard had a white puffy pillow. Frits and I played in the early morning snow as Oma, Tante Kuk, and Didi watched from inside the dining room. Our faces turned red and our frozen hands turned blue, but of all the things we could play with in Deventer, the snow topped it all, even though it didn't last and was gone by the afternoon.

Postwar Scarcity

Although Deventer seemed to Frits and me to be a place of great abundance, even luxury, we could not have known how different the town was now compared to what it had been before the war. Oma received coupons for her household for the most ordinary necessities: to purchase bread or milk, for textiles, shoes, or fuel. Everything was expensive, everything was scarce. Two weeks after our arrival, on February 28, 1946, Didi wrote Jan about her first impressions of her hometown:

> *This morning I again walked arm in arm with my mother through Deventer. The shops give a good impression from the outside, but it is only when you are inside that you really notice what is going on. We visited Bruynsteen, an old-fashioned, respectable fabric store, where in the past the shelves had been laden with bolts of the most gorgeous fabrics. Now they are laden with big empty boxes, wrapped in paper, that are standing on the display shelves, in an effort to make it look as if there is merchandise. And everywhere is a huge mess, even in the most expensive shops, and none of the shops have heat. It all looks so impoverished. The minister is supposed to have said that he hopes that he will see the day that textiles will be sold free again. Kukje bought a blouse the other day for which she had to pay 11 textile coupons. This is a lot when you realize that everyone received 15 coupons and then later another 10.*
>
> *Food supplies are better. We live in relative abundance because our pig, named Jan, has been butchered and because we also have received some extra things from people in celebration of our homecoming, such as hare, a beef tongue, and smoked sausages and so on. Otherwise meat remains scarce. Fish is plentiful. We also can get enough groceries. Bread is available, vegetables are limited to carrots, onions and beets, we can get white or red cabbage every now and then and sometimes we can get Brussels sprouts or chicory. When that is available it is a real treat for everyone, except me—Brrr! Fruit is also scarce but thankfully we have our own apples, even though it has been a poor fruit year; but for our own use there is plenty. We are lucky that we are getting double rations, that way we have more than enough for the whole family. We are entitled to 24 liter of milk each week; butter is also more than enough—it actually is really margarine; only little Frits gets butter and that is really delicious. We have received a sheet of textile coupons and we have coupons for shoes for each one of us. In this way we are doing well.*
>
> *Gerrit is back in Delft where he is now in the end stretch. He receives food from a central kitchen and he wrote that it gets worse daily. He works in a room without heat. They have coupons for coal but the delivery man claims that he doesn't have any. We recently sent him a*

large package consisting of pieces of the pig Jan, and butter and other good things, among them some of the cans that had been part of a packet I received from the Red Cross. I am so glad that I took it all along with me.

When you come to Holland you should stuff your pockets with cigarettes. Men are allowed forty cigarettes a week, women get twenty plus candy or just candy. But don't ask what brand of cigarettes ... Rhodesia—truly awful knockoffs! The boys were delighted with my cans of Gold Flake and Craven A.

The general scarcity lasted for more than a decade, and during that period, I remember that it was common to unravel old hand-knitted sweaters, wash the yarn, and then knit a "new" sweater from the old one; sometimes the yarn of several sweaters was needed to make the new one; as a result, striped sweaters became the height of fashion in postwar Holland. But the best story is one that Oma liked to tell: "An elderly couple in Olst was looking forward to the wedding of their daughter and wanted to make a nice party to celebrate, but because they did not have much money to spend, they decided to unravel their own knitted white cotton bedspread and use the yarn to knit many, many pairs of socks, which they planned to sell to raise the funds for the celebration. When they were ready to sell the socks, a neighbor approached them who wanted to buy all of them, to the great surprise of the elderly couple. When asked why he needed so many socks, his answer was 'My wife wants to knit a bedspread for the wedding of our son.'"

I have never found out if this story was true, but it doesn't matter—it offered my grandmother and her audiences a lot of cheer in the telling of it.

Our Treasure Breaks Oma's Heart

Didi immersed herself in the warmth and care of her family those first days at home. She wrote Jan after several days that she had not even bothered to unpack the old duffel bag that contained all our earthly belongings. But one day, she and Oma went upstairs to empty the bag of its contents. For the first time, Oma saw our camp clothes, bleached to a pale grey after years of washing in dirty water without soap and drying in the bright tropical sun.

Oma was appalled when Didi unpacked Frits's little sandals made from rubber tires. The *rubbertjes*, as Oma called them, were unceremoniously thrown out because they were so bad for his growing feet. Didi and Oma also found our baby books and the few letters Didi had received during the war or just after and had saved in the bottom of the bag. When they were almost done, Oma found a small tin can all the way down in the bottom of the bag with a sticky brown substance in its bottom. The sticky brown mess turned out to be Didi's last little bit of *Goela Jawa*, Javanese sugar that she had carefully saved. Sugar had been one of the most precious things we owned in the camps; we could sometimes buy it in the little camp store, and Didi had brought the few spoons of sugar all the way from Banjoebiroe, Magelang, Halmaheira, and Bandoeng to her home in Deventer.

The few spoons of brown sugar, our treasure, brought tears to Oma's eyes.

CHAPTER 13

DEVENTER DURING THE WAR

We were awakened very early in the morning of the 10th of May, 1940, by the sound of airplanes overhead. We assembled in the living room and turned on the radio—that is when we heard that the Germans had invaded our country. Oom Bart was a house guest at the time and his reaction was that he was surprised that the Germans had invaded so soon. Being an important member of the NSB [the National Socialist Movement] he probably had known of the expected invasion..."

—Tante Kuk in *Herinneringen van Kuk van Nieuwland,* February 2010

While Didi talked about our experiences in the camps on Java, Oma and the rest of the family told her about their survival in Deventer during the Nazi occupation.

Deventer is a medieval town on the eastern bank of the River IJssel, in the province of Overijssel. During the middle Ages, it was a prominent trading town, part of the old Hanseatic League, and remnants of old city walls still exist, while eighteenth-century patrician houses proudly stand in a row along the harbor. The Brink, the large town square, is surrounded by old shops, and in its center is the Waag, the old weighing station. The city is especially well known for its unique skyline, featuring the tall tower of the Lebuinus Kerk, or Grote Kerk, the big church, with its round dome. The church tower is irreverently called the *peperbus*, the pepper shaker, by the townspeople. Another church, the Bergkerk, is situated on a rise, an old river dune, and remnants of the wide moat, called the Singel, that once surrounded the old town, are now part of a lovely park system. In the past, on very cold winter days when the Singel was frozen, children learned to skate on the ice, holding onto the backs of old kitchen chairs. Oma's house was located at number 30, now number 32, in the Brinkpoortstraat, between the old market square and the Singel.

The skyline of Deventer, photograph by my cousin Hanneke

The Nazi Occupation of Holland

The Germans invaded Holland without any prior warning or official declaration of war during the night of May 9 to May 10, 1940. That night, my grandparents and their children woke up in the dark to the ominous sounds of airplanes flying in large formations from the border with Germany, less than fifty kilometers to the east of Deventer. The planes headed west, in the direction of the most populated parts of the provinces of North and South Holland. The large cities in the western part of Holland were heavily bombarded, especially Rotterdam, with its famous harbor, which was completely destroyed. The Dutch were taken by surprise and were unprepared and incapable of withstanding the huge German air force and its awful bombs. Hundreds of citizens were killed in the German sneak attack, and within days, on May 14, the Dutch capitulated and the government and Queen Wilhelmina went into exile in London, where they remained for all of the years Holland was occupied by the Nazis.

Initially, the Dutch reaction to the presence of the Nazis was one of resigned accommodation to changed circumstances, but the *Nationaal Socialistische Beweging*, NSB, the National Socialist Movement that had started in 1931 in the Netherlands, flourished. The NSB was a fascist organization that sympathized with the Nazis, and its leader encouraged the Dutch to embrace the Germans, renounce the Dutch royal family, and openly collaborate with the Nazi occupiers.

In her memoir, *Herinneringen van Kuk van Nieuwland* [*Memories of Kuk van Nieuwland*], Tante Kuk remembers that my grandfather's half-brother, Oom Bart Brascamp, was a member of the NSB and he happened to be a houseguest in the home of my grandparents in the Brinkpoortstraat when the Germans invaded the Netherlands. Oma hated the NSB, and she was furious with Oom Bart's reaction to the invasion; Oma gave my grandfather an ultimatum: either Oom Bart left, never to come back to the Brinkpoortstraat, or she would leave.

Oom Bart was never again welcomed in their home. He was convicted of treason in 1945, and his considerable collection of Chinese porcelain and other art and financial assets were confiscated by the Dutch authorities. We never met him after we arrived in Holland in February 1946, but I still own an antique Indonesian silver platter that Oom Bart had given Oma long before the war.

The primary reasons for the German occupation of the Netherlands were twofold: first was the German determination to force the Dutch economy and its workforce into collaboration with the German war effort; second was to cleanse the Dutch people of "foreign elements." As to the second German objective, the Nazis were extraordinarily successful in rounding up Dutch Jewish families; with the help of the much-celebrated Dutch bureaucratic efficiency, the Nazis gained easy access to the names, occupations, and addresses of Jewish citizens. By the end of 1941, according to www.JewishVirtualLibray.org, the Germans had established a formal deportation plan, and they began to deport Jewish families on a large scale in October 1942. By the end of the war, more than 100,000 Dutch Jews, close to seventy-five percent of the prewar Jewish population, had lost their lives.

The Dutch complicity in the deaths of so many of its Jewish citizens remains a painful wound that has not healed. As late as April 2005, Holland's prime minister Jan Peter Balkenende apologized for the country's collaboration with the Nazis as he marked the sixtieth anniversary of the liberation of the Westerbork transit camp in the eastern part of Holland.

The Death of Opa de Jong

In my grandmother's first letter to my mother, dated October 19, 1945, she wrote:

> *All of us have survived the war in good health, except for our dear Pops, who died on the first of June 1943, after he had been sick for two years. We did not write you about his illness initially because his doctor had assured us that Pops would get better and we did not want to alarm you with the news of his illness, because it was lung tuberculosis. Father indeed did get better. He was first hospitalized here in Deventer from August 1941 until June 1942.*
>
> *After first having been home for three months, Father left for Almen [a sanatorium] in September 1942. It took a while before Father was treated, but by February 1943, his treatment started, and we experienced a wonderful time of healing. Father was the success of the facility and the doctor (a careful, capable, almost pessimistic man) was elated over the great results. The seventh of May Father was declared completely cured but he died on the first of June from meningitis. Oh, sweetheart, it was so terribly cruel. All of us have suffered intensely but it was of course the worst for me. For me the war was nothing compared to this loss. It is now almost two and a half years ago and although the wounds don't heal, they become less painful and one must go on and I get so much love and help from my children.*

Coping with the War in Deventer

While Oma tried to come to terms with the illness and death of her husband, she also had to maintain her home for their children under the most difficult of circumstances. The oldest, Gerrit, was already a student at the University in Delft, while Kuk and Piet were still in high school when the war started. Fortunately, Oma's house was not too badly damaged during the war, and they were able to stay there for most of the five years of the war's duration.

For the family in Deventer, the worst happened at the very end of the war, in the winter of 1944–1945, when a severe bombing raid by the Allies shattered all the large windows in the houses on the Brinkpoortstraat. Because supplies of all sorts were scarce, especially at the end of 1944 after almost four and a half years into the German occupation, my grandmother and her family lived for weeks with makeshift wood and cardboard covers where once, large glass windows had been. Small panes of glass taken from the now empty greenhouse in the yard, once my grandfather's pride and glory, were installed here and there to allow some light into the rooms.

Pieter, Didi's youngest brother, wrote Didi:

> *Our old gymnasium is ruined; it fell during the bombardment of December 15, 1944. But the "Peperbus" still stands; it only was hit by a couple of shells in its dome, and that has been repaired already. The most important old buildings in the city, like the Bergkerk, the Big Church, Town Hall, the Police Bureau and the Waag are still standing. A bomb did fall about 3 meters from the walls of the Waag and blew literally through it; it was a huge mess. I worked days with two other boys and Lingers, the conservator, to save the collection, and we were mostly successful. As thanks we received a "beautiful certificate," signed and painted by Bokhorst.*

Of course, the family in the Brinkpoortstraat had the great good fortune of owning a farm in Olst, a brisk bicycle trip away from Deventer. The farm, called *De Stege*, consisted primarily of apple orchards, but there was usually also a pig being fattened, and the fields and orchards were great for hunting hare and pheasants. During the war, Oma received crates of apples, supplies of old apple wood for the woodstove, game in the fall, and pork sausages whenever one of the pigs was slaughtered.

The Dutch Resistance

The Dutch Resistance had become active by 1942 when the Dutch had awakened to the troubling fact that the Germans were rounding up all Jewish men, women, and children and transporting them to Germany—no one knew what was happening to the Jews there. At that time, the Germans also started gathering up young Dutch men to put them to work in German industrial centers in support of their war effort; when the young men began to resist in large numbers, the Nazis started to conduct *razzias*, an Italian word meaning "roundup," during which they would arrive in the very early morning hours to search the houses for young men in hiding. If they did not find a young man where they expected to find one, they would uncover all beds, to count how many of them were warm in excess of the number of people they found in the home. During the time of the razzias, Oom Gerrit and Oom Piet were *ondergedoken*, literally "submerged," for weeks at the time, hiding from the Germans.

In a letter dated December 13, 1945, Oom Gerrit, who was an engineering student at the University of Delft, wrote a long letter to Didi about his experiences during the war:

> *I had to leave Delft in April 1943 and would have finished my studies in September 1943! I did not see a technical book since that time and was hopelessly out of touch. This is why I am now very busy, am getting into it again and expect that I will graduate in February 1946. I will then be officially an engineer, but before then I will likely lose a lot of sleep.*
>
> *In 1943 (on about Jan. 1st) the Moffen tried to send me to the transit camp in Vught, but they were not successful in my regard. Two months later I was back here, but in April '43 we were ordered to sign a Declaration of Loyalty to the Mof and off to Germany to work for the war industry! I had no interest and went into hiding and then became the manager of the "Fruitteelt Bedryf P.J. de Jong" in Olst [Our grandfather's farm in the village of Olst near Deventer]. I worked first in Olst as manager and later as chief.*
>
> *That was all just fine until the "Organisation Todt" (bunker construction) wanted to put me to work in Sept. '44 and they were again unsuccessful. I disappeared and resurfaced in Brinkpoortstraat 30, where I on purpose never officially had registered during the war. I remained 'submerged' until April 1, 1945. We had built underground tunnels to Houck and Hesselink [two neighbors in the Brinkpoortstraat] and I informed everyone each evening about the war, having listened to the extensive news of the day on 5 different channels.*

The radio Gerrit listened to must have been carefully hidden somewhere in the house in the Brinkpoortstraat, because the Germans confiscated everything: they took cars, radios, bicycles, and anything else they could use. They plundered Holland until nothing was left. The tunnels he refers to were made through the walls of the cellars of the houses and made it possible for the neighbors to crawl through them and get together after curfew at night; more important, the tunnels allowed young men in hiding in the houses to escape when the Germans started a razzia down the block. Gerrit continued his letter:

> *The last months I was busy with espionage jobs and drawing charts for the Allied advance in Salland. Then, on April 1st, I joined the forces*

of the resistance and after many adventures I returned in the night of April 10/11 to a liberated home that was filled with weapons, soldiers of the underground, a courier and two prisoners. It all had gone well, but please ... never again! My hat off to Mother, who approved of everything and helped any way she could.

In Oma's house, they had created a hiding place in the attic, next to the bathroom. It was a small space with only a mattress, some cans of food, and some sort of toilet arrangement, perhaps just a chamber pot. One day, Oom Pieter had to hide there in a hurry; later, he could not remember how he had been able to get there, but Tante Kuk believes that he used the swing set in the attic to swing to the ceiling and drop down into the hiding space as the Germans were climbing the stairs. Years later, Piet told me that he could see the tops of the helmets of the Germans as they were walking around in the attic searching for him. His greatest fear was that he would cough or sneeze and they would find him.

Pieter also had to leave home, like so many young men, to go into hiding while he was still a high school student. He lived for a period of time with a farmer and his wife, but when they too were expelled from their home by the Nazis, he had to leave them and find his way back home. He arrived back in Deventer dressed like a farmhand, carrying a small puppy under his jacket. The little dog had also become homeless, and in that miserable winter of 1944–1945 the little dog brought a great deal of pleasure to the family in the Brinkpoortstraat. Weeks after Pieter had come back home, the house in the Brinkpoortstraat further filled up when acquaintances of my grandparents moved in temporarily after their house had been destroyed during one of the bombing raids. Because they brought a cat along, the house at the Brinkpoortstraat must have been full of life in those cold months of the "Hunger Winter."

The Hunger Winter of 1944–1945

The last winter of the war was by far the worst for everyone. Not only was food and everything else in short supply, it was unusually frigid. Tante Kuk wrote in her memoir that the cold was even worse than the pangs of hunger and that it must have been particularly bad for many people in the cities, who began to burn everything they could when fuel became scarce. They burned doors, window frames, furniture, trees, anything at all that could be used as fuel.

In one of her letters, Oma described how the family farm in Olst helped them to survive the worst days of the Hunger Winter of 1945: "We have not suffered from hunger because we had our own garden planted with vegetables and potatoes, rye and wheat and we also have not suffered from cold since we had plenty of old wood from the orchards."

Oma, the Lioness of Flanders

Oma did not tolerate fools well and had strong opinions about those she did not like. I have heard my grandmother's children refer to their mother as the *Leeuwin van Vlaanderen*, the Lioness of Flanders. I always assumed they called her that because she resembled the emblem of Flanders, a lion standing on its hind feet in water up to his chest, raised front claws at the ready, fiercely protecting those she loved, but after a quick check with Wikipedia (http://en.wikipedia.org/wiki/DeVlaamse-Leeuw), I learned that "De Vlaamse Leeuw" is an anthem written by Hippoliet van Peene in July 1847 that commemorates the 1302 victory of the Flemish urban militias against a well-armed French infantry force that included cavalry, knights, and squires. The burghers won the Battle of Kortrijk in Flanders on July 11, 1302. I now believe that Oma is called the Lioness of Flanders because of her courage and perseverance during the war, just like the burghers from Kortrijk and their leader, whose nickname was "the Lion of Flanders." The first lines of the battle song "De Vlaamse Leeuw" include the following:

They will never tame him, the proud Flemish Lion
Even if they threaten his freedom with fetters and with shouts
They will never tame him, as long as one Fleming lives,
As long as the Lion can claw, as long as he has teeth
Time devours cities, no thrones will ever last,
Armies may go under, but a people never die.
The enemy comes marching in; surrounded by mortal danger.
We laugh at his anger: the Flemish Lion is here!

Oma absolutely hated the German invaders, especially the SS, and right from the beginning of the war, she made sure that in small and large ways, she would show her contempt for them. She would resist any efforts by the Nazis to control her life and the lives of her loved ones. A familiar family story relates how she would defiantly refuse to step aside for any German whom she met on the narrow sidewalks of the old town. She would intentionally occupy the entire walkway, pushing out her elbows with shopping baskets hanging from each arm, thereby ensuring that any German coming toward her had to step down into the gutter to let her pass. But she hated the members of the NSB the most ... they were traitors.

Oma was born in Olst and fondly remembered many Jewish friends from her schooldays in the little village on the River IJssel. Once, early on in the war, when she met an old friend passing her house, she invited him in for a cup of coffee. His answer—"Aaltje, I cannot do that, now I am wearing the yellow star"—enraged her, and she told him, "In my house I decide who enters. Please come in," holding the front door wide open to let him in, for all to see. Oma was glad to help another Jewish family from Olst at another time when they asked if they could leave some suitcases at her home in the Brinkpoortstraat for safekeeping while they were about to go into hiding. Weeks later, when she was trying to rid the house of an invasion of moths, Oma looked into the suitcases and found that many of the packed clothes in the suitcases still bore the yellow star. Tante Kuk and Oma made sure that each star was removed and thrown away. Their friends survived the war and were able to retrieve their belongings when the war was over.

Oma refused to be afraid, and Kuk remembers that Oma hid several hand grenades under some mops and pails in the little cabinet under the kitchen sink. But Oma really showed her true mettle in the last months of the war. In his eulogy at Oma's funeral in 1981, Oom Gerrit related the following stories in celebration of her courage during the war:

> *In 1944 the Brinkpoortstraat 30 was confiscated by the Kriminal Polizei, and Oma found a haven with neighbors, the family Houck. We had lived 29 years in our house and had to turn it over within 16 hours. And within those 16 hours the house was empty; we removed everything. At a quarter to ten a high-ranked officer of the Grüne Polizei came to inspect the house. But he was early, Mother was supposed to turn it over at 10 o'clock. With icy calm and flaming eyes she sent the Mof packing, like a dog.*

A few months later, just before the end of the war, Oma again took matters in her own hands and refused several armed Germans entry to her house after they rang her doorbell and told her they were looking for bicycles. Oma refused them access, telling them that she had no bicycles. Faced with this fearless old woman, the Germans moved on. If they had made their way into the house, they would have found far more than bicycles, as Gerrit explained:

> *The automatic rifles, machine guns and ammunition that belonged to the Underground movement stood in the old kitchen of the sousterrain, neatly stashed, ready for use. When it came to Germans, she was not afraid of a thing!*

The Liberation of Deventer

On April 10, 1945, Deventer was liberated by the Canadians, and slowly, life became more normal. Oma wrote Didi:

> *On April 10 Deventer was liberated—we could not believe it but it was true, the Canadians were the ones who liberated us. Slowly it is beginning to penetrate our heads that we are free again and life is again very different and so much happier that it has been. We eat most everything again but the most important thing is that we are FREE. I will write you much more about this later.*
>
> *Slowly life is beginning to become normal and every week you see improvements. The factory in Olst is running full speed again. This week we were able to get beschuit, sweets and pastry and lots of nutritious items with our food coupons. Compared to last winter we are doing extremely well and even then, we were able to manage alright and because we constantly had a house full of people we were able to help each other.*

The factory that Oma refers to was the machine factory of her eldest brother, Oom Johan Aberson. About the farm in Olst, Gerrit wrote in the fall of 1945:

> *The orchards have grown a lot and we sometimes work there with six people. Since I could no longer do it all myself we have hired a salaried manager and a permanent young farm hand. We have 6 hectares in full production; one hectare recently planted and then after 22 February 1947, another 6 hectares, which are now still part of the farm. The way the revenues are now, it appears to be a profitable enterprise, but that can change.*

Pieter, Didi's youngest brother, wrote a long letter on November 25, 1945, in which he describes the mood at home, in the Brinkpoortstraat, during the aftermath of the war:

> *When you get here, dear, you will find much changed. Pops is no longer. At the time when you left, we had "heaven on earth" here and that is all gone. We are doing well together, very well actually, but the days of joy and happiness are gone. Now I am looking forward so much to the time that you and the little ones will be here. Those sweet little things that don't pay much attention to their surroundings and who don't have great demands will make us young, and that is necessary because on the whole*

I am getting quite old. However courageous Mother is she still misses Father of course a lot. Kukje thinks mostly about Cor. Gerrit has all sorts of internal conflicts, and I have, so to speak, inherited the pessimistic family trait, with the hopeless urge to worry and to unravel everything. I don't like myself very much. I used to have a girlfriend (it sounds perhaps funny, she was very young but I loved her nonetheless) who has left me for a Canadian. That is currently very much in vogue here. But I should stop complaining to you.

Oma wrote in the middle of December 1945 how the liberation was making a difference in the life of the town because the people could celebrate the feast of Sinterklaas, which had been banned by the Germans:

Last week we celebrated Sinterklaas and Gerrit came home for one day. We had a nice evening together, the four of us, and we kept on saying how wonderful it will be with the little kids next year; then we will put everything on the doormat near the front door, ring the bell loudly, and run down the basement stairs and we will sing Sinterklaas songs and will go to the IJssel to greet the saint. That has happened this year for the first time because for some time it was not allowed. Furthermore, during the war there was nothing to give, no candies, no cookies, no presents, nothing.

But now it has started again in a modest way and it was such a wonderful sight: the decorated boat, and the bells that pealed, and the cannon that issued a salvo. The Canadian soldiers in our country had made a lot of toys for the children and as a result there were six Canadians among the entourage of the Saint (Mr. Tulp who had been a hostage during the war). The whole town celebrated the fact that this was again possible.

I had not gone to see the boat because of my bad cold, but I stood at the window and received a special greeting from the saint. The school across the street is currently used as a home for old men and women, because the houses in the Begynenstraat were bombarded. You should have seen those old folks, dear, the old women were dancing and waving their hands and the saint bowed to them and Pikkie [Black Pieter] flourished his broom.

We now enjoy these things so much because they did not exist during that terrible war. And in this way there is so much: the trains are running; the streets have lights; we have gas for cooking; and lots of good bread; and enough food for everyone. And shortly you will be here with us; sweetheart, we will help you and comfort you to make your life good again, so that you will be happy notwithstanding all that has happened.

Along with all the news about their survival during the war, the letters from Oma, Tante Kuk, Oom Gerrit, and Oom Piet were filled with their plans for our return to the Brinkpoortstraat. Toys were gathered and cleaned up, Pieter made doll house furniture for me, the small children's table with two chairs was put in the dining room, and Kuk selected clothes she thought would fit Didi. Together, they were making plans for next year's Sinterklaas feast. Pieter wrote to Didi on November 25, 1945:

> *Oh, dearest, I hope you will never receive this letter and that you are already on your way home. It will be hard to leave the country in which you have experienced so much horror but also had the best time of your life. But we shall fight together for you and your kids' future. Goodbye, second sweetest of the world! Pieter Jan.*

CHAPTER 14

WHEN THE THREE OF US MARRIED OOM JAN

I'm going to love that guy like he's never been loved before.
I'm going to show that guy he's the fellow I adore.
When he's in my arms again, our dreams will all come true.
Then the years between might never have been,
We'll be starting our lives anew.

—World War II song mentioned in one of Didi's letters to Jan

With the liberation of Holland and the East Indies, normal life slowly started to return to the people who had lost so many years to that awful war. Almost everyone was mourning a loved one. Many had experienced unthinkable suffering and losses. Everyone was eager to catch up, to return to the days before the war, to a normalcy they remembered as in a dream. At twenty-nine, Didi wanted to be young again and be in love again. She was eager to start her life anew.

To tease her sister, Kuk, who was waiting to hear when she would be able to join her husband, Cor, in Batavia, Didi sang the song, quoted above, accompanied by her brother Piet on the piano, but Didi was surely also thinking of her own romance with Jan and the new life she was going to start with him soon, while she was singing her heart out next to the piano.

From a Steady Friend to a Husband

When Jan and Didi finally found each other again in December 1945, they had just a few days together before we left for Holland. They had fallen head over heels in love without having had a chance to notice the huge changes that had taken place for each one of them—life-altering changes that could not easily be reversed. Didi was now a widow with two children, Jan was a bachelor of thirty-four, and both of them had been prisoners of the Japanese for more than three years, having survived under the most difficult circumstances.

They had fallen into each other's arms next to the washbasins in the hold of the *Johan van Oldenbarneveldt* when Jan was seeing us off to

Holland on January 12, 1945, and they had decided to get married on the spur of the moment. Days later, Didi wrote Jan from the boat:

> *...I am so much looking forward to the future and to act as if we are eighteen years old. One is only as old as one feels—I feel as if I am twelve, not older, sometimes.*

After three days at sea, Didi wrote Jan another, longer, letter:

> *Oh, Jan, I am so glad and I know for sure that this is good the way it is. Because, you know, the fact that things were generally good between Daan and me was in large measure thanks to you. You were always there for me whenever I was upset about something. You always helped me and pushed me through difficulties and whatever Daan lacked, I found in you. The situation will now be different because you will no longer be the steady friend, but my husband. And therefore Jan, you must take care that you will be in charge. Don't laugh, I really mean it. We need that especially. Don't be too nice to me. I need someone who guides me.*
>
> *How wonderful it will be to have a husband whom you can tell everything and who understands everything and with whom you can talk about everything; and also to start all over again. Especially in the evening when I am in my hammock, I think about all that has been and how things will be in the future.*

When she was alone with her thoughts, lying in the hammock where she did so much of her thinking, Didi also worried about Jan, who was still in Batavia, in the middle of the dangers of the Indonesian struggle for independence and the bersiap period. She wrote Jan:

> *No mail has arrived from Java that was written after our departure and I am so afraid that that is a bad sign. It is perhaps silly, but I sometimes worry. I don't know what I would do if something happened to you. Please remember that. In the past I never thought about you other than as a friend, but with the certainty that I always could count on you. You were always available when I needed you. But now I am afraid that I could lose it all.*
>
> *Last night I had a terrible dream. I will tell you about it and perhaps I will forget it, I keep thinking about it constantly:*

I am driving up a hill together with you, and look down on a city—a city of white houses, gleaming in the sunlight under a gorgeous blue sky with white clouds. It is so clear that to the left I see a large billboard advertising some kind of cigarettes. It is wonderful and we enjoy the lovely scene. All of a sudden we hear the roar of motors in the distance and see airplanes flying towards us, perhaps 150 or so in a tight formation—it is an amazing sight until they arrive above the city and drop bombs and everything bursts apart .... I still see it so vividly in front of me—how the billboard flies up and falls down in three pieces. It was so terrible and the children were down there somewhere below—I screamed: Jan .... Jan ....! But when I looked around you were no longer there—I could not find you anywhere. I woke up with a horrible feeling and I cannot let go of it—perhaps I can now—now I have told you.

A Love Life Lived in Letters

Before Jan arrived in Holland at the beginning of July 1946, Didi and Jan had barely seen each other and had not had a moment alone to talk, but they wrote each other almost twice weekly during the spring of 1946, while they were planning their wedding day and life together. Jan saved all of Didi's letters to him, all thirty-seven of them, written between February 16 and June 10, 1946.

Didi's letters are full of bits of news and gossip, but she also wrote eloquently about her hopes for the future and included stories about Frits and me. Frits, who turned four years old in May of 1946, was a funny, easygoing little boy with a sunny smile who could disarm anyone. He was the center of attention most of the time. Didi's favorite uncle, Oom Nol, called Frits his *mannegies aape*. For years I had no idea what this meant other than that it was a hilarious reference to Frits that made everyone in the family giggle. It was only much later that I found out that *mannegies aape* means "little monkey man" in the dialect of Olst. My mother's letters are full of stories about the antics of Frits, the little monkey man.

I was a very different kind of child: on the one hand moody and watchful and easily brought to tears, on the other, sweet and caring. In April 1945, Didi wrote Jan:

You wrote that you were surprised about what I wrote about Syts's character. It is very difficult to write you about it. If you were here for a few days you would notice yourself what I mean. Syts is very sweet and there is nothing the matter with her character—she is more independent than Frits who is more a mother's child. She is of an age where she has become aware of everything she does and wants to be in the center of everything. She tries very hard but is usually not successful, while Frits usually gets everyone's attention. She tries to be like him but it never works out. It is not jealousy on her part, at least not overtly so, because she is usually very sweet to him and she is also charmed by him. She sometimes looks at him with a motherly smile on her little face when he is at it again. She is sweet, perhaps a little less sensitive than Frits is—I sometimes don't know myself; we will have to talk about this more.

I want to get back to you about Sysjepop—that is how she called herself when she was little. When I said that I thought that Frits is sweeter than she, I really meant that he is more affectionate than she and that Syts sometimes can be quite aggressive and nasty. Sometimes—it is already much less than when we had just arrived.

You know sweetheart, that little thing has been brought up in a camp until now and that has left its mark—that is not surprising. She has seen far more than she should have and understands a lot and she has learned that one has to stand up for oneself, if one wants to get somewhere. And that is why it is sometimes really sad, because she must learn to understand that everyone loves her—she needs a lot of love, that little thing, and if she gets that, all will be all right.

Frits will be fine, he wraps the whole world around his little fingers—no one can dislike him. Syts must be given a lot of help, do you understand me? And yet, Syts is quite independent and resolute; she knows her mind and goes about her own business. But mentally she needs reassurance and support. And because we all try to give that to her she is getting much better.

Though I thrived in Oma's house with the love of my family, I remained a frightened, watchful little girl, expecting disasters to happen at any moment that would destroy our happiness. One night, when Didi, who had a bad cold at the time, was tucking me in, I asked her why she was crying. She explained that the tears in her eyes were not tears of sadness but because she had a bad cold. She added that there was nothing to be sad about now we were in Oma's house. Apparently, I did not agree with her and told her that there would be plenty to be sad about when Oma died. I continued having nightmares about violent people hurting us and often worried that the people I loved would die soon and disappear out of my life. I expected the safety of Oma's house to be a temporary respite from ordinary life in camps, to which we would be returning.

The Least a Child Can Hope For

For us children, the fact that we did not have a father remained at the heart of everything. Even though we had no clear idea what to expect of a father, not having one left a huge hole in our lives. Once, when Frits saw a photograph of Didi and Daan in my grandmother's bedroom, he said to Oma and Tante Kuk, "When my father is no longer dead, then I will have a father again, and then I will love him a lot, and then I will give him a kiss."

Didi commented later to Jan:

> *He has never known his father and yet he knows that he misses something. I am so glad, Jan, that they will get a father again. That is the least a child can hope for, to have a father and a mother.*
>
> *Sweetheart, you write so lovingly about the children. I know that you will do everything to be a good father for them and that you will try your best to make sure that they will love you. Yet, I would like to give you this advice: don't try too hard in the beginning—children can be so peculiar. Often you see that they adore someone who means well but who doesn't pay much attention to them, while they don't want anything to do with people who try hard to be sweet and friendly to them. They have to know right from the start that you are the boss. I believe that you must let them find out in their own sweet time that you love them and would do anything for them.*

In the same letter, Didi wrote that I was eager to find out when Oom Jan was expected in Holland, although I did not clearly understand then that they were planning to get married. In the margin of the letter, I made a drawing of a bucolic scene of little houses, flowers, and trees, a favorite subject of my drawings. Underneath, I wrote, with my mother's help: "Oom Jan, I am glad that you are coming; a kiss from Sytsje and Fritsje and also a little kiss from Mammie."

Becoming a Family at Last

Jan and Didi were married in August of 1946 in the town hall of Deventer. Didi was dressed in a two-piece outfit that was made from a suit that had belonged to my grandfather Engelberts. Jan was dressed in the uniform of the air force. With their marriage, Didi got the husband she had longed for, we children got a new father, and Jan, who had been a bachelor all his life, gained the woman he loved. But Jan also acquired two children of four and six who, just like the adults, carried the scars of the war years.

The four of us standing on the steps of town hall on the day we married Oom Jan and minutes after Frits had declared, "The witch is now married."

The wedding ceremony was short and simple, but to four-year-old Frits, it was an obvious continuation of *Hansel and Gretel and the Wicked Witch*, a play we had just seen. When the official presiding at the marriage ceremony declared Oom Jan and our mother husband and wife, Frits, turned around in his chair at the front to face the assembled family behind us and explained in a loud, clear voice, "De heks is nu getrouwd," the witch is now married.

Weeks before the wedding, Frits and I had talked about the day when *we are getting married to Oom Jan.* After all, Didi, Frits, and I had been so close for so long, through such extraordinary circumstances, that we children were sure it was the three of us together who were marrying Oom Jan. So, at the end of the wedding day, when our mother and Jan went away on a short honeymoon after a cheerful reception in Oma's house, Frits and I were extremely disappointed and surprised that we were not invited to come along.

Pappie, a Dream Come True

A happy family of four on the verandah of Oma's house, celebrating the queen's birthday with our "tooters," August 31, 1946

After their marriage, Didi and Jan asked us what we wanted to call Oom Jan, and without hesitation, he became our Pappie. Being a part of a real family with a father, a mother, and two children was wonderful. I remember watching Didi and Pappie standing in the middle of the room, hugging and kissing each other, and me loving the sight of the two of them.

I also relished my own time with Pappie, sitting on his lap, spelling out difficult words in the newspaper he was reading and smelling on his handkerchief the benzene he used as lighter fuel. I still remember Pappie's delight in my accomplishments and my pride when I successfully deciphered a three-syllable word.

It cannot have been easy for Pappie to move into a ready-made family, living in his mother-in-law's house with very little privacy. Didi's family had loved Daan, and Pappie must have felt he had to live up to Daan's memory—a difficult task, as Daan had been such a favorite of them all. And, of course, Jan had to take on the role of father for two children who, while they delighted in the idea of a father, also were unsure how to react to one.

Frits and I had grown up in a world of women and children. The only men we remembered were the Japanese and Korean guards—men we had distrusted and had been afraid of. We had not received much discipline while growing up in the camps, and we did not have the manners Jan thought we should have. He had old-fashioned ideas about child rearing and strongly believed that children should be seen but not heard. He demanded excellent table manners and obedience at all times. Even Oma, who was a serious disciplinarian herself, had to point out to him that we were still very young and that he could not expect perfection from us.

Didi was probably not much of a helpmate in the childrearing department. She had avoided controversy all her life, hating any kind of argument, never very good at taking a point of view and sticking with it. Even when she was a young child, Didi had been known by her friends as someone with whom they could never pick a fight. She probably left most of the decisions about discipline to Jan and never argued with him about the right approach to child rearing. The adjustment for all of us must have been far more difficult than any of us had anticipated.

Of course, a father wasn't all we gained when Jan and Didi married. We also acquired more family members. Jan's mother, Oma Borgerhoff, had become *Grootje*, Granny, as she liked to be called when Didi and Jan married; she became another loving grandmother to us. Grootje remained Grootje until our little baby brother, Jan, learned to speak and turned Grootje into *Huja*, which was how she was called from then on. We also gained another aunt and uncle, Tante Tiek and her husband, Oom Jan Simonsz.

When I was a teenager living at my boarding school in the 1950s, I saw Oma and Huja often. They were very different from each other, but I adored them both. Oma in Deventer was the grandmother with whom I felt safe. At Oma's house, life was solidly predictable, comfortable, and dependable. But Huja was the grandmother who showed me what it was like to have *joie de vivre.* In Huja's rented rooms, life was relaxed and unregimented, and the mood was always cheerful, almost elegant. Huja had the reputation that she could make a feast with absolutely nothing. And when I came for a visit, Huja always asked me what I would like to have for lunch, regardless of its cost, although Huja had no money and spent her small state pension carefully. Huja was very creative and could embroider beautifully, and she knitted sweaters for us children, skills she later taught me; and she was a very good cook. But, best of all, she was so easy to be with.

Our First Sinterklaas, December 1946

On December 5, when Holland celebrates the birthday of Sinterklaas, Frits and I had our first taste of this Dutch feast in all its glory. The family in Deventer had been looking forward to celebrating this holiday with us for close to a year, ever since they had learned that we had survived the war, and they made sure that this Sinterklaas would be memorable.

A day before the saint's birthday, we put our little shoes, filled with hay and pieces of an apple, in front of the wood-burning stove in the dining room. The hay and apples were our gifts to Sinterklaas's horse, which would bring the holy man over the roofs of the town, through the chimneys of the houses, and into the rooms where the horse's treats would be waiting. The following morning, we ran downstairs to make sure that Sinterklaas had made it through the chimney into Oma's house. And sure enough! The horse's treats had been taken from our shoes and had been replaced with chocolate letters. Frits received a large chocolate *F*, and for me there was an *S*. Throughout our childhood, we would argue whether his letter had more chocolate than mine, an argument that has continued for generations of Dutch children.

Though we were already overwhelmed by the excitement of the morning and the remainder of the day, the night held still more surprises. Early in the evening, there was a huge commotion when the back doors to the verandah unexpectedly flew open and handfuls of *pepernoten*, tiny spice cookies, were thrown into the room by Zwarte Piet, Sinterklaas's attendant, as tradition had it. We screamed with delight as we ran around to collect the little nuggets. We were only sorry for Oom Piet, who had just left the room to do something upstairs and was not present when Zwarte Piet scattered handfuls of pepernoten throughout the dining room…

Throughout the evening, we received huge numbers of presents, each one more wonderful than the next. We were thoroughly exhausted from the excitement, but it wasn't over yet …. Late in the evening when we were just about ready to go to bed, the brass bell at Oma's front door rang with a clanging sound. I still see us running through the marble hallway, tripping over each other to get to the door first. When we opened the door, there was nobody there, but we found a large wooden horse on the stoop, with a real horsehair mane and tail and a beautiful leather bridle and saddle. It was the final gift from Sinterklaas. And it was beautiful.

Much later, we heard that the horse had once belonged to my mother and her siblings and had been repainted after the war by someone my grandmother knew in Deventer who had taken the trouble to collect real horsehair for the mane and tail at farms in the area. While we were standing on the stoop, screaming with delight, this wonderful man was hiding in the shadows across the street, equally delighted at the sight of us.

CHAPTER 15

OUR RETURN TO INDONESIA

Jan, when we said goodbye you had said: "perhaps I will get a job in Holland"—but sweetheart, I will settle for anything. I love the Indies but Holland is also fine with me and if you ever would want to go to America or Australia or South Africa I would cheerfully follow you—I really mean it. I will be the ever faithful wife.

—Didi's letter to Jan, written on the *Johan van Oldenbarneveldt,* January 16, 1946

Two days after the Japanese surrender on August 17, 1945, Soekarno had declared Indonesia's independence from the Netherlands, an independence he had been planning for decades prior to the war. Together with Hatta, Soekarno had been a leader in the national movement for Indonesia's independence since the 1920s, and during the war, both had visited Japan, where they had been decorated by the emperor and had met Prime Minister Hideki Tojo. During their occupation of Indonesia, the Japanese had encouraged Soekarno to make plans for the independence of the country for the time when the war would be over and a new era would begin for all of Southeast Asia. Furthermore, as early as 1942, the United States had advised the Netherlands to consider the independence of its former colony once the war would be over.

In 1945, Indonesia was not prepared to turn back the clock.

Why Didn't Didi and Pappie Stay in Holland?

Why Didi and Jan decided to go back to Indonesia after the war is a puzzling question. They had left Indonesia in 1946 and had returned "home" to Holland while postwar Indonesia was in turmoil with roving bands of revolutionaries kidnapping and killing Dutch men, women, and children. In the fall of 1945, during the bersiap period, when the POWs and internees were first leaving the camps, fighting had broken out between the Dutch, who expected to restart their former lives in the Dutch East Indies, and the young revolutionaries, who were ready to fight for their country, an independent Indonesia.

Until 1949, the Dutch continued to argue for a return of Dutch control over its former colony, but when the United States and Great Britain began to put pressure on the Netherlands, insisting that Indonesia be granted its independence, the Dutch soon realized that their return to their former colony did not guarantee a return to the old days. The Dutch did hope, however, that a different relationship between the Netherlands and its former colony would be possible to the economic benefit of both countries. While she had been in exile in Britain, Queen Wilhelmina had stated in an address, which had been prepared and read in English, that she hoped to establish a commonwealth that would include all of the Dutch overseas possessions:

> I visualize, without anticipating the commendations of the future conference, that they will be directed towards a commonwealth in which the Netherlands, Indonesia, Surinam and Curacao will participate, with complete self-reliance and freedom of conduct for each part regarding its internal affairs, but with the readiness to render mutual assistance.

Planning Our Family's Future

Although the "unrest" was troubling, various considerations figured in Jan and Didi's decision to leave Holland and return to Indonesia in 1947. First, life in Holland was hard. There was a major housing shortage, and families who had lost their homes were moved by the authorities into the homes of other families, where they had to share kitchens and bathrooms. Any family with a room to spare was affected. Another consideration for Didi was the small size of the identical row houses, built side by side along dreary streets that might be available for those who were fortunate to obtain a home of their own. Didi wrote Jan in March 1946 that she had visited a cousin who actually was one of the fortunate ones and who had just moved into one of those row houses on the outskirts of town with her husband and two little sons. Standing on her cousin's tiny balcony and looking out over all those tiny rear gardens and all the other identical little balconies and small sheds, with laundry lines crisscrossing the space in the back of the houses, she realized that she could not see us living like that. Her memories of the colonial houses in which she had lived not that long ago, with ample gardens surrounding them, became a powerful incentive for Didi to go back to Indonesia.

Second, the Dutch families who hoped to return to the Indies assumed that life there soon would become "normal" again and that the prewar life they were dreaming of would eventually return. On March 5, 1946, Didi wrote Jan, who was still in Batavia:

> *Your last letter was quite down and I really understand. It is an awful situation over there and I can imagine that you have to work against the tide. You want to do something and you cannot get anywhere because everything is against you. Do you believe it all will work out in the end?*
>
> *I often see the future in a somber light; of course it will not be the same as it was in the past, the differences were too huge. But it should be possible to find a place for <u>us</u> in the Indies—we have a right to that, even if it would be on equal footing with the Inlanders, as long as our place is not <u>under</u> them, because we cannot accept that and of course it would not be possible. It is so difficult and I easily become upset thinking of it—for you it is even worse because you are in the middle of it all.*

Third, while Didi was contemplating what life would offer them in Holland if they stayed, Pappie returned to Makassar in 1947, writing eloquently about old friends he had met there; about the soos, which was in full swing again; and about the swimming pool and its seaside patio where everyone gathered to have a cool drink in the early evening and watch the sun set behind the silhouettes of small islands across the bay. For Didi, who constantly was cold in that very frigid winter of 1947, the promise that she could be sitting in a summer dress, drinking a cool drink next to the man she loved while watching the sun go down in a blaze of pink and orange rays was a perfect dream of what the tropics have to offer, and it was very different from shivering in her mother's house next to the wood-burning stove in the dining room.

All along, Didi's fantasy had been that she and Jan would connect with their old friends back in the Indies, that the horrors of the war years could be erased, and that the carefree life of *Tempo Doeloe*, the good old past, would return. As early as January 27, 1946, while we were still sailing to Holland, she had written Jan:

> *I am so much looking forward to the future, assuming that we will return to the Indies. Tiek and Jan, Kuk and Cor, the two of us, and Mieke and Buis! Oh boy—it promises to be so much fun.*

In the final analysis, the decision to return to Indonesia was made on the assumption that life in the Indies was going to be easier than life at home in Holland, that many of their friends were going back, and that the "troubles" caused by the independence movement would be temporary and limited to a few contained areas. And of course, Pappie had a well-paying job to go to with the firm he had worked for before the war, while it was not easy in 1947 to get a decent job in Holland that would allow for some comfort and a pleasant place to live.

The Struggle for Independence, 1945–1949

When Jan and Didi decided to go back to Indonesia, the country's Struggle for Independence was in full swing and many of the towns and villages in Java and elsewhere had become dangerous places for the Dutch. Fighting continued between the revolutionaries on the one hand and the Dutch military forces on the other when Pappie returned to Indonesia in the spring of 1947. He arrived in Makassar, the capital of Celebes, now Sulawesi, when the infamous Raymond Westerling, often called the Turk, had been appointed commander of Dutch Special Forces and had been given carte blanche to subdue the bands of fighting revolutionaries in South Celebes.

Charged with restoring peace and order among various fighting groups of Indonesians in the city of Makassar and its surrounding area, Westerling took to the task with deadly energy. During a three-month assignment in Makassar, he was in charge of several massacres in which thousands of local men were killed. The exact number of men who were killed remains in dispute. Indonesia estimates a total of 40,000 dead, but the Dutch estimate is somewhere between 1,500 and 3,000 men who died at the hands of Westerling and his special forces.

Oom Buis and his family also ended up in Makassar after the war. In his speech on the occasion of Didi's sixty-fifth birthday, Oom Buis remembered "After the war you experienced a complete change and a new beginning with Jan Borgerhoff Mulder in Makassar, where, for us Dutch, life was perfectly safe, thanks to the Turk, in contrast to Java where the fighting continued much longer. In Makassar life was somewhat chaotic but quite pleasant."

The United States of Indonesia, December 27, 1949

The Struggle for Indonesia's Independence continued until the end of December 1949, when Holland had to capitulate to America's insistence that the Dutch give up any efforts to maintain control over their former colony. On the twenty-seventh of December, Soekarno became president of the United States of Indonesia, and Hatta was appointed prime minister. The new nation consisted of various states, some of which had been loyal to the Dutch during colonial times and continued to be supported by the Dutch in 1949. The Netherlands hoped that these states would have a pro-Dutch influence with the powers in control of the new Indonesian federation.

When Indonesia assumed its independence, it had not anticipated the complexity of governing a country consisting of thousands of islands with diverse populations that spoke different languages and had their own cultures. Furthermore, the country had been devastated by years of the Japanese occupation. Its infrastructure had disappeared, and its people were living in abject poverty. Soekarno was eager to design a form of democratic government that would encourage participation by the federal states in the "outer islands," many of whom continued to be ruled by their own royal families, who had cooperated with the Dutch during colonial years. The outer islands also had to accept the fact that the seat of government would be located on Java, just the way it had been in colonial times, first in Jogjakarta and later in Jakarta, the former Batavia.

While Soekarno celebrated the formation of the United States of Indonesia, he also realized that the republic needed to craft a new relationship with its former colonial power because it needed the economic know-how of the Netherlands and Dutch economic development funds for Indonesia's financial stability.

The issue of whether New Guinea was to be included in the new republic remained unresolved in 1949. Indonesia considered West New Guinea as a rightful part of its territory because it had traditionally been part of the Dutch colony. The Dutch, in contrast, considered West New Guinea as separate and distinct and did not want to include it in the negotiations. The New Guinea question would continue to be a huge area of disagreement for many years.

Unity within Diversity

While the Indonesian–Dutch negotiations were continuing, Soekarno attempted to craft a democratic society. He stated in one of his speeches:

> *If we want democracy, it should not be Western democracy, but a democracy that gives life, that is, political-economic democracy that*

guarantees social welfare! Indonesian people have spoken about it for long. People want welfare. Those who used to be deprived of food and clothing create a new world in which there is justice.

Soekarno tried to create a diverse but united country based on five primary principles that would be the driving force within the new republic: Indonesian nationalism; internationalism, or humanity; consensus, or democracy; social justice; and the belief in one God (although not necessarily one religion). He liked to think of these five principles as quintessentially Indonesian in character. While Indonesia was trying to find its way as a modern country with a democratic government that was based on these five principles, the Dutch started to come back to Indonesia in large numbers and quickly gained a strong economic presence in the country.

Returning to Indonesia

I missed Pappie very much after he left us in February of 1947, and I wrote him many letters, embellished with little drawings, to let him know that we were thinking of him and that we loved him so very much. Was I afraid that he too would disappear from our lives and never come back, just like Papa Daan had done so long ago?

But the evidence that we would follow him soon after he had found a home for us in Makassar was all around me. While Pappie was looking for a place to live, Didi assembled the necessary household goods to start a new home back in Indonesia. With astonishment, I looked at the steamer trunks and suitcases slowly being filled with sheets and towels, pots and pans, dishes, cutlery, and all sorts of other ordinary household essentials. To my family's horror, I finally asked my mother what on earth we needed all that stuff for. Didn't she remember we would not have any use for it in the camp?

After my question, Didi and the rest of the family kept reassuring me that there were no more camps in Indonesia and that we would live in a regular house together with Pappie and that we would go to school in Indonesia and that I would continue to learn to read and write.

At the end of May, we left our wonderful life in Deventer with Oma to join Pappie in Makassar. I was sad when we said good-bye to our grandmothers and the many uncles and aunts we had learned to love, and I was sad to leave the security of our life in Deventer behind us to go back to the land we only dimly remembered as one of hunger and fear in the camps. But I was also excited about going on a voyage and seeing Pappie again soon. We never had had a permanent home before, and that made it probably easier to pack up and move again.

For more than four weeks, we traveled on the *Ophir* during fairly stormy weather. The *Ophir* was an old ship that had been used as a hospital ship during the war and had been rebuilt to accommodate fewer than one hundred passengers. On this voyage, the passengers consisted primarily of young women and their children who were joining their husbands and fathers who had gone back to Indonesia ahead of them. The ship was noisy and unsteady in high seas; after a big storm, the cabins on one side of the ship were flooded so that many women and their children ended up sleeping on mattresses in the dining room. Their accommodations resembled a Japanese internment camp, with mattresses close together and laundry lines with clothing and towels strung above them. Fortunately for us, our cabin was located at the other side of the ship and remained dry throughout the voyage. Many passengers were seasick, and to make matters worse, a number of children came down with whooping cough, but Frits and I did not get sick on this trip.

Fort Rotterdam, Our New School

Once we got to Makassar, I quickly saw that it was different from the camps we had lived in. For the first few weeks, we lived in Hotel Wijnands until we could move to our home on the Generaal van Dalen Weg. While we were still guests in the hotel, I was reminded one day of the war that was no more, when I saw someone who had only one ear. I still remember his name, Mr. Kipperman, who lived in a room near ours. We saw him regularly during meals in the dining room. I was fascinated by the one missing ear and asked Pappie why it was that one of Mr. Kipperman's ears was gone. I was told that the Japanese had cut it off. Soon after, I developed a major ear infection that required a visit to the doctor. I remember being terrified that I too would lose an ear, just like Mr. Kipperman.

Soon after our arrival in Makassar, Frits and I started to go to school in Fort Rotterdam, a seventeenth-century fort built by Dutch traders, protecting the Spice Islands from invasion by the British and the Portuguese. Frits's preschool class of little children was held in the chicken coop of the fort. Going to school in Fort Rotterdam was a lot of fun, especially because the slightly bigger kids, including seven-year-old me, used to climb the stairs to the top of the sixteenth-century broad walls that surrounded the open space in the middle of the fort and walk all around on the walls, to the dismay of our teachers below.

A "Home of Our Own"

Housing was scarce in postwar Makassar, and the house we finally moved into was home to two different families, while a young couple occupied the garage. All of us had to share bathroom and kitchen facilities. Our home consisted of two adjoining rooms and a small pantry. One of the two rooms became our living/dining room; the other was my parents' bedroom. The pantry, not attached to the two main rooms and located at the back of the house, was just large enough to house a bunk bed and became Frits's and my bedroom. It was not an ideal arrangement, but it was our own home, nonetheless.

Because of continued unrest in Makassar, we had a *jaga*, a watchman, to watch our house at night. The jaga sat in an old chair in our yard, smoking his *kreteks*, clove cigarettes, making sure no one would bother us. I was always glad to see the red glow of the jaga's cigarette in the dark when I woke up at night and smelled the sweet-spicy odor of the cloves.

Our house on the Generaal van Dalen weg was located at a five-way intersection and looked out on ruined houses and yards filled with rubble. Behind our house was another ruin of a bombed house. For me and my friends, these ruins were wonderful places—we loved to play in them, climbing over the remnants of walls still standing; jumping over deep holes in the ground filled with dark, stinking water; and trying to avoid shards of glass and pieces of rusty metal. It was a highly dangerous place for young children to play in, and I am sure that Pappie and Didi had no idea that we were playing there during the "quiet hours" of the tropical afternoons when Pappie was at his office, Didi was taking a nap, and Frits and I were expected to be in our room, the stuffy little pantry, resting.

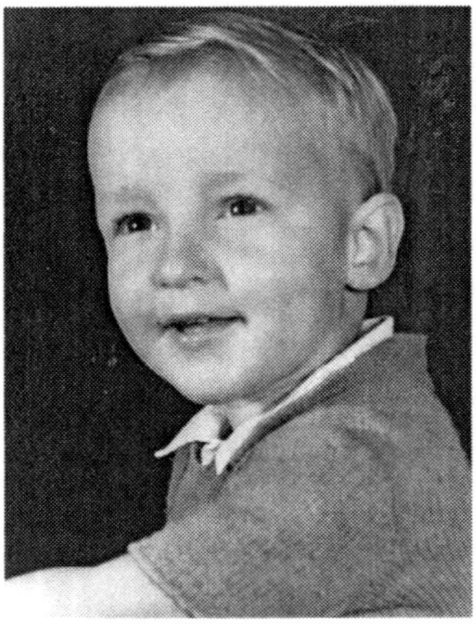

Two-year old Jantje in Deventer, 1950

The Birth of Jan, Our Baby Brother, September 28, 1948

Several months after we had moved into our house and Frits and I had established the normal routine of going to a regular school, Didi and Pappie told us that we were about to have a baby. This was a big and wonderful event for me. I was eight years old at the time, and having a real baby at home was every little girl's dream. I had looked forward to the baby's birth for a long time and was terribly disappointed when I saw our baby in his bassinette at Stella Maris Hospital a day after he was born. Our new baby was not a girl but a boy. Worse, he didn't look like the baby-food advertisement that I expected. Our baby looked much more like a tiny, shriveled old man. Apparently, I took one look at my skinny, red, wrinkled baby brother and then walked out of my mother's hospital room without even saying good-bye to her; my disappointment was too huge.

That evening at home, Pappie was upset and angry with me and told me that I had to apologize. I didn't know how to do that and finally decided to write a little note to Didi, asking her for forgiveness: "Dear Mammie. I am so sorry that I have been so mean. O, Mammie please don't think me bad anymore. Goodbye dearest, many kisses from Sytske and Frits." Didi saved the scribbled little note I wrote, and I still have it—it is part of the collection of my little messages and drawings Didi saved in my baby book.

Though little Jantje was not what I had expected initially, it didn't take long before I adored him. I loved taking care of him, and my memories of playing with him and all his stuffed animals remain vivid pleasures in my mind—but I did have one new big worry after Jantje's birth because I was afraid that my relationship with Grootje would change now that she had a "real" grandchild of her own. I had become acutely aware that Frits and I had two sets of family. We had "real" family, such as Oma and the family in Deventer, connected to us by blood, and we had "acquired" family, such as Pappie, Grootje, and Tante Tiek and Oom Jan. Would Grootje still love me the way she had before little Jan was born? I didn't have to worry—Grootje wrote a wonderful Sinterklaas poem for me several months after Jantje's birth. It reads in part:

I love Jantje just as much as I love Sytske and Frits
But I thought that they already knew that.
I will remain for all three "their Grootje."
Mr. Saint Nicholas, please bring them a nice present.
I thank you for all your troubles, Saint Nicholas,
With greetings for you and Pieterbaas

Sweet Sytske, you will always be my granddaughter
And we are both very happy about that.

Traveling between Indonesia and Holland

We lived in Makassar from the summer of 1947 to the summer of 1950 and then went back to Deventer for a six-month furlough, where Frits and I had to go to school and make new friends. We stayed in Oma's house for the duration of Pappie's vacation. When Pappie's six-month furlough was over, we left Holland again, this time for Singapore, where we arrived on January 31, 1951, my eleventh birthday. We lived in Singapore for a year while Pappie temporarily replaced the director of the Singapore office of Mirandolle Voûte, whose turn it was to go on furlough. We enrolled in the Dutch School in Singapore and made new friends. After a year, we left and moved to Semarang, where we had to get used to yet another town, another house, another school, and new friends. From first to sixth grade of elementary school education, I went to five different schools—not unusual for Dutch children of our generation in Indonesia at the time—but our nomadic life in those six years notwithstanding, we were a regular family with a father and a mother and three children, living like an ordinary family—a life of regularity with daily schoolwork, occasional reprimands, birthday celebrations, and vacations in the mountains.

The Republic of Indonesia, August 17, 1950

The United States of Indonesia lasted from December 1949 to August 1950. On the fifth anniversary of the Proclamation of Independence, on August 17, 1950, Soekarno dissolved the United States of Indonesia and created the Republic of Indonesia.

While Soekarno was busily creating a new country, it had not taken long for Dutch families in Indonesia to resume a very comfortable lifestyle. In the 1950s, the Dutch once again lived in colonial-style houses on tree-lined streets located in nice parts of towns. Dutch children attended Dutch schools, and household tasks were again performed by a Djongos, a Kokkie, and a Baboe. In the evenings and weekends, the families got together in the Dutch Club or at the swimming pool—places that even then did not admit Indonesian members.

But while the Dutch were living a very comfortable, almost colonial, life in the 1950s, ordinary Indonesian people were not benefitting from the economic revival of Dutch enterprises. Life was hard everywhere, and poverty was visible in the cities and towns. Beggars and squatters were seen walking the roads in tattered clothing and looking for handouts, and of course, the Dutch were seen as the only cause of the people's poverty and lack of economic gain. In the 1950s, the Communist Party in Indonesia became a powerful force, to the dismay of the United States.

Through it all, Soekarno continued to be seen as "the Father of the Nation," while the governing authority continued with the prime minister and his cabinet. Soekarno had enormous charismatic power and is especially well remembered for his impassioned frequent speeches in which he often mixed languages—Indonesian, Dutch, French, English, and German—but though he was a national hero and loved by most of the people, he could not control the antagonism between the various factions within the Republic of Indonesia, which then also included a powerful military establishment, and the New Guinea question was still being debated in the 1950s. Finally, under pressure from the United States and the United Nations, the Netherlands lost the argument that West New Guinea should not be considered a part of Indonesia and that a local referendum was needed to determine the wishes of the people themselves. In 1962, West New Guinea was turned over to Indonesian control.

August 1952, Leaving Home

For me, being a part of a regular family lasted only six years, from 1946 through the summer of 1952. My life in Indonesia came to an end when I turned twelve and was ready to go to high school.

I had always known that I would have to go to Holland to go to high school someday, and I had not looked forward to that as a little girl, but when the time came, I had mixed feelings. On the one hand, I was sad to leave, but on the other hand, I was excited about this new phase in my life and looked forward to seeing my grandmothers and uncles and aunts again.

Leaving my little brother Jan behind was the hardest for me. I always played with him, gave him his baths, and dressed him. Days before I left, I explained to four-year-old Jantje that I was going to Holland ahead of the rest of the family so I could buy him a bed, in anticipation of everyone joining me a year or so later. This made some sense to him then.

On my last day at home, I said good-bye to all the kind people who worked for my parents—they were another part of my extended family: Roos, the Kokkie, who cooked; Wakidjan, the Djongos, who served at table and took care of various other household tasks; Ratmi, the Baboe, who did the laundry; Ahmat, Pappie's chauffeur; and the Kebon, our gardener.

My memories of Ahmat are the most vivid of all of them because he went to the passar in the business section of Semarang, where he would buy fresh vegetables and fruit and other items on the shopping list my mother had prepared for him. When Ahmat returned to our house with a lot of commotion and loud honking of the car horn, everyone stopped what he or she was doing to see what Ahmat had bought and to hear his stories about all he had seen at the market. Ahmat was round and roly-poly and always cheerful; the moment you saw him, he would make you laugh. Ahmat was a great storyteller and always knew a lot of gossip about whom he had seen and what the latest news was from the kampongs. Sitting on the cool tile floor at the back of our house together with Roos, Wakidjan, and Ratmi, Frits and I sat listening eagerly to Ahmat telling tall tales about the goings-on downtown, while all of us laughed hilariously.

On the day of my departure, Pappie, Frits, and Jan brought Didi and me to the airport to settle us in the plane that was to take us to Jakarta. I still see them standing at the exit, my father and my brothers, waving me off. The next day, Didi took me to the airport in Jakarta, from where I flew alone to Singapore to meet up with a Dutch family, friends of my parents, with whom I sailed to Holland. After I had left for Holland, we never lived together again as one family.

Of course, before I left, I promised to write my family once a week—the same promise Didi had made when she left home in 1936. We were a family of letter writers, and even as small children, we learned to write to our relatives in Holland. Didi saved every single letter I wrote from my boarding school—they, too, are all here in Millerton.

A few days before I left, Didi and Pappie gave me a wonderful farewell present, a beautiful photobook of Indonesia entitled *Tanah Air Kita*, Our Land and Water, assembled and written by Niels Douwes Dekker. The book is a joint Dutch–Indonesian publication printed in The Hague, the Netherlands, and Bandung, Indonesia. The book's foreword explains that "never before has the need for an illustrated book about Indonesia been as great as it is at present, because after a period of misunderstanding, conflict and sensational headlines, the world wants to renew its acquaintance with Indonesia. Never before has there been such a need for the balm which the beauty and the intrinsic riches of the archipelago can lay on the wounds of the past."

For Indonesian readers, the book is a celebration of the independence of their country. For Dutch readers, it is a remembrance of a much-loved motherland in which many were born and grew up. Almost every teenager who lived at my boarding school in the 1950s had a copy of *Tanah Air Kita*.

Slightly more than a year after I had left Semarang, our family came to Holland on a furlough, and when their vacation was over and our parents and Jantje left to go back to Indonesia, they left Frits behind in Holland as well, in the same boarding school where I already lived. Didi had written Jan years earlier:

> *I am grateful for one thing and that is that we will end up in a city [rather than on a plantation], which will mean that I will have the children with me, because I have always found it an awful idea that there would come a time that they would have to leave home to attend school. I have seen too many difficult situations and there are so many advantages for staying together within the circle of family.*

Leaving us behind in Holland was hard for everyone, but it was the most difficult for little Jan, who missed Frits and me. He kept walking aimlessly around in the beginning, asking, "What should I do now? I don't have a sister, and I don't have a brother anymore. What should I do now?"

Our Vacation in Paradise, at Home in Semarang

A year and a half later, in the summer of 1956, Frits and I flew to Indonesia for a six-week vacation, courtesy of Mirandolle Voûte, Pappie's firm. It was wonderful to be back "home" again in Semarang, and Didi and Pappie made sure that this vacation was going to be especially memorable. They made sure we would visit all of the most important ancient sites in Indonesia.

We made trips to the Boroboedoer and Prambanan temples near Jogjakarta. We went to the Dieng Plateau, an ancient Hindu holy site, where Hindu temples still dot the landscape and where we saw hot water springs and geysers reeking of sulphur. We visited the mountain resort of Tretes and went to the Bromo, the extinct volcano in East Java, with its huge sand sea in the center and the smaller volcanic dome in the middle of all that ancient sand. And we spent a weekend on the beach at Pasir Putih with its broad, white-sand beaches and saw the famous coral gardens through glass-bottomed boats.

But the best part for all of us was to be together again, all five of us.

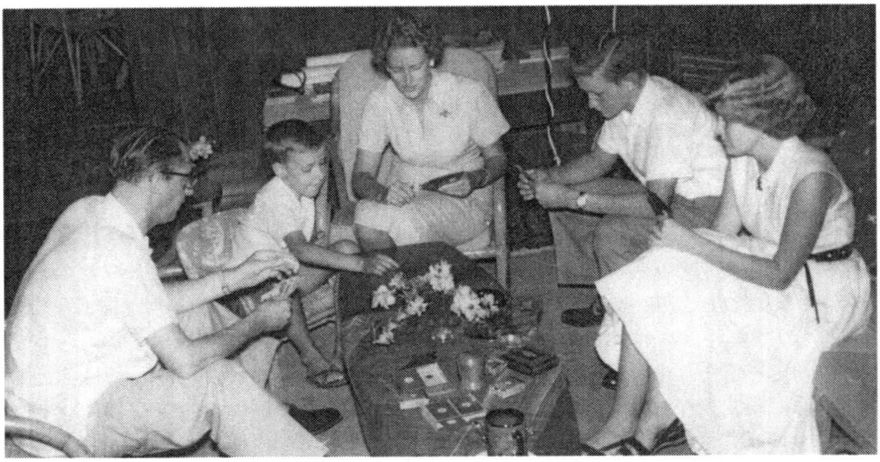

The five of us together in the living room of Djangli 22 in Semarang in the summer vacation of 1956

The End of Our Years in Indonesia

Although my memories of our vacation in 1956 are full of great experiences and free of worries, Didi and Pappie must have had concerns about the future. By 1957, Soekarno had taken control of the constantly deteriorating relationships between various interests within Indonesia and declared that Western-style democracy, which he had hoped for, did not work in Indonesia. Instead, he argued that a new type of democracy was appropriate in Indonesia, based on ancient traditions, in which decisions were made by local councils that would take the time necessary to deliberate and eventually end up with a decision acceptable to all. He promoted a democratic system in which the former five principles were reduced to one, resulting in a so-called *gotong-royong* state, a state based on mutual cooperation and consensus building that would express itself under presidential guidance. He called this new style of democracy guided democracy.

At the same time, he also planned the expulsion of all Dutch from Indonesia and the take-over of all Dutch businesses.

While Soekarno was making speeches in 1957 about the new form of democracy he was promoting, our family was on its way to Holland because Pappie was scheduled to go on another furlough. During his time in Holland in the summer and fall of 1957, many of their friends who had returned to Holland earlier urged Pappie to stay in Holland as well, but he did not listen to them.

He left on December 2, 1957, to return to Indonesia for another three-year term, working for Mirandolle Voûte in Semarang, but when he arrived in Jakarta on December 3, Jan learned that he had been on the last KLM plane allowed into the country; that all Dutch companies, including oil refineries, plantations, banks, and import-export firms had been nationalized; and that the 40,000 Dutch nationals living and working in Indonesia were being expelled. Pappie was able to stay in Indonesia for a few months longer to transfer the office in Semarang and to pack up our personal belongings there. He came back to Europe in the late spring of 1958.

Our family's connection to Indonesia had come to a permanent end.

While we had been part of the exodus of Dutch nationals, a large number of people of Dutch/Indonesian descent who had opted to remain in Indonesia after the war and had become Indonesian citizens and established businesses there also were affected by Soekarno's new policies. These mixed-blood families were no longer welcome in the country, and many decided to leave and start a new life in Holland, a country that they did not know very well and that they had not necessarily visited before then. These so-called *spijt-optanten*, who bitterly regretted their former decision to plan a future for themselves and their families in Indonesia, were marginally assisted by the Dutch to establish new homes in the Netherlands, the United States, or Australia.

History Repeats Itself

After their return to Europe, our family was not together for very long. Pappie died in April 1962 from a massive aneurism while I was in the United States working as an au pair with a family in Englewood, New Jersey.

Pappie was fifty years old when he died, and for the second time in her young life, at the age of forty-five, Didi became a widow; little Jan was not yet fourteen years old when Pappie died—almost the same age Pappie had been when he had lost his father—and Frits and I lost our second father, the only father we had ever known.

I loved Pappie, and we enjoyed each other's company a great deal, especially when I was in my late teens and early twenties, after everyone had come back to Holland and I had not left yet for the United States. In the last years of his life, when he suffered from terrible headaches and depressions, I could sometimes make him laugh and relax.

Pappie, Singapore, 1951

On April 21, 1962, a few days before he died, Pappie wrote me a long letter. He ended his letter with these perhaps prophetic words:

Dear Syts, I won't last much longer (I mean, as far as my letter is concerned. Don't misunderstand me!). Mammie has come downstairs, and is boiling the eggs for breakfast; Jan is sitting hunched over in front of the radio, as usual; and I am not hearing anything from Frits yet—Oh wait, I am hearing him in the bathroom upstairs. I expected that he was still dreaming of his Letitia, but he had more prosaic concerns, apparently.

The sun is coming through and we expect to have some lovely Easter days. Enjoy all that there is to enjoy. Much love, Pappie.

CHAPTER 16

JAPAN'S SURRENDER AND THE WAR CRIMES TRIBUNAL

Document No. 2687

I hereby swear that exhibits A, B, C, D, E, F, G, H, I, J, K, L, M, N, and O attached hereto and initialed by me are original documents duly requisitioned and confiscated from Imperial Japanese Army Headquarters for Taiwan, Taihoku, Taiwan (Formosa) and handed over by a representative of the Imperial Japanese Army in April 1946 to the British American Formosa War Crimes Team of which I was then a member.

James T. N. Cross, Major, Royal Artillery, Commanding, War Crimes Liaison Section (Formosa) Allied Land Forces, South East Asia.

Sworn before me this 19th day of September, 1946

On September 2, 1945, two weeks after the emperor of Japan surrendered and World War II in Southeast Asia had officially ended, Japan signed the Instrument of Surrender. The document was signed by a representative of the emperor of Japan and the Japanese government; a representative of the Japanese Imperial General Headquarters; and Douglas MacArthur, Supreme Commander for the Allied Powers. General MacArthur signed on behalf of the United States, the Republic of China, the United Kingdom, and the Union of Soviet Socialist Republics, and in the interests of the other nations that had been at war with Japan. Nine other countries that had been at war in Southeast Asia signed as well, including a representative of the Netherlands.

INSTRUMENT OF SURRENDER

We hereby proclaim the unconditional surrender to the allied powers of the Japanese imperial general headquarters and of all

Japanese armed forces and all armed forces under Japanese control wherever situated.

We hereby command all Japanese forces wherever situated and the Japanese people to cease hostilities forthwith, to preserve and save from damage all ships, aircraft, and military and civil property and to comply with all requirements which may be imposed by the supreme commander of the allied powers or by agencies of the Japanese government at his direction.

We hereby command the Japanese imperial general headquarters to issue at once orders to the commanders of all Japanese forces and all forces under Japanese control wherever situated to surrender unconditionally themselves and all forces under their control.

We hereby command all civil, military and naval officials to obey and enforce all proclamations, orders and directives deemed by the supreme commander for the allied powers to be proper to effectuate this surrender and issued by him or under his authority and we direct all such officials to remain at their posts and to continue to perform their non-combatant duties unless specifically relieved by him or under his authority.

We hereby undertake for the emperor, the Japanese government and their successors to carry out the provisions of the Potsdam declaration in good faith, and to issue whatever orders and take whatever action may be required by the supreme commander for the allied powers or by any other designated representative of the allied powers for the purpose of giving effect to that declaration.

We hereby command the Japanese imperial government and the Japanese imperial general headquarters at once to liberate all allied prisoners of war and civilian internees now under Japanese control and to provide for their protection, care, maintenance and immediate transportation to places as directed.

The authority of the emperor and the Japanese government to rule the state shall be subject to the supreme commander for

> the allied powers who will take such steps as he deems proper to effectuate these terms of surrender.

Frightening Rumors Prior to the Surrender

Weeks before this momentous event, after three years of imprisonment by the Japanese, the POWs and internees had begun to hear rumors that the end of the war was near. But another persistent rumor began to circulate as well: that the Japanese had plans to destroy all of their prisoners in the event that the war would be won by Japan's enemy. According to documents from the National Archives and Records Administration (NARA) in Washington, DC, the rumors were based on fact. As early as August 1944, Japan's War Ministry had issued an order to "dispose of their prisoners." This order was transmitted to the Chief of Staff of the 11th Unit (Formosa POW Security No. 10).

Only one of the War Ministry's orders has survived; it surfaced in Formosa and eventually landed in the hands of Major James Cross, quoted above.

When I learned of these documents, I asked for copies of them from NARA, and I was startled when I received a large envelope in the mail less than a week later. The material was sent by the chief of the Modern Military Records Textual Archives Services Division of the National Archives and Records Administration in Maryland.

Though I was very well aware of the content of the recently declassified documents, my hands trembled when I took the mail out of our mailbox and saw the large brown envelope that contained copies of the Japanese documents created in 1944, and that included translations that had been prepared for the International Military Tribunal for the Far East.

"To Annihilate Them All, and Not Leave Any Traces"

Sitting on the couch in our living room, I had to brace myself to open the brown envelope and read the old Japanese orders that describe the time and methods of "disposition" of the POWs. The date of the order was August1, 1944. The translator of Exhibit No. 2015, Stephen H. Green, certified that his translation was a "true translation from the Journal of the Taiwan POW H.Q. in Taiwan, entry 1 August, 1944" (Exhibit O, Doc. No. 2687, file 2015, NARA).

> However, at such time as the situation became urgent and it be extremely important, the POWs will be concentrated and con-

fined in the present location and under heavy guard the preparation for the final disposition will be made.

The time and method of the disposition are as follows:

(1) The Time
Although the basic aim is to act under superior orders, individual disposition may be made in the following circumstances:

(a) When an uprising of large numbers cannot be suppressed without the use of firearms.

(b) When escapees from the camp may turn into a hostile fighting force.

(2) The Methods
(a) Whether they are destroyed individually or in groups, or however it is done, with mass bombing, poisonous smoke, poisons, drowning, decapitation, or what, dispose of them as the situation dictates.

(b) In any case, it is the aim not to allow the escape of a single one, to annihilate them all, and not to leave traces.

(3) To: The Commanding General of Military Police

Reported matters conferred on with the 11th unit, the Kiirun Fortified Area H.Q., and each prefecture concerning the extreme security in Taiwan POW Camps.

One of the Japanese plans was to *orchestrate an uprising* among the internees in the civilian camps as well as among the prisoners in their labor camps that would have to be quashed by the Japanese through "extreme measures, which cannot be avoided in order to defend ourselves." The Japanese order stated that the Japanese at all times had to take care that these actions would have to be *justifiable* to the outside world as defensive actions for the safety of the Japanese administrations of the camps.

Although none of this occurred in Java, there were some incidents in British North Borneo and on the Filipino island of Palawan where mass murders of the prisoners did take place.

If the order had been widely carried out, none of us would have survived.

The Order to Destroy All Documents

Another document was found in Taiwan at the end of the war ordering all POW camp commanders throughout Southeast Asia to destroy all documents in their possession that might be incriminating.

Below is an excerpt of Exhibit No. 2011, Document No. 2697, certified as Exhibit J in Document No. 2687. This document was sent to the Chief of Staff, Taiwan Army. The sender was Chief Prisoner of War Camps Tokyo, POW Camps Radio #9.

> TOP MILITARY SECRET
> This Order states as follows:
>
> > Personnel who mistreated prisoners of war and internees or who are held in extremely bad sentiment by them is permitted to take care of it by immediately transferring or by fleeing without trace. Moreover, documents which would be unfavorable for us in the hands of the enemy are to be treated in the same way as secret documents and destroyed when finished with…
>
> Addressees: Korean Army, Taiwan Army, Kwantung (Manchuria) Army, North China Area Army, Hong Kong.
>
> Reference: Korea, Taiwan, Mukden, Borneo, North China, Hong Kong, Thailand, Malaya, Java.
> Each POW Camp Commanding Officer

This exhibit was also translated and signed by Stephen H. Green, who certified that this was a true translation from Taiwan Army H.Q. Staff Files concerning POWs, Vol. 7.

To what extent all camp commanders throughout Southeast Asia received the order to destroy all documents is actually not known. The date of this order is quite late—August 20, 1945—but the intent of the order seems to have been widely carried out. A major handicap during the Tokyo tribunal was the dearth of documented evidence of wartime crimes committed by the Japanese. To a large extent, the prosecutors had to rely on eyewitness testimony to learn about the atrocities committed by the administrators and guards of the POW camps and camps for civilian internees.

The Tokyo War Crimes Tribunal

The International Military Tribunal for the Far East was convened on May 5, 1946, and lasted until November 12, 1948. The tribunal was conducted at the former Imperial Japanese Army Headquarters in Tokyo. General Douglas MacArthur appointed eleven judges, nine of whom were jurists from the countries that had signed the official Instrument of Surrender.

President Truman appointed the chief prosecutor, Joseph B. Keenan of the USA. The eleven other countries that had been at war with Japan each appointed a jurist to act as co-prosecutor during the tribunal. W.G. Frederick Borgerhoff Mulder, a distant cousin of Pappie, was appointed to represent the Netherlands at the Tokyo War Crimes Tribunal.

CHAPTER 17

MEMORIES OF SURVIVAL AND LOSS

Most of the people mentioned in this story, except for Papa Daan and Oom Heb van Oyen, survived the war and went on with their lives. They were reunited with their families, got married, had babies, started to work again, and focused on forgetting the years of deprivation—and yet, sometimes, during the dark midnight hours, the people who had suffered under the Japanese had nightmares. I remember staying overnight at the house of friends of my parents and hearing my uncle's screams in the dark when his dreams had returned him once again to the long-ago war in Southeast Asia.

But most of the former POWs and internees just tried to catch up on the lost years of their youth by partying hard and working hard. In his toast to Didi on her sixty-fifth birthday on June 30, 1971, Buis Hofstee said it well when he referred to the years when we and the Hofstee family lived in Makassar from 1947 to 1950:

> *Makassar was for us a place, where, in a reaction to the war years, we led a wild life and had a lot of fun. Remember het "platje" at the soos; wine from Timor Dilly; Pension Wijnands; and the Saturday dances at the Dutch Club? We went to Malino in the mountains to get a cold nose or sailed with the lepa-lepa to Pulau Moro to have a picnic. The old colonials among us will agree that, as a youngster, one made friends for life in the Indies. But we also worked very hard and felt that we had to catch up with the lost years of the war.*

Personal Reflections

Reading the old letters and documents was difficult. I found myself often unexpectedly bursting into tears as I read the old letters from my mother and other family members that took me so far back in time. To me they are a narrative of poorly understood memories, and they are part of a history that should never be lost.

I wrote this story for my family and friends, but I also wrote it for myself in an effort to learn more about Papa Daan. So many questions remain: Did he have a sense of humor? What books did he read? Did he like classical music? What kind of a father would he have been?

Would I have liked him as a friend? There are no meaningful answers to these questions, and the letters don't shed any light on them.

All I have been able to find out from my mother is that he was a very good ballroom dancer, that he was sweet and much loved by his parents-in-law in Deventer, and that he was very proud of me, his first-born. One of his letters, written in 1938, shows that he was a responsible and caring man, even at the age of twenty-seven, when he tried to plan for the financial well-being of his family twenty years into the future, when my parents expected to be back in Holland.

I like to think that Papa Daan would have been the kind of father that I imagine Frits has been for his children, Nynke and Hidde, when they were young.

I was not yet six years old when I was told by my mother that Papa Daan had died, but I continued to wait for him in the hope that this news was one of those wartime rumors that proved untrue. In those early days after the war, there were occasional news bulletins reporting that people who had been considered lost had been found later on remote islands or in jungle outposts. For a while, I kept hoping that someone would find Papa Daan somewhere and bring him back to us. But we never had good news.

After Didi had remarried and we had started a new life and had a second father, whom I loved, I lost interest in the father I did not remember. I managed to hide any thoughts of Papa Daan far from my day-to-day life. As a little girl, I was not able to reconcile the fact that I had two fathers: Papa Daan, who had left me and had disappeared, leaving no memories behind, and Pappie, who was present in my life and whom I loved.

Burying Papa Daan Forever

Many years later, I symbolically buried Papa Daan one day during a psychodrama workshop I participated in as part of my psychology studies. I was then in my early thirties and already had lived in the United States for more than ten years. As I piled mattresses and sleeping bags on top of the young man I had selected to play Papa Daan in the personal drama I was acting out, I accused him of deserting me and of haunting me all my life. I shouted that I wanted to get rid of him once and for all and that I would bury him forever. The experience was as intense as it was unexpected. After it was over, I went home to my solitary apartment, unaided by the support I should have had to deal with these uncovered emotions.

The timing of my participation in the psychodrama workshop was particularly poor because Didi arrived not long afterwards for a long-planned three-week visit to Brooklyn, where I lived at the time. I had looked forward to her visit, but I was so self-absorbed and raw inside at the time of her arrival that Didi, who had come with love, wanting to take care of me, received the brunt of the pent-up feelings that had finally been exposed. Didi's visit was not a success—she offered love and kindness and got back anger and accusations. A few days before she left to go back home to Holland, I shouted at her: "Don't try to mother me; I don't need you now! You always acted as if we had a normal family, but we never did—our family was make-believe!"

After my angry outburst, I felt great remorse and worried about Didi after she had left for Holland—I worried that our relationship was torn apart forever. But though our relationship had changed, we both agreed later that it had changed for the better, and we became friends. Better yet, after the workshop, I started to become interested in Papa Daan and he slowly returned to become a presence in my life.

When I was in my mid-fifties and visiting Didi in Holland, she handed me an envelope with the words: "Here is something for you from Frits and Tjits" and then left the room to get dinner started in the kitchen. As I sipped my glass of genever in my mother's living room, I opened the small packet and found photographs of Papa Daan's grave that had been taken not long before by friends of Frits and his wife. To my great surprise and my mother's consternation, I burst out in tears when I saw the pictures of Papa Daan's grave beautifully decorated with flowers. It was the first time in many years that I had cried about this father who had left me so very long ago. It was then that I decided that I wanted to visit his grave.

Finally Finding Papa Daan

On November 29, 2004, precisely sixty years after Papa Daan's death, Jon and I arrived in Kanchanaburi, Thailand, to visit my father's grave in the vast war cemetery in the center of town. His grave is located in Plot 7, Row D, in the section where most other Dutch POWs are buried. It was late in the afternoon, and long shadows fell behind us as we walked the path to Grave 8. Within minutes, we found the gravestone bearing Papa Daan's name and I had an overwhelming and unexpected sense of relief. Here was Papa Daan—finally, after all these years. I could touch his gravestone and feel its warmth after it had been baking in the sun all day. I did not say anything much to my long-lost

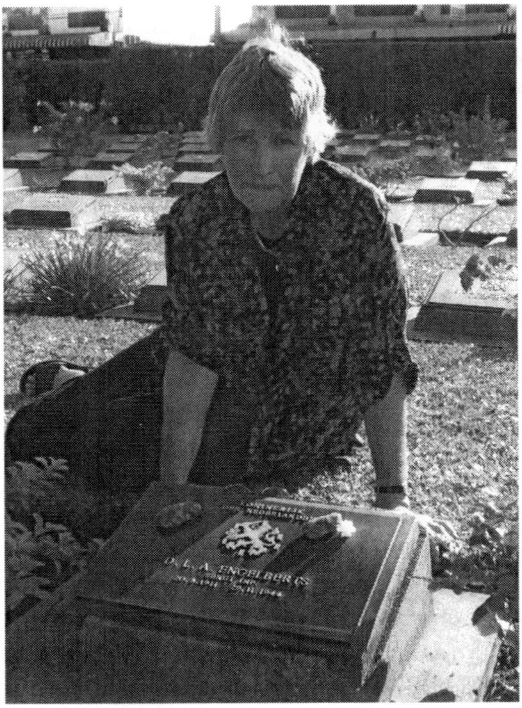

Sia at Papa Daan's grave in Kanchanaburi, on the anniversary of his death, November 29, 2004.

father; I just rubbed my fingers over his name, and then we put two little stones on his grave. One was of beautiful, polished granite, a stone that I had found somewhere in Maine; the other was an ordinary stone from our garden in Millerton. Then Jon thanked Papa Daan for having me so that he and I could marry.

We sat quietly at Papa Daan's grave and took it all in: the beautiful setting, the carefully manicured gardens, the flowering bushes, the sunshine, and especially the care that these graves are receiving. This graveyard is serene and at the same time full of vitality. I had been so afraid I would find a forlorn and somewhat remote place overgrown by tall grasses and covered in weeds, like the old Chinese burial grounds that still dot the countryside in Indonesia. What we found instead in Kanchanaburi is a place that is a balm for grief. Sitting next to Papa Daan's grave gave me the closure I had been looking for, but it was different from what I had expected. Instead of saying goodbye to Papa Daan, I had found him, and I welcomed him into my heart. Papa Daan is in good hands and is not forgotten. I now know where he is; I can always come back. I know the way.

Remnants of War

After so many years, remnants of the war are still a part of me. I still cannot throw out any food and will eat leftovers, even when I am not hungry, so I don't have to toss the food on the compost heap in the back of our garden. Not infrequently, when I'm walking in a park or hiking in the Berkshire Mountains near my home and come across a tangle of weeds or bushes, I startle myself with the involuntary thought, *this would be a good hiding place.* Having talked with Didi at length and having read our baby books, the letters, and the accounts written by Herbert van Oyen and Meindert Bolhuis about our flight into the jungle, I know that such hiding places saved our lives in early March 1942.

I now believe that the telling of the story has helped me come to terms with the remnants of fear and anxiety that linger in my subconscious. Perhaps it will be easier now to understand the flashbacks that come out of nowhere, the unaccountable feelings of sadness I have felt periodically since my early childhood, the adult depressions that come and go, and the sporadic outbursts of anger that well up unexpectedly.

I know that I am not the only so-called camp child who has had to cope with insecurities, depressions, and angry outbursts. A paper by Dr. Bekkering and Dr. Bekkering-Merens titled "De Japanse kampen: nog geen verleden tyd," [The Japanese Camps: Not Yet History] and reprinted in *Informatie en Coordinatie Orgaan Dienstverlening Oorlogsgetroffenen (ICODO)*, 1987, describes the problems of the 60,000 camp children who had survived the war and returned to Holland. The Bekkerings, who themselves had been in Japanese internment camps as young children, were among the first Dutch therapists in the 1980s who treated increasing numbers of patients in their forties who had been in Japanese camps as very young children. The therapists noticed that the people who had been under the age of five during the camp years had been particularly vulnerable. They believe that those children had been too young during the war to process their experiences in a meaningful way and suffered the consequences decades later.

Another writer and former camp child, E. de Kruyf, wrote in an article titled "Kinderen uit het Jappenkamp: De jongste generatie van '40–'45" [Children of the Japanese Camp: The Youngest Generation '40–'45], published in 1981 in the monthly magazine *Maandblad Geestelyke Volksgezondheid (MGV)*, about the difficulties the youngest camp children still experience in adulthood. She wrote, "The young camp child, regardless of the particular war he or she was in, is like an unclear photo-negative that never has been properly developed."

The children in the camps had inexplicably and without forewarning lost their fathers and had been exposed to the cruelty of other men, the Japanese and Korean camp guards. They had known fear without understanding the danger they were in. They saw the complications of disease without comprehension and witnessed death all around. The children lived with unspeakable uncertainties and witnessed sights without having the inner strength to deal with them. Camp children, such as I, had no basis for hope, because they had no prior reference sources and could not imagine another life.

Sadly, mothers and other adults were themselves depleted by the harsh life under the Japanese in the camps and lacked the energy to be safety nets for their children. Besides, the prevailing wisdom at the time was that very young children would have no memory of their wartime lives and thus would not be affected in the long run.

Years later, Didi once told me how badly she felt about her lack of understanding of what it was we children needed in those days and as we were growing up. My reaction—"But, Mam, you were so young then, almost a child yourself"—has helped us both understand that my search for our past was not intended to assign blame but was an effort to better understand our shared history.

And, of course, Didi cannot be blamed. She was in her mid-twenties when the war broke out, and for years, she had no idea where my father was or if he was still alive. She had given birth to Frits in May of 1942 under difficult circumstances, and she remained in poor health throughout the war. She suffered variously, and sometimes in combination, from dysentery, beriberi, edema, malaria, hepatitis, and, of course, chronic and severe malnutrition. She was physically exhausted and focused most of her energies on Frits, who had been a sickly baby and remained a frail little boy for all of the camp years.

I have talked recently with a few other Dutch friends who were camp children and who had lived at Louisa State, the boarding school in Baarn, Holland, where I lived from 1952 through 1957. Most of the teenagers who lived there in the 1950s had been in Japanese internment camps as very young children, and several of my friends had lost a parent in the camps. Karen, one of my friends, who also lost her father, compares herself to a bonsai tree, alive but with foreshortened roots and clipped branches—a tree trying to break away from the confinement of the container she is in. Karen wrote her account, "Groeien de weg van een bonsai kind" [Growing, the Journey of a Bonsai Child] in 1998.

The children at our boarding school, like the adults everywhere else, never talked about the war. The only common question among us children was "In what camps did you live?" The names we offered in answer to that question were so familiar: Adek, Tjideng, Tjihapit, Ambarawa, Banjoebiroe, Halmaheira, Lampersari, and Makassar. The names would roll from our lips and, without any further elaboration, created a common history that bound us together. Nothing more needed to be said.

Didi's Death, November 16, 2011

The last decades of Didi's life were happy ones. When the farm in Olst was sold and she and her siblings all shared in the proceeds, she was able to buy a lovely apartment in Bussum with a view over a small park with gorgeous beech trees and a pond with ducks that were always busy and chattering. She also learned to drive and bought a small car, which added enormously to her ability to enjoy herself. She had several close friends who referred to themselves as the Gang of Eight. She took painting lessons and thoroughly loved having her grandchildren visit her; she was a wonderful grandmother to Nynke, Hidde, Mascha, and Lidwien.

Didi and Emily, one of her very closest friends, became interested in the teachings of Krishnamurti, and both of them attended several of his lectures. Didi also started to write her own thoughts down—thoughts and ideas that were important to her. Some of these writings express her contentment with her life. After her death, I found a small notebook in which she had written the following:

O—hier te wonen—	*Oh—to live here—*
Mist om de vijver	*Haze over the pond*
Zweem van aarzelend zonlicht	*Hint of wavering sunlight*
Besef—ik woon hier.	*Realization—I live here.*

Didi in the garden of the Wildhoef, September, 2011

On November 16, 2011, Didi died at age ninety-five. For years, she had told me that she would reach the age of ninety-five, and she was true to her word. In that last year of her life, Didi lived at the Wildhoef in Bloemendaal, a nursing home for elderly people. She was happy there and loved her big, bright room and the warm attentions of the young staff. She laughed a lot and was almost always cheerful. She also loved to walk with Frits in the lovely grounds of the home and always looked intently at the dancing fountain in the pond that she could watch from her favorite chair in her room.

I had been warned by Frits and Jan that Didi's death was near, and I arrived in time to hug my mother and tell her that I loved her and that it was alright for her to let go now. Didi's three children and two daughters in law, four grandchildren, and two great-grandchildren, Jelle and Yuscha, all came to see her in those last weeks. Max, Didi's third great-grandchild and Mascha's son, was born forty-five minutes after her death. Didi had known that Max was on the way, and that news had been a joy to her. I like to think that Max and Didi met each other on the way in and out of life, giving each other a high five in the passing. Didi's death was quick and peaceful.

APPENDIX

PROCES VERBAAL

Van de belevenissen van H.D. van Oyen. Echtgenote en twee zoontjes van 6 en 5 jaar, Mevr. Engelberts en dochterje van 2 jaar, Meindert en Ankie Bolhuis resp. 8 en 6 jaar oud gedurende het tijdvak van 1 t/m 17 maart van het jaar 1942.

Ondergetekende ontving op het hoofdkantoor van Djasinga de mededeling dat de hoofdadministrateur moest vertrekken en dat de ondernemingszaken zo goed en zo kwaad als dat ging door den Heer Oesmansjah en ondergetekende afgehandeld moesten worden. Daartoe ontving ondergetekende een bedrag aan geld van den Heer Oesmansjah ongeveer groot f. 15,000 (dit bedrag is bij benadering - daar aantekeningen zoals later zal blijken, verloren gingen), nl. een bedrag van ongeveer f. 2,400, voor de gewone betalingen (f.400 Tjigeloeng, f.1,000 Gedeh en f.1,000 Tjipelar) een bedrag van ongeveer 9,400 guldens voor 2 maanden extra betaling van Mantris en Boedjangs (f.2,200 Tjigeloeng, f.3,300 Tjipelar en f.3,900 Gedeh) en nog een bedrag van ongeveer 3,200 gulden voor salaris Europeesche staf voor February en voorschot t/m Mei '42.

Al het borongan tuinwerk (nieuwe oogst) voor zoo ver dit nog niet aangenomen was, werd zoo snel mogelijk getaxeerd en ingeboekt gedurende de nacht van 28 February op 1 Maart en op 1 Maart gedurende de ochtend. Toen kwam ook Mantri (opzichter) Joesoep van Tjigeloeng zijn remise halen van 2,600 gulden die hij, zoals hij mij op 13 maart op Djasinga mededeelde, geheel uitbetaald kreeg. Tevens kwam de Heer Kok op mijn verzoek de Koleang remise halen, groot 3,328 gulden. Feitelijk was dit bedrag voor twee maanden extra betaling, en zou de gewone remise op 2 maart gevolgd zijn.

Daar de Heer Oesmansjah mij verzocht met de uitbetaling van de twee maanden extra te wachten totdat ook hij geld genoeg had (op 2 maart zou ondergetekende een remise uit Buitenzorg gehaald hebben, bestemd voor bevolking en bonus staf). Van de ontvangen 3,328 gulden verrichtte de Heer Kok de gewone betaling van ongeveer 3,328 gulden,

940 gulden op Koleang, gaf den Heer Biele 1,017.20 gulden en zichzelf f. 818,50 zodat deze Heren hun volle salaris t/m Mei '42 genoten hebben. Het restant f. 586.97 werd door den Heer Kok aan schrijver dezes na zijn terugkomst in Buitenzorg afgedragen waarover later verantwoording afgelegd zal worden.

Van 's middags 1 tot zes werd door ondergetekende op de afdeling Simpang betaald, nl. de gewone remise, waarmee ongeveer een bedrag van 2,600 guldens gemoeid moet zijn geweest. Tusschendoor werden volgens het van te voren opgemaakte schema de reistvoorraad grootendeels onder de vaste Boejangs (arbeiders) verdeeld. Om zes uur n.m. zond ondergetekende zijn auto beladen met privé barang weg naar Tjileungsa; na een half uur kwam de chauffeur echter terug met de boodschap dat de eigen troepen hem bij de kruising bij Ngasoeh niet lieten passeren. Schrijver besloot toen het de volgende morgen nog eens te proberen en dan de auto op Haoer Bentes te laten wachten, zodat hij zich altijd nog bij de dames in Tjileungsa zou kunnen voegen.

Om 8 uur 's avonds ontving schrijver het telefonische bericht van de hoofdadministrateur dat het Japanse leger reeds tot Tjipanas gevorderd was, en dat hij dus zo snel mogelijk naar Tjileungsa moest zien te komen. Schrijver gaf dit bericht dus direct door aan de vernielingsbrigade en aan de Heer Kok op Tjimaratja. Van vaandrig Brom hoorde schrijver niets meer; wel kreeg hij een zenuwachtig telefoontje van vaandrig Braams dat Brom bij de Wedana (district administrateur) geweest was en dat die volkomen zijn hoofd kwijt was en dat hij, Braams schrijver dezes adviseerde den nacht in het bosch door te brengen. Hierna belde schrijver den Heer Oesmansjah op die ook niet wist wat te doen; hij stond op het punt naar de kampong te gaan met vrouw en kinderen.

Toen schrijver daarna de heer Kok op belde om nadere instructies te geven was de telefonische verbinding verbroken, zowel met Djasing als met Tjigeloeng.Vermoedelijk is dat op order van de vernielingsbrigadecom-mandant op Djasinga gebeurd, althans voor zoo ver op te maken is uit de waarnemingen die de Heren Kok en Biele later op Djasinga deden, en uit de mededeling van den Heer Brom tegenover Mevr. Marcus in Buitenzorg waartegen hij vertelde dat de Japanners hem vlak op de hielen zaten, en dat hij de telefoondraden doorgesneden had. Door dit moedige optreden was schrijver dezes van alle communicatie afgesloten, reden waarom hij besloot tegen zijn oorspronkelijke plan in nog dien nacht naar Tjileungsa te vertrekken. Alle menschen die hij kon bereiken, dat waren dus fabrieks Boedjangs en Mantris kregen twee maanden salaris uitgekeerd en de bonus, waarna schrijver zich klaar maakte om met de Austin en de Ford via de Bendyweg door, zoo dicht mogelijk by Kampong Koening te komen.

Het vertrek van Simpang vond plaats om ongeveer 12 uur 's nachts gedurende een zware regen die reeds vanaf 's morgens geduurd had. Hierdoor kwam het dat al vrij spoedig de zwaar beladen auto's in de modder bleven steken. De tocht naar Kampong Koening werd daarna volbracht met een vijftal koelis en in Kampong Koening werden nog 5 koelis aangenomen, zoodat schrijver 's morgens om 5.30 uur op Tjileungsa arriveerde. Dat was dus de morgen van 2 maart, dien dag en om 12 uur 's middags werd Djasinga pas bezet door de stoottroepen, begeleid door rampokkers uit Bantam. Het bedrag dat ondergetekende naar Tjileungsa meenam, in den hoop het later nog aan de bevolking en de staf uit te kunnen betalen, moet dus ongeveer bedragen hebben: f. 15,000 - (f. 2,600, Tjigeloeng; f.3,328, Koleang; en f.2,000 Simpang) = f. 7,928, vermeerderen met f. 1,410, welk geld door diverse menschen aan schrijver dezes toevertrouwd was.

2 Maart. Direct bij aankomst op Tjileungsa ontmoette schrijver de hoofdadministrateur, die zich op weg begaf naar Tjisaraen. Schrijver ontving gedurende het korte onderhoud de dank voor al hetgeen hij nog voor de onderneming gedaan had. Hij deelde de hoofdadministrateur mede dat hij nog geld van de onderneming bij zich had, en dat hij van plan was dit zoo mogelijk eerst te verbergen en daarna alsnog uit te betalen, waarmede de hoofdadministrateur het volkomen eens was. Schrijver ging toen eerst wat slapen en gedurende de middag sorteerde hij het meegenomen geld en maakte een staat op in duplé; één ging in de kalt in het Tjileungsa huis, één droeg schrijver bij zich. Dien dag gebeurde niets bijzonders.

3 Maart. Schrijver begeeft zich naar het bosch om een gunstige kampeerplaats uit te zoeken en hij blijft daar tot 's middags met Mijndert Bolhuis. Etenswaren en geld worden door de bedienden naar het botenhuis bij Pintoes Ajer getransporteerd en van daaruit door schrijver en zijn echtgenote naar het bosch gecanood. Het wordt in drie porties verdeeld: het zilvergeld, ongeveer 9 zakken, wordt verborgen onder een klamboe die van tevoren met aarde vuil gemaakt was, en daarna geheel afgedekt met stenen en rivierslijk. Het papiergeld wordt gedeeltelijk opgeborgen in mijn geldkistje waarin zich alleen polissen en diplomas bevonden en voor de rest onder de dames en schrijver dezes verborgen. 's Middags om ongeveer 2 uur kwam mijn vrouw plotseling buiten adem aangerend.met de boodschap dat ongeveer 200 Japanse soldaten op 2 K.M. van Tjileungsa waren. Zoals later bleek is dit doorgestoken kaart van de Indonesiërs geweest. Vermoedelijk waren

de Kok Roesdi, de Kebon (tuinman)van de Heer Terpstra en de Kebon van schrijver in het complot betrokken. Hoe het ook zij, wij zetten zoo goed mogelijk de tent op en brachten de nacht in het bosch door.

4 Maart. Daar de dames in de haast zijn voorraad insuline en injectiespuit vergeten hadden was schrijver wel genoodzaakt terug te keren naar het Tjileungsa huis, en indien er geen Japanners meer te zien waren, te trachten zijn obat te halen. Daartoe begaf schrijver zich alleen gewapend met een geweer met 5 patronen en gekleed in zijn badpak naar het huis in Tjileungsa, waar hy na enig sluipwerk kon waarnemen dat uitsluitend de bevolking bezich was het fabriekshuis te plunderen. Schrijver ging terug en haalde zijn geweer dat hij eerst bij het huis van de administrateur verborgen had, en drong toen nadat hy zich bliksemsnel langs de helling naar beneden had laten glyden, van de achterzyde het huis binnen. De rampokkende Tjileungsa menschen waren zoo verrast dat ze eerst bleven staan waar ze waren. Daarna een algemeen 'sauve qui peut' zonder dat schrijver waarschuwingsschoten had hoeven te lossen. Het huis was reeds grotendeels leeg, voedingswaren en medicijnen lagen overal verspreid. Schrijver slaagde er echter nog in het hoognodige waarvoor hij gekomen was bij elkaar te krijgen. Terug gekomen bij de tochtgenoten werd afgesproken om de volgende ochtend in het huis van de Heer Terpstra te trekken, daar wij dachten dat dit huis door de bevolking gespaard zou worden. In het bosch bleef het nog rustig.

5 Maart. Schrijver gaat reeds bijtijds op verkenning uit om te zien of het huis van Mr. Terpstra nog bewoonbaar is. Op de waarnemingsplaats aangekomen ziet hij dat ook dit huis practisch leeg gehaald is; de bevolking sjouwt met bedden, pannen etc. De barang wordt gedeeltelijk eerst naar de garage beneden gebracht en daarna verder gebracht naar de kampong huizen achter de fabriek in de Tjileungsa kampong. Als schrijver voldoende waarnemingen gedaan heeft lost hij enige schoten in de lucht. Van de vyf schoten ketsen er drie. De twee knallen hebben tot gevolg dat een geweldige hoeveelheid inheemschen zoowel uit het huis van Mr. Terpstra als uit het huis van de fabriek naar buiten rent. Daar schrijver meent dat iedereen weg is gaat hij het huis van Mr. Terpstra binnen en vindt daar in de logeerkamer aan de achterzijde nog een tiental onbekende inheemschen met getrokken bedog (hakmes). Nogmaals lost hij een waarschuwingsschot waarna ook dit laatste stel helden de benen neemt. In de keuken staat de oude Kokkie van de Heer Terpstra bijeen te halen wat van haar gading is. Pas als ik vlak bij haar ben neemt ze de benen. Veel te redden was hier niet meer, alles was reeds weg of vernield, met

uitzondering van een schilderij dat schrijver in het bosch verborg. De antieke zware meubels stonden er nog, echter zwaar beschadigd door bijl en bedog.

Schrijver gaat terug naar het bosch en een paar uur later gaat de bevolking hier tot een aanval over. Plotseling weerklinkt een schreeuw en dicht bij de tent valt een schot. Zooals van tevoren afgesproken, laten de dames en de kinderen zich in het ravijn achter de tent glijden, waarbij gemene schrammen opgelopen worden en schrijver gaat er op uit om de aandacht op zichzelf te vestigen. Na korte tijd ziet hij daar waar hij 's morgens de rivier is overgestoken, een grote groep inheemschen bezich de mondvoorraad te plunderen. Hij vestigt de aandacht op zichzelf door een revolverschot in de lucht te lossen en het lukt: ze volgen hem. Na ongeveer twee uur door het bosch gezworven te hebben kan schrijver de weg naar het ravijn waar de dames en kinderen zich verborgen hebben, niet meer terugvinden, doch hij gaat thans op de rivier af. Na een moeilijke tocht door een dicht struikgewas hier aangekomen, springt hij juist in de kali (riviertje) als er een schot weerklinkt, dit was op hem gelost. De schutter verraadt zich door op dode takken te trappen, waarna schrijver vuur geeft in die richting. Vervolgens volgt hij de rivier totdat hij na een half uur komt bij de plek waar hij eerst de inheemschen heeft waargenomen. Alles is thans rustig, ze hebben trouwens hun doel bereikt: het eten is weg en de plaats waar het geld en de patronen verborgen waren is ontdekt. Dit kan alleen doordat er een spion in het bosch geweest is, toen het geld daar verstopt werd. Vermoedelyk waren er onder koelies van Simpang reeds verraders geweest (Roesdi en Rasin).

Onder de gegeven omstandigheden is het ondoenlijk het kamp dat ze nog steeds niet ontdekt hebben, te handhaven. Reden waarom besloten wordt 's nachts na maan opkomst naar Pasir Madang te trekken. Zooveel wij dragen kunnen wordt meegenomen, de kinderen allemaal een deken en een blikje voedsel, de vrouwen een volle rugzak. Schrijver draagt Sytske Engelberts (2 jaar) en zoo gaan we nog steeds vol goeden moed op stap in de hoop ons bij de Landmacht te kunnen voegen die ergens op Tjiseroea moet zitten. Het geweer gooi ik weg in het bosch, daar de patronen tegelijk met het geld in handen van de bevolking viel. De kist met papiergeld en polissen verbergt schrijver in het bosch. Dien nacht trekken we bij heldere maan tot dicht bij de afdeling Pasir Madang. Hier slapen we op een tuinweg, op atap (strips van gewoven palmbladeren) die schrijver haalt van loodsjes die langs de grote weg staan. Hoewel er een ontzettende hoeveelheid muskieten zyn slapen de kinderen een paar uur goed, daar we ze geheel toe kunnen dekken met de meegenomen dekens.

6 Maart. Des morgens vroeg na water gehaald te hebben, laat schrijver de vrouwen en kinderen achter op een kleine lapang (open veldje) vlak tegen Pasir Madang aan en hij gaat er zelf op uit om de zaak te verkennen. Het Pasir Madang huis is ook volkomen leeg. Hij ontmoet daar echter een paar menschen die vroeger onder hem op Tjibrani gewerkt hebben. Eén ervan loopt naar Tjibrani om de Djongossen Sarim en Brani te halen. Deze komen inderdaad, echter op hetzelfde moment verschijnt een troep rampokkers, ongeveer 150 in aantal zoodat de bedienden weer de benen nemen. De rampokkers met hun geweren en bedoks. Schrijver dringt aan op onderhandelingen en herkent pertinent de Loerah (dorpshoofd) van Tjileungsa. Ze bedreigen hem, en schrijver werkt op het gevoel door hun te vertellen van de kinderen. Het lukt, en dan terwijl we terug lopen blijkt dat een klein groepje gebruik gemaakt heeft van de tijd dat schrijver stond te onderhandelen, om de dames en kinderen te beroven van alles wat wij nog bezaten: nl. dekens, blikjes insuline en geld. Alleen de portefeuille die schrijver in een theestruik verborgen had is aan hun aandacht ontsnapt. 3,000 Gulden in de rugzakken is echter hun buit. Wij trekken verder met Etjon en Abdoel van Tjibrani en krijgen op Pasir Madang drinken van de vroegere Kok Kasim en de Kebon van Pasir Madang. Dan moeten we ons echter verstoppen in A.2., Tjibrani want volgens de menschen zyn de Jappen vlak by. De gehele dag blijven we verder onder de thee zitten. 's Middags komt Pa Laimin, waroenghouder van Tjibrani ten tonele die zich voordoet als een goede vriend en die belooft goed te zullen zorgen. Hij wekt vertrouwen doordat hij in het geheel niet over geld praat.

Des avonds begint het hard te regenen. Doordat we allen ontzettend koud en nat zijn, zoekt schrijver op den tast de weg naar kampong Pasir Madang en komt na een moeilijke tocht in het pikkedonker aan bij het huis van Kasim. Deze weigert de familie te halen, zijn huis zit trouwens vol gedroste landwachters van Djasinga. Schrijver gaat terug met wat eten en warm drinken. Intusschen is het droog geworden en de maan is opgekomen, dus trekken we er op uit om een loods te vinden op de Hoema (land in aanbouw) op de A.1., Pasir Madang. Dit lukt, het is echter een open loods. Even later komen de landwachters om ons naar een andere loods te brengen, ook op een Hoema aan de kant van Bolang. Hier is het ontzettend koud. We kunnen echter een vuur maken en terwijl de kinderen trachten te slapen, houden de volwassenen het vuur brandende. Schrijver scheept met veel moeite de landwachters af, die geld eischen. 's Morgens om 5 uur staan ze echter al weer voor onze neus en moet schrijver mee.

De portefeuille met geld is er nog en 7 menschen graaien er ieder 100 gulden uit. Schrijver moet wel toegeven want voor, achter, en opzij staan menschen. Ze denken dat schrijver slechts 100 gulden over heeft, doch in de achterzak van de portefeuille zit nog de 1,400 gulden van Van der Vijzel, Bolhuis en hemzelf.

7 Maart. Schrijver gaat terug naar den loods op de Hoema waar Kalis verschenen is met de boodschap dat we ook daar niet kunnen blijven. We besluiten dan verder te trekken en gaan dien dag naar het bosch van A.3. waar we een schuilplaats maken om te kunnen overnachten, met behulp van boschwacht A.3., Hoesdi, die met eten is komen opdagen. Tegen den avond komt Laimin die zoogenaamd de gehele dag naar Mr.Terpstra is wezen zoeken, echter zonder succes. Hij maakt zoo'n betrouwbare indruk en belooft zooveel hulp dat ik hem 200 gulden in bewaring geef, met de belofte dat hij het mag houden als hij een goede schuilplaats voor ons maakt in de tuinen van Tjibrani. Nauwelijks heeft hij echter het geld in handen of hij begint te zaniken dat hij gehoord heeft dat ik nog veel heb en dat ik hem dat ook maar beter kan geven. Van eten en verdere hulp spreekt hij niet meer. We werden echter steeds bespioneerd.

Des avonds regent het zwaar. Herbert en Loetje liggen bovenop hun moeder, Sytske bij haar moeder en Ank en Meindert bij mij. Zoo trachten we de kinderen warm te houden terwijl we zelf in een modderpoel komen te liggen. Door het fosforiseren van het bosch is vooral Meink erg bang, de anderen zijn te moe om er veel van te zien. Dan denkt Mevr. Engelberts dat het mis gaat met de baby. Schrijver gaat er dus op uit om hulp in Tjibrani te halen. Hier wordt zijn mening bevestigd dat Laimin dubbelspel speelt. Hij gaat het eerst naar de Warong. Laimin wil hem weg hebben onder het motto dat er Japppen in de Kampong zijn en hij tracht schrijver wijs te maken dat de Djongossen er niet meer zijn. Schrijver doet eerst of hij weggaat en gaat dan verder de kampong in, waar hem blijkt dat Sarim en Bari in hun huis zitten. Met moeite en belofte krijgt schrijver 4 menschen bij elkaar die Mevr. Engelberts willen dragen. We gaan terug naar het bosch in A.3.

Nauwelijks daar aangekomen komt er echter een boodschapper om te vertellen dat er rampokkers zijn in het huis van Sarim, zodat het viertal hem weer in doodsangst smeert. Nog geen 5 minuten daarna wordt een aanval gedaan op ons kampje waarbij schrijver een leverancier herkent die hij nog kort tevoren in Kampong Tjibrani gezien heeft. Voorlopig onderhandelt hij slechts met vier menschen, de beide dames hebben echter ook de indruk dat het hele bosch vol menschen zit. Schrijver onderhandelt meer dan 1 uur met de kerels en daar zij blijkbaar volkomen op de hoogte zijn van de toestand, en ook weten van het geld dat bij Pintoes Ayer verborgen is, besluit schrijver hen de plaats te zeggen. Temeer daar hij vermoedt dat de menschen het geld toch al wel ontdekt zullen hebben en om de groep er van af te brengen het kampje te onderzoeken. Schrijver vreest dat ze het geld in de portemonaie zullen ontdekken en hem dan zullen afmaken daar hij gezworen heeft dat er geen geld meer bij hem te vinden is. Eindelijk verdwijnen ze dan richting Pintoes Ayer. Na een wacht uitgezet te hebben en gedreigd te hebben de volgende morgen vroeg het kamp naar geld te onderzoeken.

8 Maart. Goede raad is duur. Gooien we het geld weg, dan wordt het gehoord. Verbranden we het, dan komen ze er ook op af. We trachten het papieren geld dan op te eten, gelukkig is het echter veel te veel zoodat we er spoedig genoeg van hebben. Mijn vrouw weigert het te vernietigen en we verstoppen het in de voering van de regenjas. De volgende morgen blijkt er dan echter geen sterveling meer te zijn. Maar spoedig komen dan weer Tjibrani menschen opdagen met verhalen over Jappen die dicht bij zitten. We hebben er echter genoeg van en zeggen dat ze dan de Jappen maar hier moeten halen. De wachter van de afdeling Tjimaratja speelde hierbij een belangrijke rol. De onderhandelingen 's nachts hadden tot doel de rampokkers over te halen tegen het bedrag dat in de kist zat, ons met de kinderen door de linies heen te helpen. Daar we niet beter wisten uit alle leugenverhalen dat er nog steeds gevochten werd.

Echter verschijnt dan weer het viertal van 's nachts die ons naar Tjileungsa brengen. Dat is dus op 8 maart. We slapen dan in de achterste logeerkamer van den heer Terpstra op den grond. Later blijkt hier een hoeveelheid menschelijke uitwerpselen te liggen, we zijn echter te moe om weer te gaan verhuizen. Des avonds om 11 uur wordt ik weer opgeklopt om naar de kist met geld te gaan zoeken. De afspraak is om te delen: zij het geld en ik de polissen. Schrijver piekert er nog over om ze naar een verkeerde plek te brengen, besluit dit er echter niet op te wagen, wat achteraf beschouwd goed gezien is. De kist wordt gevonden en wordt vlakbij het huis nog even verborgen. Bij het huis staan een 30 rampokkers die zoogenaamd niets met het viertal te maken hebben. Met andere woorden: het was doorgestoken kaart. Indien er in het bosch niets geweest was hadden de heeren behoorlijk onder ons huisgehouden. Schrijver weet echter waar het geld en de kist moeten zitten zoodat er thans wellicht nog iets van terecht komt, daar men het wel zogenaamd zal bewaren totdat alles veilig is. In het Tjileungsa huis wordt het besluit genomen om thans zoo snel mogelijk Dr. Sahit te bereiken, daar het been van mijn vrouw zeer ontstoken is en het gebrek aan insuline sedert 7 dagen op de schrijver een funeste invloed begint te krijgen. De volgende morgen wordt met 5 koelies richting Tjileungsa vertrokken, welke kampong inderdaad bereikt wordt in een stralende regen. Wij worden vriendelijk in een kamponghuis verzorgd gedurende 1 nacht. Alvorgens van Tjileungsa te vertrekken vraagt schrijver Mahadi de postzegels die overal rondom het huis van Mr.Terpstra verspreid liggen, te verzamelen en te bewaren. Op weg naar Tjisoesoe komt nog een inlander achterop met het verhaal dat hij een brief had van Mr.Terpstra die hij ons alleen mocht geven als we nog in het huis waren. Het lijkt ons erg onwaarschijnlijk dus gaan we door.

11 Maart. Via Haoer Bentes bereiken we Kampong Koening waar we door Mantri Atra feestelijk onthaald worden. Hij beweert dat de Mantris Doerahim en Garoet myn verborgen barang direct gerampokt hebben zoodra ik vetrokken was. In hoeverre deze mededeling van deze man betrouwbaar was zal de toekomst leren. Hoewel we volop te eten gekregen hebben en vele vrouwen uit de Gedeh fabriek steeds maar huilen, wil niemand ons onderdak voor den nacht geven. Vermoedelijk bevindt er zich in de huizen veel barang van Gedeh en bovendien zyn er deserteurs in de huizen, dus verder naar Simpang en slapen dien nacht in het huis van Doerahim, het enige huis dat nog in tact is. Daar mijn vrouw zware koorts krijgt en er een lange stoel is blijven we er twee nachten, drie dagen. Voor Mevr. Engelberts en mijzelf maak ik 2 banken van awi (?) en rubber om op te slapen.

De fabriek en de huizen bieden een troosteloze aanblik. In de fabriek is van weegschalen, gereedschappen of iets dergelijks niets meer te zien. De machines die stuk konden, zijn stuk gemaakt en groenbemesters en zaden liggen over de gehele vloer verspreid. In de huizen is niets meer, zelfs de deuren en ramen zijn verwijderd, de vloeren zijn opengebroken. In schrijver's huis staat alleen nog de schuilkast en een stukgetrapte lampenkap. Zelfs wc en vaste wastafel zijn naar buiten gesleept en daar stuk geslagen. Zeer veel kampongmenschen komen op de proppen met eten en drinken.

Na twee dagen trekken we verder naar kampong Bodjong waar de Wedana van Djasinga zit en waar we dan heer Oesmansjah weer ontmoeten. De Wedana doet niets voor ons, duidelijk bevreesde als hij is voor de bevolking. Alleen zijn zwager die ons ook reeds kleren en eten bracht op Simpang, durft iets te ondernemen. Diezelfde middag vertrekken wij naar kampong Soekamanah waarbij we langs het huis van de hoofdadmin-istrateur en de Sawah boulevard komen. Overal dezelfde troosteloze aanblik. Van het telefoonkantoor is ook niets meer heel. Het inheemsche bezoek is overstelpend en verschrikkelijk. Daar we behoefte aan slaap hebben en steeds weer gestoord worden, willen we slapen in de tweede kamer van de nieuwe beding (loods). Het groene zitje van de hoofdadministrateur is tot onzer beschikking gesteld door de machinist van Tjimaratja, en 1 fles whisky en 1 fles cognac. Mian Djali, Chauffeur van den heer Telstra en dito Pieter, Baboes etc. etc. komen met eten. Mantri Atra en Joesoep die ons reeds bij Bodjong tegemoet kwam, allen komen ze. De volgende dag trekken we verder naar Dr. Sahit.

14 Maart. De dysenterie begint zich te openbaren op weg door de rubbertuinen naar Toge. Ook de huizen daar zijn geheel leeg. De kinderen en mijn vrouw die thans reeds een week blootsvoets gaat, kunnen haast niet meer lopen. De kinderen worden grotendeels gedragen door de 9 man die Mr. Oesmansjah ieder 5 gulden heeft moeten betalen om ons naar Tjigoedig te brengen. En dan bij den brug van Toge staan auto's met Japansche soldaten. De inlanders blijven een beetje achter terwijl ze eerst de gehele weg gerend hebben, zodat we ze nauwelijks bij konden houden. We gaan naar de soldaten toe. Ik word zwaar gefouilleerd op wapens door een officier, de kinderen geheel niet, de dames eventjes. We maken met moeite ons doel bekend en dan maken de Japs een opelette voor ons leeg die vol wapens was en brengen ons naar Dr. Sahit. Hier moeten we naar het huis van Mr. Zeeman, waar ik zeer lang zoo goed en zoo kwaad als het gaat ondervraagd word. Het einde is dat ik een soerat (permit) krijg voor vrije doortocht voor mezelf en mijn zeven tochtgenoten.

15 Maart en volgende dagen. Voor de rest kan ik kort zijn. We worden liefdevol door de dokter en zijn vrouw gedurende ruim twee dagen verzorgd. Volop eten en goede nachten zijn vooral voor de kinderen zegenrijk. Op de 17de wagen we de reis naar Bogor die wonderlijk vlot verloopt en niet zoo erg kostbaar is als we verwacht hadden. Daar wacht ons het geheel ongeschonden huis van de familie Bolhuis en het medeleven van vele nauwelijks bekende Europeanen, zodat we weer spoedig in onze kleren zitten. Tot 22 maart ligt schrijver ziek thuis daarna is hij naar het R.K. hospitaal verhuisd tot het eind van de maand. Langer kon hij het niet uithouden.

Dit is het onvolledige en onopgesmukte relaas van onze lotgevallen. Schrijver heeft slechts enkele feiten vast willen leggen om hier later op terug te komen, vollediger, en aanklagend, tegenover een regering die zoo slecht op de hoogte was van wat in het volk omging, en die zoo weinig juiste maatregelen getroffen had. Het heeft weinig nut achteraf te zeggen of iets goed of slecht is, maar als Hollander mocht ik verwachten dat er dapper gevochten zou worden. Indien dit gebeurt was geloof ik dat ook voor ons alles anders gelopen zou zijn. Dan zou de inheemsche bevolking niet ook los geslagen zijn, want onder de honderden rampokkers boven waren enkele werkelijke raddraaiers en de rest waren meelopers die er na een week reeds genoeg van hadden en spijt hadden. Die zullen er binnenkort net zozeer de dupe van zijn als wij, Europeanen. Wel wil ik hier nog even vastleggen dat hoewel de hoofdadministrateur en Mr.Terpstra tegen ons in Tjileungsa gezegd hebben "U zult ons nog wel eens zien", de oorspronkelijke afspraak luidde dat wij er in geen geval op moesten rekenen hulp van de landwachters te mogen verwachten.

Note: Het Process Verbaal van Herbert van Oyen, was opnieuw bewerkt en omgezet in "Word" door Lidwien.

NOTES AND REFERENCES

CHAPTER 2: PREPARING FOR WAR

P. 31 "In the years leading up to the war" N. Beets. *De verre oorlog: lot en levensloop van krygsgevangenen onder the Japanner*. Boompers Drukkerijen, 1981, p. 35–36

P. 34 "The Dutch Forces, poorly trained" John Keegan. *The Second World War*. Penguin Books, 1989, p. 262–263

CHAPTER 5: DAAN AND JAN BECOME PRISONERS OF WAR

P. 59 "The military administration needed a relatively large work force" Shigeru Sato. *War Nationalism and Peasants, Java under the Japanese Occupation, 1942–1945*. M.E. Sharpe, 1994, p. 155

P. 59 "Although there are no exact numbers" Paul H. Kratoska, Editor. *Asian Labor in the Wartime Japanese Empire, Unknown Histories*. M.E. Sharpe, 2005, p. 197

P. 60 "The knights of bushido made mockery" Max Hastings. *Retribution, the Battle for Japan, 1944–45*. Vintage Books, 2009, p. 548

P. 62 "The detailed instructions from the Japanese" J. Van Dulm et al. *Geillustreerde Atlas van de Japanse Kampen in Nederlands-Indie, 1942–1945, Deel I*. Asia Maior, May 2002, p. 6

P. 63 "The Japanese amassed the vast Asian labor force" Ronald Searle. *To the Kwai and Back, War Drawings 1939–1945*. The Atlantic Monthly Press, 1986, p. 116

P. 66 "They perished by the thousands without ceremony" Henk Hovinga. *Asian Labor in the Wartime Japanese Empire, Unknown Histories*, edited by Paul H. Kratoska. M. E. Sharpe, New York, p. 214

P. 66 "Soekarno was haunted by his role" Theodore Friend. *Indonesian Destinies*. Harvard University Press, 2003, p. 29

CHAPTER 6: OUR INTERNMENT IN CAMP TJIHAPIT, BANDOENG

P. 77 "We had learned that the Japanese" www.historyplace.com/unitedstates/pacificwar/tline

CHAPTER 7: INTERNMENT IN AMBARAWA AND BANJOE-BIROE

P. 84 "The nutritional value of daily rations" J. Van Dulm et al. *Geillustreerde Atlas van de Japanse Kampen in Nederlands-Indie, 1942–1945, Deel I.* Asia Maior, 2002, p. 17

P. 85 "Battle had not devastated Java" Theodore Friend. *Indonesian Destinies.* Harvard University Press, 2003, p. 34

P. 86 "An outer estimate, three million dead in Java alone" Max Hastings. *Retribution, the Battle for Japan, 1944–45.* Vintage Books, 2009, p. 14

P. 87 "An estimated 15,800 internees" Van Dulm et al. *Geillustreerde Atlas van de Japanse Kampen in Nederlands-Indie, 1942–1945, Deel I.* Asia Maior, May 2002, p. 145

CHAPTER 8: THE END OF THE WAR—FREE BUT NOT SAFE

P. 94 "These one family homes" Van Dulm et al. *Geillustreerde Atlas van de Japanse Kampen in Nederlands-Indie, 1942–1945, Deel I.* Asia Maior, 2002, p. 136

CHAPTER 9: PAPA DAAN'S DEATH IN CAMP TAMARKAN

P. 105 "From the website I found copies" www.gahetna.nl/collectie/inventaris.

CHAPTER 10: JAN'S SURVIVAL AND RETURN TO JAVA

P. 112 "I Googled the following search request" www.mansell.com.

P.112 "The site recommended a book written by a Dutchman" www.mansell.com.

P. 113 "Evidence developed during" Van Dulm et al. *Geillustreerde Atlas van de Japanse Kampen in Nederlands-Indie, 1942–1945, Deel I.* Asia Maior, 2002, p.19

P. 114 "Jan told the men that it appeared that" J. A.Wormser. *De nacht van de rijzende zon, een Hollandse krijgsgevangene in Japan, 1942–1945.* J. H. Kok, p.155–156

CHAPTER 13: DEVENTER DURING THE WAR

P. 141 "Initially the Dutch reaction" Geert Mak. *The Eeuw van mijn Vader*. Atlas, 14th edition, 2004, p. 270

P. 142 "With the help of the much-celebrated Dutch" www.JewishVirtualLibrary.org.

P. 146 "I learned that De Vlaamse Leeuw" wikipedia.org/wiki/ DeVlaamse-Leeuw

CHAPTER 15: OUR RETURN TO INDONESIA

P. 163 "Charged with restoring peace and order" wikipedia.org/wiki/South_Sulawesi_Campaign

P. 164 "If we want democracy" Theodore Friend. *Indonesian Destinies.* Harvard University Press, 2003, p. 31

P. 169 "But while the Dutch were" Tineke Helwig and Eric Tagliacozzo. *The Indonesia Reader, History, Culture, Politics.* Duke University Press, 2009, p.330

P. 173 "Instead, he argued that a new type of democracy" Jean Gelman Taylor. *Indonesia: Peoples and Histories*. Yale University Press, 2003, p. 337

CHAPTER 16: JAPAN'S SURRENDER AND THE WAR CRIMES TRIBUNAL

P. 176 "Only one of the War Ministry's orders" National Archives and Records Administration, Washington, DC. Exhibit O. Doc. No. 2687. File 2015, NARA

P. 178 "One of the Japanese plans was" Van Dulm et al. *De Geillustreerde Atlas van de Japanse Kampen in Nederlands-Indie, 1942–1945, Deel I.* Asia Maior, 2002, p. 19

P. 178 "Another document was found" National Archives and Records Administration, Washington, DC. Exhibit J. Doc. No. 2687. File 2015, NARA

BIBLIOGRAPHY

Beets, N. *De verre oorlog: lot en levensloop van krygsgevangenen onder de Japanner* [*The distant war: destiny and course of life of prisoners of war under the Japanese*]. Boompers Drukkeryen b.v., Meppel, 1981.

Beevor, Anthony. *The Second World War.* Little, Brown and Company. 2012

Bekkering, P.G. and Bekkering-Merens, M. "De Japanse kampen; nog geen verleden tijd" [The Japanese camps; not yet history"]. Stichting Informatie en Coordinatie Orgaan Dienstverlening Oorlogsgetroffenen, Utrecht, June 1987, pages 19–31.

Bolhuis, M. "De Vlucht" [The Flight]. Unpublished Manuscript, Gouda.

Brugmans, I.J., De Graaf, H.J., Joustra, A.H., and Vromans, A.G. "*Nederlandsch-Indië onder Japanse bezetting. Gegevens en documenten over de jaren 1942–1945" [Dutch East Indies under Japanese occupation. Information and documentation from the years 1942–1945*]. Uitgave T. Wever, Franeker, 1960.

Daws, Gavan. *Prisoners of the Japanese: POWs of World War II in the Pacific.* William Morrow and Company, Inc., 1994.

Dekker-Belgraver, Wil. "Indisch Kampkind; een eigen gezicht?" [Camp child of the Indies; a profile of its own?]. Stichting Informatie en Coordinatie Orgaan Dienstverlening Oorlogsgetroffenen, February, 1986, pages 11–27.

De Kruijf, E. "Kinderen uit het Jappenkamp, de jongste generatie van '40–'45" [Children of the Japanese camps, the youngest generation of '40–'45]. Maandblad Geestelijke Volksgezondheid, April 1981.

Friend, Theodore. *Indonesian Destinies.* Harvard University Press, 2003.

Hastings, Max. *Retribution: the Battle for Japan, 1944–45*. Vintage Books, 2009.

Hellwig, Tineke and Tagliacozzo, Eric, Editors. *The Indonesia Reader, History, Culture, Politics*. Duke University Press, 2009.

Keegan, John. *The Second World War*. Penguin Books, 1989.

Kratoska, Paul. H., Editor. *Asian Labor in the Wartime Japanese Empire, Unknown Histories*. An East Gate Book, 2005.

Mak, Geert. *De eeuw van myn Vader [My Father's Century*]. Uitgevery Atlas. Fourteenth edition, January 2001.

National Archives and Records Administration. Document No. 2687; Exhibit O, No. 2015 and exhibit J, No. 2011. Washington, DC.

Penders, C.L.M., *The West New Guinea Debacle: Dutch Decolonization and Indonesia, 1945–1962*. University of Hawai'i Press, 2002.

Sato, Shigeru. *War, Nationalism and Peasants: Java under the Japanese Occupation 1942–1945*. An East Gate Book, 1994.

Van Dulm, J., Krijgsveld, W.J., Legemaate, H.J., Liesker, H.A.M., and Weijers, G. *Geillustreerde Atlas van de Japanse Kampen in Nederlands-Indie, 1942-1945, Deel I en Deel II* [*Illustrated Atlas of the Japanese Camps in the Dutch East Indies, 1942–1945, Volume I and Volume II*]. Asia Maior, 3rd edition, May 2002.

Van Oyen, H.D. "Proces Verbaal" [Formal Complaint]. Unpublished Manuscript, Buitenzorg, March 1942.

Wormser, J.A. *De nacht van de rijzende zon. Een Hollandse krijgsgevangene in Japan, 1942–1945 [The night of the rising sun, a Dutch prisoner of war in Japan, 1942–1945]*. Uitgeversmaatschappij J.H. Kok.

http://www.historyplace.com/unitedstates/pacificwar/tline-bw.html

http://www.jewishvirtuallibrary.org/jsource/vjw/netherlands.html

http://www.//en.wikipedia.org/wiki/devlaamse-leeuw.html

http://www.mansell.com/pow-index.html

http://www.indischekamparchieven.nl/en/general-information/per-island/java.html

http://www.indischekamparchieven.nl/en/general-information/bersiap.html

CPSIA information can be obtained at www.ICGtesting.com
Printed in the USA
BVOW05s0009131214

379198BV00002B/50/P